How an Island Lost its People

Improvement, Clearance and Resettlement on Lismore, 1830-1914

Robert Hay

THE ISLANDS BOOK TRUST

Published in 2013 by The Islands Book Trust

www.theislandsbooktrust.com

Copyright remains with the named author. Other than brief extracts for the purpose of review, no part of this publication may be reproduced in any form without the written consent of the publisher and copyright owner.

© The Islands Book Trust 2013

ISBN: 978-1-907443-56-5

Text © Robert Hay

All rights reserved. No part of this publication may be reproduced, stored in a retrieval system, or transmitted in any other form or by any means, electronic, mechanical, photocopying, recording or otherwise without the prior written permission of the publishers. This book may not be lent, hired out, resold or otherwise disposed of by way of trade in any form of binding or cover other than that in which it is published, without the prior consent of the publishers.

The Islands Book Trust
Ravenspoint Centre
Kershader
South Lochs
Isle of Lewis
HS2 9QA

Tel: 01851 820737

Typeset by Raspberry Creative Type
Cover design by Raspberry Creative Type
Printed and bound by CPI Antony Rowe

By the Same Author

Lochnavando No More. The Life and Death of a Moray Farming Community, 1750-1850. 2005.
Lismore: The Great Garden. 2009.

Contents

List of Illustrations		7
Introduction		9
Chapter One	War, Debt and Famine: Argyll in the 1840s	15
Chapter Two	Allan Duncan MacDougall	37
Chapter Three	The Improvement of Baleveolan	61
Chapter Four	James Auchinleck Cheyne	101
Chapter Five	The Lismore Clearances	115
Chapter Six	How Lismore Lost its People – and Held on to Some of Them	169
Chapter Seven	Legacies	189
Appendix 1	The Baleveolan Estate Community in the 1830s	193
Appendix 2	The Baleveolan Estate Community at the 1861 Census	197
Appendix 3	The Fiart Community 1841-61	201
Appendix 4	The Craignich Community 1836-71	205
Appendix 5	The Kilcheran Community 1841-71	211
Appendix 6	The Baligrundle Community 1841-61	217
Appendix 7	The Achnacroish Community 1841-71	221
Appendix 8	The Tirlaggan Community 1841-71	225
Appendix 9	The Killean Community 1841-61	229
Appendix 10	The Portcharron Community 1841-61	235
Appendix 11	Lismore Households Visited by Commissioners of the Poor Law Inquiry in August 1843	239

Appendix 12	Full Text of the Letter from Captain Pole to Sir Edward Coffin, 3 October, 1846 (*Treasury Letters, 1847*)	243
Appendix 13	Biographies of Cheyne's Tenants on Lismore	247
Appendix 14	Three Lismore Families	263
Appendix 15	The Kilcheran Cottars	269
Selected Bibliography		279
Sources		281
Acknowledgements		291
Index		

List of Illustrations

Plate 1. Idealised image of mixed farming in the lowlands of Scotland, showing a fully enclosed arable landscape with grassland and livestock production as integral components of the rotation. Autumn, Kinnordy by James McIntosh Patrick. Reproduced by permission of [tbc]

Plate 2. Part of the original Baleveolan Estate. The southern fields of Balimakillichan.

Plate 3. Portcastle Farm, with traces of rig and furrow in the foreground.

Plate 4. Illustration from James Smith of Deanston's pamphlet 'Remarks on thorough draining and deep ploughing'. W. Drummond & Sons, Stirling 1831.

Plate 5. Rev. Gregor MacGregor, parish minister of Lismore, 1836-1885.

Plate 6. Drystone dyke on Baleveolan estate built in the 1840s.

Plate 7. Signatures of Allan MacDougall (a) and James Cheyne (b) from business correspondence.

Plate 8. The abandoned township of Achanard, reproduced by permission of John Raymond.

Plate 9. Fields on Fiart township.

Plate 10. Kilcheran House in 1970. © Crown Copyright: RCAHMS. Licensor www.rcahms.gov.uk

Plate 11. Baligrundle township from above Baligrundle 2 farmhouse.

Plate 12. The abandoned township of Portcharron.

Plate 13. Bachuil, where the Napier Commission met in the Baptist Chapel in 1883 (undated early aerial photo-

	graph from the Lismore Museum Archive).
Plate 14.	Duncan MacDonald's sawpit at Port Ramsay.
Plate 15.	Cottar houses with mortared walls and gable hearths at Killean.
Plate 16.	Certificate of membership of the Highland Land Law Reform Association for John McDonald, Lismore, 1880s (from the Lismore Museum archive).

Introduction

Hugh Anderson, master mariner and song writer, was born on Lismore in 1837 around the time of its peak population (c. 1,500 in 1831). He was nine years of age when the potato famine struck and, before he left for a distinguished career at sea, he had witnessed a distressing haemorrhage of people (net loss of a quarter of the population between 1841 and 1861). Later, he expressed his continuing grief at what had happened to his community in the song *Oran do Lios Mòr:*

> Ach leis mar thanaicheadh do shluagh,
> Le bàs 's le fuadach bàirlinnean,
> An diugh cha dùraic mi dol suas;
> 'S ann bhiodh a'chuairt 'na chràdhadh dhomh.

> But the way your population has been thinned
> By death and notices of eviction,
> Today I don't dare to return
> Because the visit would be too painful

In the twentieth century, this theme of great loss still featured in the compositions of the Livingstone and MacDonald bards of Mull and Lismore. In *An t-Eilean Àlainn* (The Beautiful Island), the classic song written in 1947 by James MacDonald, the exiled islander looks back to a time when Lismore was both more populated and farmed more intensively:

> Nuair dh'èireas grian air sa mhadainn shamhraidh,
> Gur iad do chlann-sa bu mhiann bhith ann,
> Ach tha iad sgaoilte air feadh an t-saoghail
> 'S chan eil ach caoraich ri taobh nan allt.
>
> Tha 'n còinneach fàsach a' cinntinn nàdar,
> 'S chan fhaic thu làrach nan daoine ciùin;
> Le feudach 's bàirlinn chaidh 'n cur thar sàile,
> 'S an t-àl a dh'fhag iad, cha till iad ruinn.
>
> Na cluaintean àlainn a dh'fheum iad fhàgail
> A'dol nam fàsach gun bhò, gun chloinn,
> 'S na dailtean prìseil a threabh an sinnsear,
> Chan fhaic thu nì annt' ach luachair dhonn.
>
> When the sun rises on a summer morning,
> Your children would long to be there,
> But they are scattered throughout the world
> And there are only sheep beside the streams.
>
> The wild moss is growing freely,
> Erasing traces of the people's homes;
> With expulsions and summons they were sent abroad
> And their descendants will not return to us.
>
> The beautiful pastures they had to leave
> Growing wild without cow or child,
> And the precious fields their fathers ploughed
> Empty now but for brown rushes.

INTRODUCTION

If allowance is made for the conventions of Gaelic poetry, and a Highland tradition of nostalgia, MacDonald had some justification in what he wrote, since the population of Lismore was still declining, coming dangerously near to falling below 100 by 1980. Nevertheless, in assuming that the loss of people had been principally the result of evictions, without taking into account other factors such as the potato famine, changes in agricultural practice, the lack of alternative employment on the island, and the positive opportunities offered by the mainland and the empire, both bards paint a simplistic picture. Similarly, James Cheyne, the Edinburgh lawyer and accountant, who did carry out clearances on the island in the 1840s and 1850s, is, even today, singled out as responsible for the depopulation of Lismore, although he was active on Lismore for less than a decade, and there were no clearances on half of the island.

This book attempts to evaluate the roles of: the traditional landowners (whose reckless lifestyles led to bankruptcy and the acquisition of their lands by commercially-minded entrepreneurs); the new breed of accountant trustees (for whom financial probity was paramount); the Highland Potato Famine; James Cheyne, the clearing landlord; events elsewhere on Lismore, particularly on the Baleveolan estate factored by Allan MacDougall; the differing fates of tenants and cottars; the lack of alternative employment for the young; and the opportunities elsewhere, particularly in the central belt of Scotland.

The story is set against the background of national and global changes (Chapter One). The combination of higher crop yields following agricultural improvement in the Lowlands, enhancement of communications and transport, and the arrival of cheap food from the colonies undermined the role of Lismore as a major source of cereals for the West Highlands. From the middle of the 19th century, the island began its evolution from arable farming to mainly livestock production from grass. As a result of these changes, the need for labour diminished, even on the uncleared, more intensively-farmed, areas of the island. Faced with all of these threats to their lifestyles, and in a system of landowning that still permitted the landlord almost free rein, both tenants and cottars had few choices. For many, the only action open to them was to leave the island.

It is difficult to establish a balanced view of the factors affecting Lismore's population because of the shortage of primary sources. For example, the only accessible documentary evidence for Cheyne's activities was collected by the Napier Commission thirty years after his death, and there is a lack of personal and estate papers that could be cited in his 'defence'. The main sources of information are the census and other official records. However, the rich seam of information about Allan MacDougall's factorship on Lismore in the 1840s and 1850s, from the Dunollie archive and the Bachuil ground officer letters, provides a context for the times, and illustrates alternative approaches to the problems of the day. What is known about MacDougall and Baleveolan estate is presented first (Chapters Two and Three) to provide the groundwork for understanding the contemporary events on Cheyne's estate (Chapters Four and Five).

A century and a half later, legacies of Cheyne and MacDougall's activities can still be found in the landscape of Lismore but, in the case of the cleared townships of the south east, the legacy could have been much more evident had the Board of Agriculture not intervened in 1914 (Chapters Six and Seven).

The story presented here is important to Lismore and Argyll but it has a much wider reach, addressing the social problems that affected not only the Highlands of Scotland but also most of the poorer rural areas of Europe. Including full case histories of the tenants, their families and cottars, and the underlying changes in population, it is a uniquely detailed history of a Highland Clearance event. It is offered as a contribution to the evolving understanding of the traumatic events that affected many communities in the nineteenth century.

Chapter One
War, Debt and Famine: Argyll in the 1840s

War and Debt

In Argyll, the social turmoil of the first half of the nineteenth century finally destroyed any certainties that had survived the '45 rebellion and its aftermath. Twenty years of war with France raised the prices of grain and meat to unprecedented levels and led landowners to have unrealistic ideas about the incomes that could be generated from agriculture in the longer term. The buoyant trade in livestock also provided extra momentum for the clearance of people from the uplands to make room for extensive sheepwalks. The subsequent economic depression, with rent levels maintained, or even raised, plunged the tenant class into chronic arrears.

The war destabilised society in other, less direct, ways. The landed class in Argyll already had a long connection with the British army, enlisting hundreds of men for service in the Seven

Years' War, in North America and in the expanding empire. Although full records are lacking, it is known that many more men were recruited into the navy. In the titanic struggle against Napoleon, the demands for manpower involved an even higher proportion of the men of the area. Of the 689 men recruited by Captain Duncan Campbell of Lochnell to the 98th (Argyll) Highlanders in 1794, at least a third were resident in Argyll, as were most of the thirty officers. Over thirty officers with the name of Campbell served in the Waterloo campaign alone, the most prestigious of whom was Lt Gen Sir Colin Campbell (1776-1847; 'Colin Melfort', a younger son of Campbell of Melfort), the only member of Wellington's staff not to be wounded in the battle. Meanwhile his brother Patrick (1773-1841), who reached the rank of vice admiral in the Royal Navy, was an important mentor to his kinsman John MacDougall in his rise to admiral rank.

Argyll men were particularly involved in the various stages of the Peninsular campaign in Portugal and Spain. The Argyll Highlanders, now renumbered the 91st regiment of foot, participated in the events of 1808/9, which culminated in the retreat to Corunna, but they were back in 1812, playing a part in driving the French out of Spain in 1813. Losses of all ranks were extremely high, but some individuals prospered. For example, the Lismore landlord, Duncan Campbell of Barcaldine (1786-1842), who had enlisted in the Scots Guards as a teenager, acted as aide-de-camp to his cousin Sir Alexander Campbell, another of Wellington's commanders. At the Battle of Talavera (1808), Barcaldine is reputed to have 'had three horses shot from under him' and was rewarded for his courage by a baronetcy. Captain Alexander (Sandy) MacDougall, eldest son of the chief of MacDougall, was not so fortunate. In July 1811, he wrote home from Portugal to describe his excitement at dining with Wellington and his commandant (cousin Colin

Melford) but, early in 1812, the news came that he had been killed at the storming of Cuidad Rodrigo. Lieutenant Neil MacDougall (of Ardentrive), Sandy's cousin and husband of his sister Isabella, was wounded at the Battle of Castalla on 12 April 1813 and died the following day.

A career in the military could be very expensive. It cost around £400 (around £30,000 today) for Sandy MacDougall to be commissioned at the lowest rank (ensign) in the 69th Regiment of foot in 1803; Duncan Campbell of Barcaldine would probably have had to find at least double that amount for his start in the more fashionable Scots Guards. Once engaged, the annual income would have been modest, possibly £100 per annum. Promotion to a captaincy in the guards might involve as much as £4,000 but, during a conflict as long as the Napoleonic War, promotion could be free, with junior officers moving to replace those killed in action (but not those who died of disease). There was also the possibility of promotion for conspicuous gallantry. Nevertheless, whether in peacetime or war, there were the additional expenses of providing uniforms and equipment of the correct quality and style; and keeping up with the lifestyles of their affluent peers. In general, the officer class was restricted to those who could afford to find the initial cost, and live on relatively low pay, although luck and ability could allow younger sons such as Colin Melfort to rise through the ranks. The ultimate reward, for senior officers, was to be awarded a lucrative sinecure at the end of their career. For example, Melfort was, successively, Governor of Nova Scotia (1834-1841) and Governor of Celyon (1841-1847). Fortunate naval officers, of course, could accumulate fortunes in the form of prize money, following the capture of enemy ships.

The assimilation of Highland landowners into the British establishment was already well under way by this time but it could only have been intensified by the close bonding they experienced with men from wealthy and influential families in these dangerous and arduous years. Their wives were more likely to come from the south country and, like the sisters of the unfortunate Sandy MacDougall, they would set their hearts on wintering at Cheltenham or Bath rather than Edinburgh. Their lifestyles were becoming more expensive and they looked to their estates to finance them; for example, the rents on the Barcaldine lands on Lismore were increased by fifteen per cent in 1824, at a time when tenants were finding it difficult to meet the existing levels.

One important development, which commonly led to bankruptcy, was the post-Napoleonic enthusiasm, across Scotland, for building. Most of the leading landowning families in Argyll already had substantial Georgian mansions to replace their traditional fortified houses. Some, such as the Campbells of Airds, were content with such old-fashioned accommodation (Airds House, which replaced Castle Stalker around 1740) but others developed grander ambitions in the nineteenth century. For example the Georgian house of the Campbells of Lochnell was completely remodelled in castle style with extensive offices, from around 1820, only to be almost completely destroyed by fire in 1853. Barcaldine House, built around 1710 to replace Barcaldine Castle, was subjected to considerable alteration between 1815 and 1840, and plans were drawn up by the architect James Gillespie Graham to remodel the whole house in one of the fashionable gothic styles. A grand walled garden with glasshouses was constructed but, in the year of Sir Duncan Campbell's death (1842), the estate debts were so great that it had to be sold.

The Dunollie MacDougalls, careful with their money, could be quite superior about their ambitious neighbours:

CHAPTER ONE

Dugald Gallanach [Dugald MacDougall of Gallanach] is building a great edifice in the form of a castle, it will outdo everything in this part of the world, he has bought the furniture of his principal bedroom at a sale for 120 guineas, its original cost was 300 guineas so if every thing will be in proportion it must be a fine affair ... Coll's family are at Bath, he is at home <u>turning his house</u> into a castle which is the present <u>rage</u>, the Barcaldines manoeuvring their old house which is neither castle or cottage. I suppose when you build, which I think will depend a good deal upon prize money, to differ from them all it must be in the form of a man of war. *Louisa Maxwell MacDougall to her son John, 1814*

The Fate of the Lismore Landlords

From the mid-eighteenth century onwards, therefore, life was becoming more expensive for Highland landlords: building fashionable houses; adopting more expensive lifestyles; travelling more extensively; wintering away from home; sending their children away to expensive schools; paying exorbitant commission fees and expenses for their sons in the army or navy; and financing the marriages of their daughters. Meanwhile, apart from the temporary boom during the French Wars, when grain sold for up to three times the pre-war level, the incomes from many of their estates had not risen to meet the new level of expenditure.

Table 1.1 Changes in Land Ownership on Lismore, 1750-1850

Township	1751 Valuation	1850s
Fennachrochain	Duke of Argyll	Sold 1852 by Sir John Campbell of Airds to Alexander Haig of Blairhall
Achinduin	Duke of Argyll	Duke of Argyll
Cloichlea	Donald Campbell of Airds	1852 Airds to Haig
Balimenach & Baligarve	Donald Campbell of Airds	1852 Airds to Haig
Kilandrist	Donald Campbell of Airds	1852 Airds to Haig
Balnagown	Donald Campbell of Airds	1852 Airds to Haig
Baligrundle	Colin Campbell of Glenure	Sold 1845 by Sir Duncan Campbell of Barcaldine to James Auchinleck Cheyne
Achnacroish	Colin Campbell of Glenure	"
Killean	Colin Campbell of Glenure	"
Portcharron	Colin Campbell of Glenure	"

CHAPTER ONE

Baleveolan	John Campbell of Baleveolan	Donald Campbell of Baleveolan
Balimakillichan	John Campbell of Baleveolan	"
Kilcheran	Neil Campbell of Dunstaffnage	1842 Barcaldine to Cheyne
Fiart	John Campbell of Combie	1842 Sold by Charles Combie to Cheyne
Achanard	John Campbell of Combie	"
Frackersaig	Archibald Campbell	1852 Airds to Haig
Craignich	Coll MacDougall	1845 Combie to Cheyne
Achuran	Dugald Campbell	1852 Airds to Haig
Tirefour	John Campbell	1852 Airds to Haig
Tirlaggan	John Campbell	1845 Barcaldine to Cheyne
Half Bachuil	Duncan McLea (Livingstone)	Alexander Livingstone

The result was a spectacular cascade of bankruptcies, and the concentration of land into many fewer hands. In the first half of the nineteenth century, the number of proprietors in Argyll fell from 156 to 73 and much of the area came into the possession of entrepreneurs from elsewhere. In a letter to his brother John, Allan MacDougall describes the situation clearly:

> As a warning to Highland Chiefs the sale of half Glengussie estate is just going round the papers ... In fact there are more highland properties now lost by the proprietors apeing the style of men in the South of three times their income than used to be lost by rebellion against the Throne or their superiors or the ware-fare they waged amongst each other .... So much for what our poor father used to call 'your style & your comfort', a few Lowland Lairds and English Squires may to the end practice a life of both, but I cannot name a Highland Laird that has in my experience indulged in both that has been able to stand it. *Allan MacDougall to John MacDougall, October 1835*

Nowhere was this trend more obvious than on Lismore. Comparison of the landowners in the 1751 valuation with those of the 1850s (Table 1.1) shows that only four of the twenty one land units were still held by the same family, and that the rest of the island was owned by only two new proprietors, who had no history of landholding in the West Highlands: James Auchinleck Cheyne, a lawyer and accountant from Edinburgh; and Alexander Haig of Blairhall in Fife, of the whisky dynasty, from whom it passed to his kinsman, the Rev. James Alexander Fell of Penkridge, in Staffordshire. These changes arose out of the serious levels of debt incurred by three families of Campbells (Airds, Barcaldine at least twice, and Combie) but Table 1.1 also bears witness to the difficulties of another, Campbell of Dunstaffnage, who sold Kilcheran to the Roman Catholic Highland Seminary in 1803, not long after building a substantial house there. These transactions were to have very serious consequences for the tenants and cottars on the land (Chapter Five).

The People

International events had other, more subtle, effects at all levels of society. From the 1790s, letters among the moneyed classes reveal their anxiety that the revolutionary spirit unleashed in France in 1789 might infect the lower classes in Scotland. At a time when they were already treating their tenants primarily as a source of income for their expensive lifestyles, they were also developing fears for their property and privilege.

The outlook of the lower classes was also changing, under the combined pressures of: increased population; rising rents and arrears; rural unemployment; and greatly improved transport and communications. Regular steamers plied between coastal communities and Dumbarton, Greenock and Glasgow, where there were opportunities for employment; and although the French wars took a great toll of the young men, many returned home with a new view of the world and its possibilities. The Rev. Gregor MacGregor's private record book includes the marriage of a Peninsular veteran of the 94th Foot who had battle honours from Badajos, Cuidad Rodrigo, Salamanca and Toulouse. The ties of society were weakening. Chiefs and landowners may have wished the people to remain passive and deferential but there was no turning back for those, aware of the causes of the widespread bankruptcies amongst the upper classes, who felt freer to think for themselves. Many of them decided to grasp opportunities elsewhere.

At least from the 16th century onwards, and probably from much earlier, there were no resident landowners on Lismore. It is also not clear to what extent their tacksmen (principal 'middle class' tenants) lived on their holdings on the island. A surviving 1629 tack for Baleveolan from Sir Duncan Campbell of Glenorchy to Archibald MacGilleune stipulated that he must 'mak his actuall dwelling' there, suggesting that residence was not automatic. Certainly, the fact that Alexander Campbell of Clenamachrie was absent from Baligrundle (tack 1707 for twenty one years) was an important factor in the trouble that he faced in securing the rights to water for his corn mill. Under these circumstances, it is not surprising that the lesser tenants and cottars on Lismore were independent-minded, and prone to defiant behaviour. In spite of a relatively sparse documentary record, there is good evidence of a lack of deference in the early decades of the nineteenth century.

The primary response to agricultural depression, for those that could, was emigration. Families had started to leave Lismore for the Carolinas from the 1770s; a kinship group of Carmichaels was particularly successful, giving rise to a strong lineage of soldiers and businessmen in the Southern States. Movement to the United States was checked by the War of Independence and the French Wars but, after Waterloo, significant Lismore colonies developed first on Cape Breton Island, Nova Scotia, and then in Upper Canada, in the newly-opened lands west of Toronto. These emigrants were not forced from the land and, in spite of their modest origins, some proved to have very adequate resources. For example, Archibald Black, a tenant in the marginal township of Achanard, who emigrated to Cape Breton around 1820, had, by 1823, bought a farm of 270 acres there for 85 Nova Scotia pounds (slightly less than £85 sterling).

Meanwhile, there was a steady stream of other islanders to the central belt, particularly Glasgow, Dumbarton, Greenock and Paisley, in search of work in the expanding industries of the Industrial Revolution or in domestic service. There was also a well-established pattern of seasonal migration of young men and women to work in the lowland harvest and the herring fisheries. In some cases, this led eventually to permanent migration; for example, there is an island tradition that Lismore men were in demand because of their skills in horsemanship.

The net result of these movements was that the population reached its peak around 1830. Numbers for the parish of Lismore, which included the detached portion of Kingairloch on the mainland, were 1638 in 1821, rising to 1790 in 1831, but Rev. Gregor MacGregor records in his return to the New Statistical Account for Scotland (1841) that the 1831 figure for the island alone was 1497. By 1841, it had fallen to 1148 and, by 1851 to 1010. Rapid decline began, therefore, *before* any substantial forced clearance of tenants and cottars by the Cheyne family in the 1840s and 1850s (Chapter Five). Under the pressures of the times, islanders chose to move to other places which, although harsh, offered the opportunity, denied at home, to make their living. In addition to the factors 'pushing' them off the island, there were strong 'pulling factors' (availability of land without oppressive landlords, the benefits of regular income, and encouragement by earlier migrants).

Any idea that those who stayed behind were passive is contradicted by the evidence. If deference had been the pattern of behaviour in earlier years, by the early decades of the nineteenth century the people had learned to combine to try to resist the will of the landlords. The ability of Baleveolan tenants around 1800 to employ their own legal support to oppose Campbell of Baleveolan is discussed in Chapter Three. Further south, the township of Achanard had been cleared of its families (possibly as many as fifty people) by 1790, but the parish records show that by 1810, it had been re-occupied by five or six families from the surrounding townships. A similar number of families, mainly squatting cottars, remained until Achanard was completely cleared in the 1840s (Chapter Five). Meanwhile, Donald McColl, the miller on Baligrundle, was facing another form of resistance in 1817. He had to petition the help of the landlord, Campbell of Barcaldine, to get the tenants to pay their mill dues:

> Humbly sheweth that the tenants absolutely refuses to pay the dues of barley which your Honour hath ordered to your Petitioner proportionalee to a one peck per every bole of what they would sale – and do they so stubbornly stood against what your Honour ordered. Your Petitioner then only demanded what they use formerly to pay which they also refused. Therefore your Petr. hopes that your Honour will compell the said tenants to come to terms of satisfaction to your Petitioner and as in duty bound ...

However, the most spectacular event was the deforcement (physical resistance) of law officers trying to serve a notice of eviction on the MacColl family in Baligrundle in 1843 (Chapter Five). In a subsequent riot at Achnacroish, a crowd of fifty or sixty islanders liberated Malcolm MacColl from arrest, and sent the police packing. Eventually, two months later, the procurator fiscal, in person with a team of eleven policemen, managed to arrest the ringleaders, who were later sentenced at Inveraray Sheriff Court to sixty days in prison. MacColl avoided arrest, and eventually emigrated to Canada.

The New Statistical Account of Scotland confirmed that the Lismore people were not to be trifled with:

> Every sept or clan [in the parish] stands by itself to support one another against any other sept or clan that may wish to encounter them; but although they sometimes in this way quarrel when at home, yet when abroad at markets they are very faithful to one another, and woe betide the unfortunate stranger who may attempt to insult the least of them.

Strong character and good health were, of course, necessary for survival under the very basic conditions that all islanders lived. Many of the landless cottars, in particular, were in a state of abject poverty (Chapters Three, Five , Six).

Agricultural Improvement in Argyll

By the 1840s, farming in the Lowlands of Scotland had largely settled into a pattern that would persist for a hundred years. Celebrated in early twentieth century art (Plate 1), a fully-enclosed landscape, producing meat and milk as well as crops, had become possible because of the rapid and revolutionary introduction of subsoil drainage from around 1830. The age-old rigs were ploughed out, allowing the benefits of liming, fertilisers and new crops to be exploited, and the appearance of the countryside was determined by the new rotations: operation of the classic 'six-year shift' meant that the farm area was a mosaic of cereal crops, 'green crops' (potatoes, turnips), and grassland. For at least two years out of the six, grass leys were grazed by livestock. This diversification of products gave greater stability to farm incomes, and the amalgamation of smaller holdings into tenanted farms of 100-200 acres meant that there were fewer people to be supported directly by agriculture. Until the agricultural depression that set in around 1875, lowland farmers, housed in greater comfort than they had experienced in the past, enjoyed a period of relative prosperity. Displaced men, who failed to secure employment as ploughmen or general farm servants, were obliged to take their families to the towns and cities in search of work.

North of the Highland Line, and in the islands and the uplands, agricultural improvement tended to lag behind, principally because of the challenges posed by the environment. In more favoured areas that resembled the lowlands in climate and topography, for example in Dunoon and Kilmun parish, Kintyre, Islay and Gigha, landlords were transforming their farms in line with lowland ideas. Elsewhere in Argyll, 'Improvement' was mainly consolidation of holdings, with small crofts proliferating to accommodate displaced tenants; and the development of extensive sheepwalks, with associated improvements in sheep and cattle stocks by breeding programmes. Much of this was driven by the major landlords, Argyll and Breadalbane, who also encouraged local farming clubs, but both Campbell of Baleveolan and Campbell of Barcaldine were active in establishing sheep enterprises in Lorn. Indeed, Barcaldine had a wider interest in sheep ranching, leasing cleared land in Sutherland for sixteen years from 1794. Even though this had caused emigration from Argyll to the central belt and the colonies, substantial populations were still dependent upon an agricultural economy that was fragile, and subject to crises such as the poor harvests and cattle epidemic of the 1830s.

Improving landowners have been criticised for their lack of attention to the arable areas of the Highlands, but this is wisdom in hindsight, since the tools and management necessary for intensifying crop production and increasing income in this demanding environment were lacking at the time. Subsoil drainage was just being introduced in the 1840s, and it was difficult to justify the capital expenditure for marginal areas. Even in the potentially productive machair lands, the growing of higher-yielding crops was hampered by a lack of understanding of the micronutrient deficiencies associated with the high levels of shell lime in the soil. Bere barley and black oats were tolerant of these conditions but the new, and potentially higher-yielding, varieties of barley and oats were not. The most appropriate management for productive land in the wet west was to minimise cultivation and concentrate on permanent grass, with conservation and storage of feed for overwintering stock. However, until the advent of silage-making technology in the twentieth century, Highland farmers faced a serious challenge in making hay in such a wet and variable climate. Consequently, in the first half of the nineteenth century, much of the arable cropping that continued followed age-old practice, barely beyond the level of subsistence. The land was cropped to continuous cereals (normally alternation of bere and oats), with some potatoes, under traditional infield (wintertown) and outfield arrangements. Runrig was still in operation in some areas, even on Islay.

Farming on Lismore

The Isle of Lismore was an exception to this pattern. It is low-lying and, to a certain extent in the rain shadow of Mull, so that rainfall is generally lower than on the surrounding mainland. The fact that its geology is dominated by ancient Dalradian limestone of high purity has three important consequences for agriculture. First, because of the many sink holes carrying away drainage water, some parts of the island are freely draining; secondly, the soils tend to be relatively shallow, allowing the recycling by plant roots of calcium dissolved from the underlying rock; and thirdly, once suitable fuel (charcoal or coal) was available to kiln the limestone, there was a local source of agricultural lime. Since excessive soil moisture and soil acidity were the major factors limiting crop production in the West Highlands, Lismore was a much more practical area for arable farming than most of the mainland and, until the mid-nineteenth century, every suitable parcel of land was under the plough, the main problem being the extensive reefs of limestone where the bedrock reaches the surface. Visitors to the island remarked on the fact that so much of the land was under cultivation, and traces of rig and furrow can still be seen throughout the island, even in uninhabited areas, such as Alastrath.

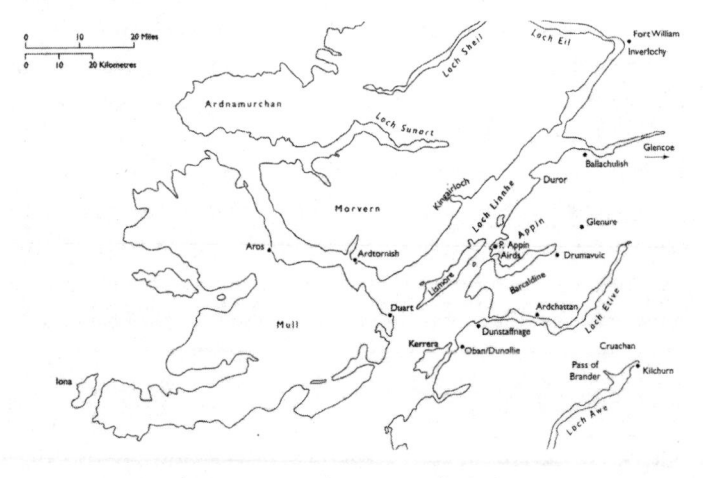

Fig. 1.1 Map of Lismore and Surrounding Area

Lismore estate documents (rentals, plans, estate correspondence) show that multiple tenancies had been abolished on all the Barcaldine and Baleveolan estate townships by 1840. Estate maps for the Combie lands (Achanard and Fiart, 1815; Craignich 1836) show complete subdivisions, with a separate steading on most of the holdings. Land on the island had been allotted to individual tenant families, as farms and crofts, and the age-old division into infield and outfield had disappeared. Subsoil drainage was just being introduced, and lime was available from Kilcheran, Park and Sailean. Letters to the

Baleveolan ground officers make it clear that the island tenants held strongly to the tradition of continuous cereal growing, alternating bere and oats. Some land was devoted to potatoes, but the tenants were resistant to the idea of introducing rotations including turnips and sown grasses and clover. Rents had been converted to cash, although the Baleveolan tenants also supplied oatmeal, milled on the island, and the proprietors continued to demand labour services, particularly from cottars. However, from the mid-nineteenth century onwards, the role of Lismore as an exporter of grain to the mainland would be undermined progressively by the crop surpluses generated in the lowlands, improvements in transport and communications across the country, and, ultimately, by the flood of imported products from the colonies that followed the repeal of the Corn Laws (Chapter Five).

Since the farms were only partly enclosed and most had limited areas of grazing, there was still a need for herd boys and girls to keep the cows out of the corn. Cattle numbers at this time were generally low, estimated by the parish minister at 500 in 1846, and there were around 200 sheep. As recorded by James Cheyne in 1846, the tenants still relied on a few 'generalist' Highland black cattle, as yet unimproved by the introduction of Shorthorn or Ayrshire genes. They provided the family's needs (dairy products and a little meat) and the occasional beast for sale. The island retained its reputation as a breeding ground for horses with good bone, raised on limestone grassland. The Caledonian Mercury newspaper of 27 January 1820 records the Highland and Agricultural Society prize of three guineas awarded to Mr Carmichael, Lismore, for the best three-year old colt or filly, and there was considerable demand for Lismore horses at the Oban sales at least until the 1850s.

Across the island, before any effects of the potato famine were experienced, many tenants were chronically in arrears of rent, associated with the post-war economic depression, and the fact that some landlords had actually raised rent levels. Chapter Three explains how the factor of Baleveolan estate acted to deal with these arrears. One result of the agricultural depression was widespread illicit distilling, adding to the value of the bere produced on the island by converting it to whisky. Particularly in the 1820s, Lismore was recognised as a major centre for trafficking in spirits but, by 1840, the trade had been largely undermined by the success of commercial distilleries and the activities of the excise officers. The financial position of some tenants *after* the start of the potato famine was particularly precarious. For example, in 1853, many of the surviving tenants on James Cheyne's estate had arrears of around three times the annual rent (Chapter Five); William Black, who moved from Fiart to a smaller holding on Craignich (15 acres, £16 rent), had accumulated arrears of £66 (Appendix 13).

In summary, with much of the island passing into new hands, the farming community had experienced the first stage of improvement (rationalisation into individual holdings; use of lime; start of introduction of subsoil drainage) but further developments were hampered by a sluggish agricultural economy, by widespread rent arrears, and by the reluctance of tenants to embrace new ideas (particularly rotations involving new crops, and the enclosure of individual fields). As communications improved elsewhere, the additional costs and difficulties associated with farming on an island became more important. Even in 1832 it cost 9/6 per horse for the ferry (an open rowing boat) across the narrows to Port Appin, and this more than doubled (to £1 5s) if the horse was shod. The lack of a suitable ferry to carry livestock caused distress throughout the century, particularly in view of the trend towards more pasture and livestock production:

The tenants have had to give up breeding horses as it was not possible to obtain the services of entire horses [stallions] through the want of a large boat for their conveyance to and from the island. Neither the steamer nor the pier accommodation in Oban and Lismore is suitable for horses. *District Clerk to the County Clerk for Argyll, 1911*

Famine

Throughout the Highlands and Islands, by the 1830s, the agricultural economy was in recession and many of the coastal communities were also affected by the collapse in the market for kelp. However, much worse was to follow. Winter came early in the three years 1836-8, snow lay late into the spring, with extreme temperatures, and the summers were cold and wet. These extremes were almost certainly related to the major eruption of the Coseguina Volcano in Nicaragua in 1835, which threw clouds of dust into the upper atmosphere, and the resulting poor harvests of both cereal and potato crops precipitated some areas into famine. Food shortages were worsened by the failure of the fisheries in Scottish waters. This was a global problem, resulting in distress across the world from the USA to Japan, and it has been cited as a major cause of emigration from Scandinavia. In the Highlands and Islands of Scotland it was a dress rehearsal for the potato famine to come a decade later, exposing the vulnerability of the food supply. Following a public appeal, which raised the extraordinary sum of £50,000, food was distributed throughout the area, including Lismore. In 1838/9 this prevented widespread starvation and saved the day, but only for the time being. A greater threat was on the horizon.

The arrival of the potato crop from the Andes in the sixteenth century, and its subsequent adaptation to growing over long days in cooler northern latitudes, had provided a bountiful new source of food by the late eighteenth century. The potato gave a high yield, earlier in the season than grain, and there was no need to take it to the mill. It became the staple for the poor, but wide areas of monoculture of the crop provided an ideal environment for the evolution and spread of disease. Epidemics of the most damaging fungal pathogen, *Phytophthora infestans,* devastated crops in the eastern states of the USA in 1843 and 1844: the resulting disease, late blight, caused rapid defoliation of the potato plants, stopping any further growth of the tubers. In wet conditions, spores from the leaf infections were washed into the soil where they infected the tubers. This could be latent at harvest, but when the stores were opened later, the potatoes had turned into a stinking mess. At the least, the disease caused a reduction in yield but, more commonly, it resulted in a total loss.

Blight crossed the Atlantic very quickly, possibly by tubers carried by ship, possibly simply in an aerosol carried by the wind. In 1845, it spread like wildfire through France, Belgium and the Netherlands, reaching the British Isles by the autumn. The tragic consequences for Ireland have been very fully documented but the impact on the Highlands and Islands was also very severe. There are reports of up to one third of the crop in Argyll being affected in the first year of the epidemic, although the MacDougalls at Dunolllie appear to have been careful and fortunate:

> The potato disease has scarcely proved so bad as was anticipated, but the continual wet is much against those [potatoes stored] in pits and of course many have not houses to store them in, particularly as they require to be thoroughly dried and placed in layers. Ours have not gone much since the first and the pigs and poultry have been fed on the diseased ones after cutting out the

CHAPTER ONE

affected parts. *Sophy MacDougall to her husband John MacDougall, 1845*

It was not till 1846 that the full implications were revealed. An even more virulent race of *Phytophthora* destroyed virtually all of the potato crops in the country, and serious crop losses were to continue well into the 1850s. The worst effects were experienced in the poorer areas of the Highlands and Islands where the potato was the sole staple. To add to the misery of the times, the winters were unusually severe and there was a collapse in cattle prices from 1847 (Chapter Five).

The crisis stimulated another extraordinary response from the public, with nearly £16,000 raised by the Free Church of Scotland by May 1847 from across the UK and from concerned communities as far away as Canada and India. Rapid mobilisation of emergency supplies of food, and help for outlying communities to seek paid work on the mainland, saved the Highlands and Islands from the degree of mortality experienced in Ireland. Meanwhile, the Lorn Presbytery of the Established Church of Scotland organised collections for a range of *other* charities, including support for the conversion of the Jews; its ministers, led by Rev. Gregor MacGregor (Plate 5), the Lismore parish minister, ordained fast days in 1846 and 1847, with the conviction that the epidemic was a visitation on a sinful population. The ministers of the Free Church would have agreed but that did not prevent them from mobilising an astonishingly effective aid programme.

There were serious consequences even for less vulnerable areas such as Lismore with its greater emphasis on grain production. In October 1846, on the advice of Rev. Gregor MacGregor, Government officials reported that the island potato crop had been entirely destroyed; that 600 of the inhabitants were entirely dependent upon the potato for food;

and that at least 400 of them (more than a quarter of the population) would shortly be destitute. There was enough food on the island to feed its people but the cottars did not have the means of earning the money to pay for it, and the landowners were reluctant to help. Meanwhile letters were arriving from Cape Breton Island describing similar problems caused by blight amongst the Lismore emigrants.

As explained in Chapters Three, Five and Six, the impact on Argyll generally was lessened by the fact that the population was already in decline and the proximity to the central belt offered the possibility of seasonal and permanent work. However, the epidemic had an important influence on the opinions of the ruling classes who were coming to the conclusion that the communities over much of the Highlands and Islands were unsustainable. The detailed analysis that followed the earlier crisis in the 1830s ('Remarks on the Evils at present affecting the Highlands & Islands of Scotland; with some suggestions as to their remedies') included a range of possible remedies: improvements in tenure and the legal basis of landholding, better education, improved communications, better approaches to the support of paupers, capital investment in employment, and emigration. However, public opinion was now moving strongly in favour of emigration as the key solution. In relation to the two estates studied here, it is highly likely that James Cheyne was influenced by this point of view. As a result of his actions in converting much of his island landholding to a sheepwalk, many islanders were forced to leave, mainly for the central belt of Scotland. Meanwhile the factor of another Lismore estate, Allan MacDougall, was doing all he could to keep his better tenants, to guide them towards more profitable farming, and to alleviate the worst effects of the famine.

Chapter Two
Allan Duncan MacDougall

Allan Duncan MacDougall, later to act as factor for the Baleveolan estate on Lismore for twenty four years, was born in Edinburgh on 2 April 1798, to Louisa Maxwell Campbell, wife of Patrick MacDougall, a lawyer and Writer to the Signet. He was their ninth child (out of twelve) and fourth son; as three of his sisters had died young, the children at that time included Isabella (born 1783), Alexander (1785), John (1789), Patrick (1791) and Lucy (1795). In the same year, the family moved to the ancient seat of the family at Dunollie House near Oban, where three more daughters were born (Ann Colina (1799), Mary Jane (1801) and Colina Katherine (1804)). In 1801, Patrick, aged fifty nine, succeeded his father as 24th Chief of MacDougall. When young, he had not expected to inherit the title, but his older brother John died in 1775 in Bombay, in the service of the East India Company.

Allan's life and personality must have been formed, at least partly, by the influence of the powerful personalities that surrounded him in his family. His father, who had by all accounts led a dissolute life in Edinburgh, continually in debt, underwent a dramatic change in character on becoming chief. Faced with the responsibilities of the estate, and the high costs of launching his children, he became extremely parsimonious with money, and very controlling of his wife and family. Nevertheless he could be realistic, providing rent relief to his tenants in times of difficulty and, acting carefully, he escaped the bankruptcy experienced by so many of his neighbours. Allan's mother, nineteen years younger than her husband, was a woman of spirit and opinions.

He had to live up to the reputations of his heroic older brothers. The eldest, Captain Alexander (Sandy), was killed during the storming of Cuidad Rodrigo in Spain in 1812. The next, John, was sent to sea as a midshipman aged thirteen in 1802, when Allan was four; he did not return home for ten years and then only on compassionate leave on the death of his brother. By a combination of ability, willingness to seek out opportunities to display real courage in action, and the support of kinsmen in the service, John eventually rose to the rank of admiral, accumulating a modest fortune in prize money. As Chief from 1825, he was probably as firm with money as his father had been, causing real difficulties for his impecunious siblings. Allan's third brother, Patrick, was also a man of action, reaching the rank of colonel in the army. Faced with the anxieties and grief associated with three sons in the armed forces, Louisa Maxwell was protective of Allan:

> You rejoice in war but alass little do you know what your poor mothers and fathers feel. But we must trust in Almighty God. 'Tho' his arm is strong to smite it is likewise strong to save.' May God Almighty watch over you my dearest boy in the hour of danger. I trust Allan will be neither soldier or sailor. You need not wonder,

my dear, that our late severe loss [the death of Sandy] should make us all have serious thoughts. *Louisa Maxwell MacDougall to her son John, 4 May 1812*

Another factor of relevance to his later actions on Lismore is that Allan was of proud Highland stock. In medieval times, the MacDougalls had been the dominant family in the west, controlling most of the original 'kingdom' of Somerled and building a chain of mighty stone castles along the seaboard of Argyll. Losing their position owing to their opposition to Robert Bruce, and in spite of their active involvement in the 1715 Jacobite rebellion, the family held on to lands in Lorn around Dunollie and the Island of Kerrera. They viewed themselves as part of the old Highland aristocracy and were, up to this time, relatively unaffected by the prevalent anglification of the landed gentry. Patrick had been fostered in the traditional way with a modest clansman, ensuring that he had a full grasp of Gaelic, and the family was imbued with MacDougall history and tradition. Allan's mother was a Campbell of Achallader, cadets of the Breadalbane Campbells, used to keeping the peace on the borders of Rannoch Moor. He would have understood the loyalties binding Highlanders of all ranks and appreciated the values of the Lismore tenants; and he was also able to draw on the accumulated knowledge and experience of a family that had a particularly strong interest in farming practice. His notebooks from the 1820s show that he had a interest in trees and horticulture and may have been responsible for landscape and planting at Dunollie at that time.

However, possibly the most important factor in Allan's life was religion. Louisa Maxwell was a very devout Presbyterian. In describing the attitudes of the English (Anglicans) to Sir Walter Scott, she wrote:

They will scarce allow him any religion which provokes me. I tell them he does not kneel, stoop or stand as often as they do – for our blessed and pure form of worship is pure, simple and from the heart, without parade or show. *Louisa Maxwell MacDougall to her son John, 28 January 1828*

Her response to life was stoic:

We must just console ourselves with the Christian Maxim that all things are ordered for the best by the wise disposer of all events. *Louisa Maxwell MacDougall to John, 30 November 1817.*

Allan was close to his mother. Raised in an atmosphere of piety, he developed into a tortured soul. Private notebooks, rediscovered only in the winter of 2012 in a wooden box in an attic at Dunollie, reveal a lifetime of obsession with his 'manifold sins'. On 25 October 1828, he wrote:

Hear me good Lord. How extraordinary it is that the Lord should yet preserve me who have so much deserved death and judgement. Which is his will that I should live. I trust it is that I may continually glorify him. In that idea there is more happiness than if worlds were now laid at my feet.

and, in January 1833, he resolved 'To endeavour with all thought & resolution to spend the days, hours & moments of this year as becomes a man & a Christian'.

Raised in this challenging environment, it is not surprising that, during his adult life, he displayed an unusual combination of honour, generosity, good technical knowledge, and poor judgement. Something of his character can be seen in his signature (Plate 7a) – carefully and clearly written and completely consistent across the years, in official and private letters – in contrast to James Cheyne's signature, which could show signs of hastiness (possibly impatience) at times (Plate 7b).

Early Years

In 1808, the MacDougalls followed the habit of other Argyll families by sending Allan (aged ten) to the Grammar School at Perth, where he lodged with William Dick and his family. Letters to Dunollie show that the Dicks were also protective of a young man who seems to have been far from robust, and susceptible to infections.

By 1815 he was apprenticed as a lawyer to the family man of business: John Young W.S., whose offices were at 32 Castle Street in Edinburgh. Patrick was a close friend and former colleague of Young, and his eldest son, Sandy, had boarded with the Youngs when at school in the capital. We lack a physical description of the young Allan, but his personality was clearly puzzling to his parents:

> Allan I think is a most singular character, I do not know what to make of him, he does not want abilities, but they are most singularly placed and it is difficult to say how he may come on in his profession. *Patrick MacDougall to his son, John, 1820*

> Allan does not want good sense altho' odd on some ways but he is very affectionate and good tempered. *Louisa Maxwell MacDougall, 1820*

Not long after he started in Edinburgh, there were two important developments. Receiving no salary for his work, and living on an allowance, by 1816 he was already seriously in debt. Thus began a lifelong problem that would feature in begging letters to his father and, later, to his brother John, after he had succeeded to the chieftainship. There is no suggestion in the extensive family correspondence that Allan was a heavy drinker or gambler; it seems that he simply could not manage money. A letter from John Young to Patrick MacDougall indicates that he was popular with his peer group and enjoyed an active social life, with its associated costs:

> You will please caution Allan not to make my house a place of call for his companions & friends. I detest idle interruptions and strangers in the writing room. *Young to Patrick MacDougall, 11 October 1816*

Secondly, early in 1816, Young wrote to Dunollie to say that Allan was ill. He had been unable to throw off the after-effects of a cold, and had a range of symptoms. Patrick, mindful of his own dissolute years and the rather lax sexual mores of the family (Captain Sandy had left at least one illegitimate child), must have rushed to conclude that his son was suffering from venereal disease, because the eighteen-year old's reply is very much to the point:

> I cannot dear father after your truly parental letter proceed further without thanking you for an advice the want of which as you say ruined the constitution of thousands. But thank God led as I may have been into the committing of many follies I have never yet suffered from a connection with the opposite sex. I pray therefore you do give yourself no uneasiness as to the cause of

my present confinement. *Allan to his father, 23 February 1816*

A week later he was slightly better:

Allan continues much the same as when I wrote you last though rather better, but his breast pains him now and then. I suspect the skin is off on part of the passage into his stomach and he must continue to feed with [softened] meat and drink. *Young to Patrick MacDougall, 29 February 1816.*

Clearly part of Allan's condition was a digestive problem and there is a temptation to conclude that he was suffering from stress. With his illness lingering, he was finally sent home to Dunollie in April to recuperate and, in spite of a series of letters from Young asking when his apprentice would be back to work, it was not until early November that he returned to Edinburgh. The view was growing in the family that he was a hypochondriac.

As soon as he was back in Edinburgh, living costs came to the top of the family agenda:

After a great search I have got myself settled here [Jamaica Street] in lodgings at 7/- a week which are as cheap as I could find and I think them a great bargain my rooms are a sitting room and a small bed closet off it and I have had particular recommendations for them and the landlady from an old lodger. I enquired about the boarding houses but find I would not get myself tolerably boarded for my whole annuity. ... I am conveniently situated for the office. *Allan to his father, 11 November 1816*

... I find you think my lodging extravagant. I would be indebted to anyone who will discover me cheaper. I have seen one or two from 7 to 8 shillings but what you are saved in lodging you are charged in living. There are lodgings under the same roof with Mr Young he thinks I should take a room there and I am of the same opinion but altho it is the garret story and a small garret room with a concealed bed I would not get it under 12 shillings a week which is more than my purse can afford. My reason for wishing to be so near him is that it does not at all agree with me going out at night to the office especially in this dreadful weather as I am so apt to take colds. I believe this is partly Mr Youngs reason. *Allan to his father, 19 December 1816*

Allan settled back into his work and studies, attending law classes at the university:

I cannot let as good an opportunity pass without writing you a few lines although I have very little to say except that I am well, and well worked to the bargain. Wharrie's absence in the country is greatly the cause of my hard labor, for three weeks past I have not been to bed a night before 11 oclock and I am sitting by my Law notes at 5 o clock in the morning. The watchman rouses me and my landlady rises and gives me a fire so I sit very comfortably. *Allan to his father 3 December 1818*

By 1820, nearing the end of his apprenticeship, he was clearly in financial difficulties and his relationship with Young was wearing thin:

CHAPTER TWO

I was driven a few days ago from want of cash to ask it from John Young. His answer was 'your father is abler than I am to give it to you'. As that would not dine me or satisfy my landlady upon consulting who would give me it <u>as a favour</u> I applied to John Bowie from whom I borrowed £15 promising to refund it by the 20th of next month. Whatever Mr Young owes me I think I owe him very little for favours or friendship. I will keep silent till the 8th of July when my indentures are out we shall then I hope have an understanding. *Allan to his father, 28 June 1820*

But seriously I should remain in town this season at least if I could afford it. It is very amusing spending a few months in the country but to return and spend such a winter as this last is more than I desire and what my credit wont stand my present desire is if Mr Young will make me no allowance to get up my indentures and get into an office where I hope by my own exertions to get quit of the debt that had been burdening me for the last 4 years. I was much assisted by your advice and I believe it prevented a rupture altho I often think want of spirit only prevented it long ago. *Allan to his father, 13 July 1820*

In 1822 he came close to destroying his legal career before it had hardly started, by actions that were unprofessional at the least. He had been persuaded to provide part of the security for a bill of £35 but, when Wharrie, a clerk in Young's office, disappeared, he found himself liable for the full amount. He then 'borrowed the sum of my bill from some money put in my hands to keep' and it was only the arrival of a greater sum of money from his father for other business that allowed him to return the money. Although his integrity was compromised, John Young was understanding, and the matter blew over. Allan confessed to his father, who had lost £35 in the process: 'I cannot call my conduct less than criminal and oh! what a dreadful pang it gives me to say so'.

1824-1850 Lawyer in Edinburgh

On qualifying in the law, practising for a few years, and paying the appropriate fee, Allan became a Writer to His Majesty's Signet (W.S.) in 1824, following his father into the elite company of Edinburgh solicitors. By 1823, his brother, Commander John MacDougall, had returned to Dunollie on half pay, taking up the running of the estate from his ageing father, who died in 1825 and Allan began to assume the role of family 'man of business' from John Young, who died in 1828. Their correspondence shows that the relationship could be tense at times, but Allan was trusted to negotiate John's marriage settlement with Miss Sophy Timmins of Cheltenham in 1826 and 1827 ('you are now entitled to the interest of £5,000' – an indication of the resources she brought to Dunollie) and to deal with the financial aspects of the extension of Dunollie House in the 1830s, which over-ran the original estimate of £840 by £200. Nevertheless, there were signs that Allan's inability to manage his personal finances continued, at least in the 1820s:

> I hope my dear Father you are continuing better and gaining strength for this winter. Assist me to do the same by sending me an order for £100. You know all the money I can command is in a cash account for £500 which I pay very smartly for to the Bank. *Allan to his father, 20 November 1824*

CHAPTER TWO

The arrival of John's bride at Dunollie in 1826 precipitated the final dispersal of the family. Patrick was already abroad with his regiment, and Louisa Maxwell decamped with her four unmarried daughters to rented accommodation in York. Meanwhile John was drawing away from the other members of his family in terms of his social status. Although he had, so far, reached a modest rank in the navy, he was a leading figure in the Celtic Society, leading one of the four Highland companies that greeted George IV on his visit to Edinburgh; and in 1824, he was appointed to the Royal Company of Archers (The King's Bodyguard for Scotland). By 1842 he was a leading guest at Taymouth Castle during the visit of Queen Victoria, and on visiting terms with the Duke of Argyll. These activities drew heavily on his financial resources, which were stretched by an expensive programme of building, a large family to launch on the world, and four needy sisters (one widow and three spinsters).

Around 1828, Allan entered into a legal partnership, Baxter and MacDougall W.S., which would deal with MacDougall business for the next twenty years from 32 Castle Street, Edinburgh (Young's former office). His partner, Charles Baxter, born into an Edinburgh merchant family in 1785, described himself as a writer or solicitor but had not achieved signet status. He was already at work as a clerk in John Young's practice when Allan started his apprenticeship. Although Baxter had no children, he had taken his wife's niece and nephew, Edmund and Agnes Cockshoot or Cockshute, into their household. Edmund, choosing to adopt the Baxter name, was apprenticed to Allan MacDougall, and on 11 July 1837, was appointed a writer to the signet. He was a man of ability, prospering in the law and ultimately achieving the rank of Auditor to the Court of Session. His son, Charles Baxter (1848-1919), also a writer to the signet, was a close friend and executor of Robert Louis Stevenson, who dedicated Catriona to him.

In spite of his partnership with the energetic Baxters, the business of the law did not make Allan's fortune. In a letter to his brother John, part of a continuing correspondence about his indebtedness, he wrote:

> Nothing in the world would have led me to write you a second on the subject – but you very much mistake what I have said if you suppose me independent – I am only struggling to be so & have been for 6 years, and I would now be <u>in the way</u> of being so, were I not obliged to my partner for a Cautioner – I am now as dependent as ever I was six years ago, and God now only knows the result – I am not ungrateful for the assistance you have already given me, and I may live to prove it perhaps not so soon now as I expected.
> *Allan to John, 16 February 1836*

In view of Allan's history of difficulty with money, it is significant that it was his partner, Charles Baxter, who wrote to John MacDougall in 1838 to report that:

> Allan and I with the addition of Edmund have entered into a new contract of co-partnering for a period of ten years, the former one having expired. I am glad to say that for the last few years our business has been gradually & steadily increasing, and with every prospect of still doing so.

Explaining that continuation of the practice necessitated the establishment of £800 credit with the National Bank, he asked John to provide part of the security. The continuation of the

CHAPTER TWO

partnership suggests that John did oblige, but Allan continued to struggle, as later events were to show.

Meanwhile there had been important family developments, which led to Allan's long involvement as factor to the Baleveolan Estate on Lismore. The owners of the estate, a branch of the Campbells of Barcaldine, lived at Druimavuic ('Ridge of the Pigs') on Loch Creran on the mainland, but preferred to refer to themselves as the Campbells of Baleveolan (a more romantic name, said to commemorate a tragic Norse beauty). In the 1820s, the laird of Baleveolan, Colonel Colin Campbell, and his sister, both childless, nagged their younger brother Peter (otherwise Patrick) continually about the continuity of their family line. At the same time, Allan's sister, Ann Colina, had failed to secure a husband on her visits to Edinburgh and Cheltenham and had been overtaken in the marriage stakes by her younger sister, Mary Jane. Eventually, in 1827, Ann (aged 28) managed to 'overlook his age and appearance', in the words of her mother, and a marriage of convenience was arranged with Peter Campbell. Allan drew up an impressive contract of marriage, establishing the right of Peter's eldest son (if any) to inherit the Druimavuic estates, in line with the entail set up by his grandfather John Campbell in 1756. Colin Campbell intended to share the house at Druimavuic with the newlyweds, allowing them to draw the Lismore rents, but he died in the following year.

The marriage did not last for long. Peter did his duty in producing a son and heir for the Campbells of Baleveolan in 1829, and then promptly died as a result of a 'fall from a horse'. Looking after the interest of his nephew, the infant Donald Campbell, John MacDougall assumed the day-to-day management of the estate, leaving the legal work to Alexander Lambert, writer in Oban. When John was recalled to active service in the navy (1833-1836), Allan took over the factorship of Baleveolan, actively guiding and managing the tenants by his many letters from Edinburgh to the Baleveolan ground officers, and occasional visits.

In 1840, the family faced another crisis. Ann decided to take possession of all her resources and marry again:

> Ann I am sorry to say will now require all her cash and you will have no peace until it is paid. She has not a fraction in my hands which until this hopeless union took possession of her mind she always had. We must make up our minds to put the best face upon her conduct we can, but I quite approve of her getting full time to ponder over her lamentable infatuation. *Allan to John, 2 March 1840*

Her intended husband, George Locke was thought to be highly unsuitable:

> I have failed in my endeavours towards restraining your unfortunate sister from ruin and disgrace. I went to see her and it is sad to say that I left her as I found her. ... The man she is about to adopt is as deficient in his external appearance as he is low in his mental qualifications, without the slightest pretensions to a gentleman either by birth or education, in short as ... says he is a wretch you would kick out of your way. Income £35 a year. *Charles Munro (Ann's brother in law) to John MacDougall, February 1840*

Undaunted, Ann proceeded with the marriage, which, as the family correspondence testifies, appears to have been quietly successful. The Lockes certainly showed limited interest in Lismore and left the business to Allan. His work as factor for them and Ann's son is the subject of Chapter Three, which shows that he kept himself very well informed about the agricultural developments of the day. The archive at Dunollie has several signed books from his library, showing that he was familiar with the writings of Sir John Sinclair and Arthur Young, amongst others. Following his election to the Highland and Agricultural Society in 1829, he was appointed as a livestock judge for Mid & Nether Lorn.

A Life in Decline, 1846-1876

The early 1840s saw Allan engrossed in legal work, agricultural Improvement and family support, keeping an eye on John's children (Alexander, Patrick and Sophy) who were at school in Edinburgh. Although she had been exiled in England for many years, the death of his characterful mother in 1841 must have been a serious blow. Even when close to her death she had still been fussing round him:

> You will receive a basket containing 4 fowls 2 ducks a small tin butter a little honey comb & a roll of mutton & a few eggs. *Louisa Maxwell MacDougall to Allan, 12 November 1841.*

He found little time for breaks in Argyll, and lived as a lifelong bachelor in an apparently modest way. In 1841, he was lodging with Mrs Grizel Welton at 49 Castle Street, not far from the office. His fellow lodgers were two servants Isabella Horsburgh (aged 50) and Helen Watson (aged 24); brickmaker William Cruikshank (aged 75) and Jean Wilson (aged 10). Nevertheless, in Edinburgh he was surrounded by a network of Argyll kinsmen and friends of his illustrious brother; the correspondence of the time suggests that he was active in maintaining his many contacts and social activities. For the time being, the costs of his lifestyle seem to have been under control, and there is no reason to believe that he was in any way incompetent or unprofessional. However, his life was about to unravel.

When Captain John was recalled to active service yet again in 1845, he was concerned about leaving his wife Sophy in sole charge. His brother, Colonel Patrick, now retired from the army, was of the opinion that a woman could not manage the estate and threatened to take charge at Dunollie. John seems also to have had some reservations about the support given to Sophy by Baxter and MacDougall. Allan's diary for 1845 shows that his financial state was no better and that he was prone to introspection; his 'resolutions' included:

11 Feby	To buy nothing on credit from this day
7 March	To take nothing on credit from this day
12 Jany 1846	To eat no fish or shellfish; to take walking exercise 2 hours daily

and he was particularly diligent in recording the text of each Sunday's sermon. By the middle of the year, his health had collapsed and he retreated to Dunollie, accompanied by a female servant, Ellen (probably Helen Watson, his fellow lodger). According to the local doctor, there was nothing seriously wrong with him, consistent with the family opinion that he was a hypochondriac: 'the doctor has fine times of it, six visits last week!' Allan simply needed a more regulated life, but Dunollie correspondence reveals his erratic patterns of eating, exercise and social contact. On one occasion he had packed his belongings to leave but, changing his mind, he left his luggage for a considerable time before unpacking and settling back into Dunollie. His diary records that, during a period of illness in January 1846, he was put out of his room for visitors. However, to the despair of Sophy, he stayed on until June 1848 when, with the return of Captain John from China, he moved out to Sims Hotel in Oban and then to stay with MacDougall relatives at Ardincaple House on Seil, at least from August 1848 to January 1849.

In spite of his poor health and irregular lifestyle, Allan remained attentive to his duties as factor of Baleveolan (Chapter Three). In these years of the Highland potato famine, he wrote regularly from Dunollie to his ground officer, John McColl, with detailed instructions for the help and control of the tenants, and kept in touch with his partners in Edinburgh. For a short time in the summer of 1850 he was back at the office in Castle Street, dealing with estate business but, on the night of the 1851 census (30 March) he was again staying at Dunollie. The surviving correspondence indicates that he did not return to work as a lawyer in Edinburgh and the postal directory for 1852/3 lists the firm as C&E Baxter W.S. at 32 Castle Street. It is likely that, owing to his indifferent health, there was no renewal of the ten year partnership agreement with the Baxters that had expired in 1848.

In his early fifties, Allan was single, homeless, and apparently without regular income. His affairs were in crisis early in 1853 when Charles Baxter wrote to John MacDougall to report that Allan was in danger of being imprisoned for a debt of £400. He appealed to John and his sisters not to desert him and to make

> an effort not only to raise sufficient funds to pay his debts (which are not of great account) but also by giving him employment, and remuneration for it, to place him in a position to support himself in time to come. *Charles Baxter to John MacDougall, 20 January 1853*

Baxter was clearly appalled that Allan's family, and nearby relations, had been using him to manage and improve their estates, without any thought of paying him for his work:

> since Allan left Edinburgh now upwards of five years, altho he has been much occupied with the Improvements of Ardincaple (draining etc) and working the slate quarries, besides drainage at Dunstaffnage, and other employment at Dunollie, he has never charged or recd a shilling for his extra labour, from any person. Indeed as I understood from him, he has been greatly out of pocket in consequence, and attributes his present difficulties chiefly to losses he has sustained in working the Ardincaple Quarries [on Seil Island], which have turned out, he says, a very losing concern.

Baxter's solution:

> I have no doubt he could be most usefully and beneficially employed on the Dunolly, Dunstaffnage, Ardincaple & Baleveolan Estates under the immediate superintendence of yourself, Sir Angus Campbell, Capt McDougall Ardincaple & Mr Locke.

This does not seem to have been taken seriously by the family but Allan's affairs settled down, at least for the time being. He was able to write to John on 23 April 1853 with the news that 'I have been at length able to quiet all the parties to whom I am due money & they like myself hope for better times'.

Until the autumn of 1856, he was resident mainly at his sister's house, Druimavuic, looking after the Baleveolan estates on Lismore and on the mainland, writing letters to John McColl the island ground officer, arranging building work on the

CHAPTER TWO

mainland, and keeping contact with his former partners in Edinburgh for legal work. He acted for C&E Baxter in the letting of Druimavuic House from 1855, since Ann was no longer resident (she had moved to Shrewsbury and died in 1858), and her son Captain Donald Campbell was serving with his regiment in the Crimea. This was a short lull; by December 1855, he was writing to his creditors explaining that he could not repay his debts ('I will in time be able to pay my debt to you & be the most thankful man in life') and, approaching sixty years of age, he was starting to look in earnest for paid work:

> My dear Sir
> An influential friend in the present govt to whom I applied for employment in any way connected with Agriculture has asked me to send my certificates as to qualifications. I am thus moved to trouble you to give me your opinion of my knowledge & practice in Draining
> *Extract from draft letter to D Campbell 28 Dec 1855*

His difficulties were compounded by the fact that his sister and her son had left him in charge at Druimavuic without arranging funds to pay for his work on the estate, and the necessary supplies:

> I have yours of the 9th July [1856]. There is no person I can apply to that would be security for your debt and Capt Campbell has treated every letter I have written him on the subject as he has done your own by taking no notice of them. ... Had I for a moment supposed he and his Edinr agents would have refused to pay your amount, it would never have been incurred, for not by

one single item of it have I been benefited – and your disappointments in regard to its settlement have solely arisen from the great disappointments I have myself met with. Had I the fourth part of the money I lost within the last five years, by the Glasgow agent recommended to me, or the fifteenth part of the cash I have lost within the same period, by the non-payment of accounts and money due to me, you would have long ago received the amount of your account. The result of my successive losses, have been, to leave me alas! nothing in the shape of personal effects, except the gold chain you will receive in a separate packet in the same post which conveys you this. It was purchased from the first goldsmith in Edinr & cost me £12 when new. The personal value I cannot tell you, you can learn. *Draft Allan MacDougall at Baleveolan by Bonawe, to Messrs Drysdale & Co., 33 Queen Street Glasgow (seedsmen & nurserymen)*

This letter, which confirms the honourable (but at times naïve) approach that Allan took in much of his work on Lismore, shows that he was in a very poor way. By the end of 1856 he had effectively lost control of the Lismore tenants and the Baxters had to intervene (Chapter Three). Allan sent his last letter as factor to John MacColl as ground officer in May 1857.

Retreating to Dunollie, and a series of lodgings in the Oban area, Allan tried to set himself up as an insurance agent:

Dear Sir

We are in receipt of yours of 19th curt. And have sent you by post a supply of stationery as requested. Mr Archd Campbell saddler is our agent for Oban, but that need not interfere with you as there is plenty room for both, the district being large. We hope to have some business from you soon and are Yours faithfully, H & J G Harrison. *United Kingdom Provident Institution, 17 George Street, Edinburgh. 21 Nov 1857*

He was to receive fifteen per cent commission on first premium, five per cent on renewals, on lives insured for £50 to £5000, but this was a false start. By spring 1858, he was writing to his brother for help in a new (clearly impractical) venture, as agent for Messrs Adam & McGregor 'to the wool growers in the West Highlands':

I am, as I have before intimated you, entitled to claim all my expenses in travelling upon Adam and McGregors business, until the 14th July next. My employers are very well pleased that I have not been putting them to expence on this account, but I consider it to be of the highest importance to me, that I soon begin to attend the chief markets, and to take an early opportunity of visiting such places as I think hold out prospects of benefit to myself and my constituents.

If I had the means to do this, I feel a firm assurance, that before autumn, I would find my branch of the wool business, well worth industry bestowed upon it, to a person in my present circumstances. If I had a credit at the National Bank, Oban, for £40 I could employ it twixt this, and the 14 July next, in going these rounds, and as the firm which employs me, cannot refuse to pay my advances, I would be able by Martinmass to refund the money drawn from the bank, and thus free my cautioner, from the necessity of putting his hand in his pocket to assist me. *Allan to John, 16 Aprl 1858.*

The underlying problem was that Allan had already borrowed heavily from his brother:

> I expressed in writing my deep regret at the amount of my debt to you, and my inability to pay it, and since July last when you introduced that subject in conversation, I repented the unhappiness I felt at being unable to acquire the means of paying you and said it was I believe greatly occasioned by the bad health I had suffered from for many years. Can I now say more in reply to your remarks, than that I believe, as my general health is greatly improved ...

In his work for Messrs Adam & McGregor Wool Brokers, Leith, he had made contact with nearly 250 potential suppliers but, whether or not he was fleeced in the process, he soon departed from Edinburgh in search of paid work:

> When you were so kind as ask me what I would require to come here to look for employment, I told you I though I would have little chance of success, if I could not command from £20 to £30. With the sum you have given me, I have done my utmost to obtain employment but have not yet succeeded. I still however think I would succeed if I had £10 more. *Allan at 14 Hope Street, Edinburgh, to John, 22 March 1859*

Moving on to Glasgow during 1860, his failed attempts to set himself up in the wine trade and in the manufacture of 'chemical manures' in a period of economic depression resulted in a flood of begging letters to his brother John, his youngest sister Colina and the Baxters, in the spring of 1863:

> I am preparing to meet my extreme of poverty – what gives me most pain is the inability to meet the just claims of the good people who have been furnishing me with the necessities of life. *15 April 1864*
>
> I hope you will now for the <u>last time in this life</u> help me, to let me pay my lodgings. *18 April 1864*

The MacDougall family had other issues to face, and Allan disappears largely from the correspondence from this point, probably because John's successors did not keep Allan's letters. Having achieved the rank of Rear Admiral, John died in 1865, to be succeeded by his son, Captain Alexander, who himself died in 1867 and was followed as 27th Chief by his brother Charles. Allan held on until 31 July 1876, dying of 'general debility and old age' at Gartnavel Royal Lunatic Asylum, Partick, Glasgow, aged 78. In spite of his hypochondria, he had outlived all of his siblings.

Chapter Three
The Improvement of Baleveolan

Allan MacDougall's determination to improve the farming on Lismore, and deal with the chronic arrears that burdened the tenants, has been almost entirely forgotten, whereas the clearing activity of James Cheyne during the same years is still fresh in the minds of islanders. Until recently, it was only because of the survival, by chance, of eighty six letters to the ground officers of the Baleveolan estate on Lismore that we knew what MacDougall was trying to achieve between 1833 and 1845. However, the opening of the Dunollie archive in 2011 has now made available not only a wide range of MacDougall's correspondence at different stages in his life (Chapter Two), but also, against all expectations, the continuation of his ground officer correspondence from 1846 to 1857. It is not clear how the thirty six letters to John McColl at Portcastle on Lismore could have made their way back to Dunollie, but they provide further evidence of MacDougall's activity during the potato famine and subsequent years.

The Baleveolan Estate on Lismore

The history of Lismore is inextricably bound up with the history of the ruling Campbells. John Stewart, Lord of Lorn (including Lismore), was killed in 1462, without a legitimate male heir. He intended that the lordship should pass to his brother Walter, rather than his two daughters Isabella and Janet, who had married the two leading Campbells of the day (Colin, 1st Earl of Argyll, and his uncle, Colin, Lord of Glenorchy). However, Walter was unable to cope with the warring factions in the area and, in 1470, agreed to a legal transaction, by which Lorn was surrendered to the Campbells in exchange for land in the East of Scotland. Argyll became the feudal Lord of Lorn and, in recognition of Janet Stewart's claim, the Lords of Glenorchy (later Earls of Breadalbane) gained possession of one third of the lordship; this portion included the Lismore townships of Balimakillichan (including Portcastle and Creckanbreck), Portcharron, Baleveolan (including Sailean), Killean, Achnacroish (including Newfield), Tirlaggan and Baligrundle with Tirewin. As has frequently been observed, the Campbells gained more from the marriage bed and the law courts than by the sword.

By 1751 (Table 1.1), the Breadalbane lands on Lismore had passed through the hands of Patrick Campbell of Barcaldine to his heirs. His son, Colin Campbell of Glenure (the "Red Fox" of the Appin Murder), received Baligrundle, Achnacroish, Killean and Portcharron, leaving Baleveolan and Balimakillichan (together known as the Baleveolan estate) for his kinsman John Campbell, on the distaff side of the family. John's landholding on the mainland was at Druimavuic, next to Glenure, but the family chose to use the title of Campbell of Baleveolan.

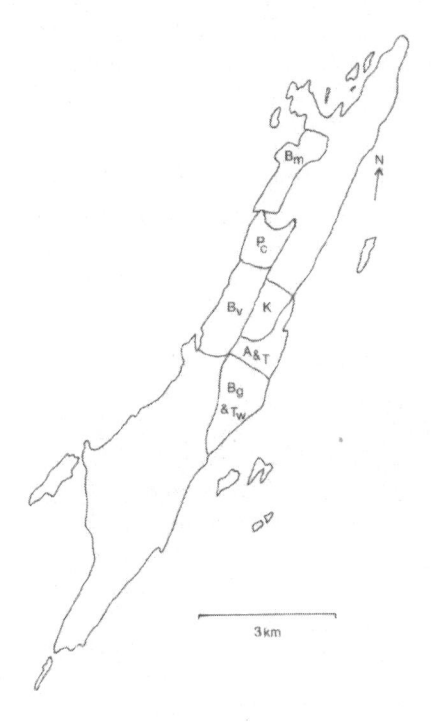

Fig. 3.1 Sketch Map of the Lord of Glenorchy's Lands on Lismore, 1470

(A&T Achnacroish & Tirlaggan; Bg &Tw Baligrundle & Tierewin, with the islands; Bm Balimakillichan, including Creckanbreck & Portcastle; Bv Baleveolan with Sailean; K Killean; Pc Portcharron)

The Baleveolan Estate and its Community in 1830 (Appendix 1)

Taking on the role of factor, Allan MacDougall found himself responsible for a community of over 150, tenants and cottars, indigenous people of all ages. The estate had been transformed by the first wave of improvement, principally the abolition of runrig and multiple tenancies. Demarcation into infield and outfield had disappeared, and each of the original townships had been divided into distinct farms and crofts with single tenants. Around half of the total of approximately 600 acres (250 ha) was good ploughland, free of ridges of limestone and steep slopes, but cliffs separated the lower-lying Portcastle and Sailean from the undulating higher upper areas (Fig. 3.2; Plates 2,3). However, the land still lay in rig and furrow, with some enclosure, including head dykes dividing the arable from rough grazing. All of the tenants had rights to grazing on the common land between the Baleveolan and Balimakillichan townships.

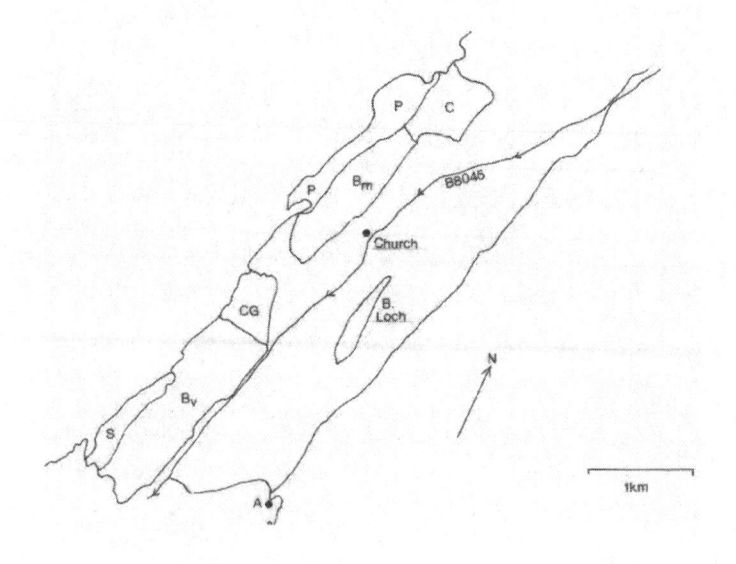

Fig. 3.2 Baleveolan Estate
(A Achnacroish; Bm Balimakillichan; Bv Baleveolan; B Loch Balnagown Loch; C Creckanbreck; CG Common Grazing; P Portcastle; S Sailean)

The Druimavuic Campbells did not have a particularly good record as landlords on the island. Between 1798 and 1801, the laird, Donald Campbell, had tried to evict several of his tenants in Balimakillichan and Baleveolan without recognising their legal rights. He and his Inveraray lawyer, AR Bell, were confident of the strength of their position, although Bell did warn Campbell:

> You'll please observe, that a party of the Military cannot be applied for until a Sheriff officer shall first try to Eject the defenders, & unless he is deforced [resisted with violence], Which I suppose the defrs [defendants] dare not attempt. *Bell to Campbell of Baleveolan, 25 May 1799*

However, the islanders that he targeted turned out to be highly resourceful. They employed their own lawyer, who established that, although the tenants did not have written tacks, the payment in advance that had been demanded on entry (a grassum) gave them security of tenure over the period of their lease. The struggle in the court at Inveraray continued for three years, by which time Campbell had lost interest in the process. In due course, the McGlashans, McKenzies and McLachlans departed from their tenancies, and the last of the McKeichs were removed from Creckanbreck in 1831. However, the next generation of Blacks and McIntyres were still on the estate in the 1830s and memories of their treatment by the Campbells must have played a part in their responses to the changes instituted by the estate factor.

By 1827, when Peter and Ann Campbell took possession of the estate on Lismore, the tenancies were still on a verbal basis. The tenants were summoned to the mainland in person twice a year at or after Martinmas (28 November) and Whitsunday (28 May) to pay their rents in cash (£460 in total; 1831 rental) but they were also required to deliver forty five bolls of oatmeal (milled on the island at Balnagown) and two bolls of oats for horses each year, for the use of the landlord's family or for sale. The business of the estate was conducted through a ground officer, based on the island. The individual farm rents, at something over £1 per acre, were in line with those for generally inferior land in Baligrundle (Chapter Five). Most of the cottars on the townships were expected to pay £1 each year but they were liable to be summoned to Druimavuic to provide labour. The exception was John McCorquodale, the Baleveolan publican, who was charged £3 10s for his 'dram shop'. Although the requirement for tenants and cottars to supplement their rent by providing other products in kind had been largely abandoned, Ann Campbell would, from time to time, send for hens and eggs, or a cow for slaughter.

Appendix 1 combines information from the 1841 and 1851 censuses and the 1831 and 1844 rentals to outline the communities of Baleveolan and Balimakillichan in the 1830s. All of the people on the estate were from indigenous Lismore families, and most of the tenants were middle-aged men with younger wives, and several young children at home. Three generations were crowded into some dwellings. These were the survivors of the attempted evictions around 1800 (Blacks and McIntyres) and new blood, from elsewhere on Lismore, introduced since then. Their farms were relatively small (mean area around thirty acres), but slightly larger on the generally better land of Baleveolan. The exception to the rule was Coll Livingstone, the Baron of Bachuil (hereditary keeper of the staff of St Moluag) who had fourteen acres freehold at Bachuil in addition to a partnership with his brother Duncan on Balimakillichan. He acted as ground officer for the estate up to his death in 1842, when he was succeeded by his son Alexander. From 1846, this role was filled by John McColl, brother of the tenant of Portcastle.

CHAPTER THREE

The Lismore cottars provided essential services to the island: the 1841 census lists carpenters and joiners, a wright, smiths, millers, a mason, quarrymen and lime burners, tailors and a shepherd. The island still had seven handloom weavers, producing woollen cloth, and four of them were on Baleveolan estate, together with a shoemaker and a publican. The widow Mary Stewart and her son John (Appendix 1) would later prosper as general merchants, building the substantial Hawthorn House in the 1860s. However, in 1832, she was still very poor, writing to the Baleveolan factor:

> Now as your petitioner has got liberty to build the house; she presumes to ask liberty from you to take few of the stones in the broken wall of the old house formerly possessed by the tenant on the farm to make up her house, as it requires more stones when built of new. *Petition Mary Stewart to Allan MacDougall, 26 June 1832.*

In general, the people were not to be underestimated. In particular, they were well informed about the world outside Lismore and beyond Scotland, many were literate, and the census returns show that they sent their children to school. Several belonged to families that had taken, or would take, the decision to emigrate to the New World for a better life. Duncan McDonald, writing from Cape Breton to his brother Gilbert at Frackersaig on Lismore in the 1840s and 1850s, was continually asking about his kinsman John Mòr (John McKellaich the Baleveolan tenant) and sending news of their relations to the Graham cottars. In the same period, five of the younger Livingstones (Bachuil and Balimakillichan) set off for Illinois. Later, in the 1870s and 1880s, John MacDugald, cottar on Balimakillichan, handloom weaver, and Sunday School

Superintendent at Achuaran for thirty years, featured in a long correspondence with members of his family in Glasgow and America, mainly Minnesota.

Allan MacDougall as an Improving Factor

With the return of his brother John in 1833 to active service in the navy, Allan MacDougall took over the factorship of Baleveolan, looking after the interests of his widowed sister Ann and her son, Donald Campbell. He inherited a situation in which most of the tenants were in arrears: seven of the eleven could not meet their payments due at Martinmas 1834, the deficit amounting to over £29 (12% of the half-year total). By Martinmas 1840, they were all in arrears (over £138 or around 62%) and there were arrears of meal delivered. The Livingstones had failed to pay their full rent, even though Coll was ground officer, and the Buchanans were in a difficult position, owing more than half a year's rent. Across the Highlands, tenants were in trouble following a series of poor harvests affecting all crops, almost certainly related to the major eruption of the Coseguina Volcano in Nicaragua in 1835 (Chapter One). There was real hardship on the island, necessitating the distribution of food aid by the parish minister in 1838.

In the first few years of his factorship, MacDougall tried simply to secure the income from the estate and to ensure that the tenants took care of the land. In his first letters to his ground officer, he took a firm line about the recovery of rents from tenants and cottars:

> You will be so good as intimate to the tenants that I am to collect the rents upon Wednesday the 26 of June.

CHAPTER THREE

I have put off the day to give the tenants as much time as possible to prepare for you will mention to them as I have now to make up my accounts. I can take nothing but the full rent. *Allan MacDougall to Coll Livingstone, 27 May 1833*

I propose collecting the arrears here upon Monday the 26th Augt of which you will inform the tenants – You will also be so good as say to the cottars that those who wish to work out their arrears will come here [Druimavuic] either upon Wednesday or Thursday first to do so. Those who prefer paying will either come then or upon the 26th and those who do neither you will warn off the land. *Allan MacDougall to Coll Livingstone, 8 August 1833*

In the face of a worsening situation, he continued to insist on full payment but, by 1838, with arrears mounting, he had to face up to the fact that the financial position of the tenants meant that there could be no early resolution.

Three options were open to him. The simplest would have been to evict the tenants out of hand, but this would have meant the total loss of the arrears owing; and in the poor state of the agricultural economy at that time, it might have been difficult to find suitable replacements. On the other hand, the parish minister claimed that the Lismore rents were high because of *competition* for a restricted supply of tenancies. The second option, also involving the removal of the tenants, would have been to follow the trend elsewhere and turn the estate into an extensive sheepwalk. This would also have resulted in the loss of arrears and required a considerable investment in stock and enclosure. MacDougall chose a third way, presumably with the agreement of his sister:

> You will also inform the tenants that they must each have made some improvement on their lands before next collection, otherwise they need not look for their getting much delay in paying their arrears. Tell them that as I have done so much for them, I now want to see how much they will do for themselves. Let each tenant therefor shew you what improvements he intends making on his possession, and then shew you it when made, and you will report the improvement made by each tenant at the collection in June. I will then be able to judge how long they should get to pay their arrears.
> *Allan MacDougall to Coll Livingstone, 20 January 1838*

According to his plan, the tenants would carry out approved schemes of improvement on their farms (drainage, enclosure, tree planting), under the direction of the ground officer. Their work would then be valued and set against their arrears. In principle, this would be to the benefit of both sides: for the tenant, relief of debt, and for the owner, the recovery of arrears of rent in the form of capital improvement of the land. However, it committed the tenants to additional heavy labour, over and above the work of securing the annual harvest. MacDougall had embarked on the difficult role of improving factor, but it is clear that his sister had little idea of the physical demands made on the tenants:

> We wish you to send those of the tenants that are short in arrears to do some work about the place. I suppose most of the potatoes are now planted so they cannot have much to do they better come on Monday the 6th.
> *Ann Campbell Locke to Alexander Livingstone, 1 May 1844*

CHAPTER THREE

Draining

The primary limits to arable crop production in the West Highlands were soil acidity and excessive soil moisture. Lime was available in large quantities from Kilcheran, at least until the 1820s, and there was an early lime business based on Baligrundle. It is not clear how active the Kilcheran kilns were after the departure of the seminary (see Chapter 5), but the Park lime works, at the north end of the island, were in operation from at least 1830. The Sailean quarry and kilns on the Baleveolan estate would become a major industrial site in the second half of the century but, as shown by the difficulties MacDougall experienced in securing lime in 1847 (see below), production at that time was sporadic and not under the management of the factor. Major developments were under way in the 1850s: in 1855, Allan MacDougall employed Dr Thomas Anderson, an analytical chemist in Glasgow, to assess the potential of Lismore lime for building purposes; and, the next year, John MacIntyre was planning a new quay for lime export from Sailean by sea. Over the coming decades, the commercial success of the MacIntyre family in providing paid employment at the Sailean lime works for up to sixteen men, as well as cargoes for the fleet of Lismore sailing smacks, was to be a crucial factor in the economy of the island.

Liming the arable land had become standard practice on Lismore, removing one of the primary limits. With a good grounding in agricultural practice, MacDougall, therefore, gave priority to drainage on the estate. The arable land was managed as rig and furrow, with the ridges, normally around two metres between furrows, aligned with the slope of the land so that excess water was carried away by the furrows. This was an unsatisfactory solution for three reasons. First it involved the laborious repairing of the rigs each Spring when the soil was wet and difficult to manage. Secondly, the furrow was wasted land, usually infested with rushes and other weeds, and thirdly, without a systematic arrangement to carry the water away, it was common for higher ground to flood lower areas. In the 1830s, the system devised by James Smith of Deanston was being introduced into the lowlands and MacDougall was keen to bring this state of the art technology to the island, providing a copy of Smith's pamphlet to his ground officer in 1844. The approach, which became standard across the country, was to develop an array of parallel underground drainage channels, which discharged into a main drain that carried the water away to the nearest watercourse. The channels, dug below existing furrows so that they were thirty inches below the soil surface, were to be filled with twelve inches of stones of diameter less than three inches, and the tops sealed off to prevent the channels becoming clogged by soil. On more affluent estates, files of hollow ceramic tiles replaced the bed of stones (Plate 4).

Introducing this technology to Baleveolan estate took time, and MacDougall was still urging the tenants to make progress in his last years as factor. He insisted that any drainage scheme should be approved before the work started, and carried out to a high specification; and even called on the parish minister to make sure that the ground officer was taking his instructions seriously:

> ... it is found that furrow draining is the best, that is, to put the drain in the hollow betwixt the ridges, one is put in every furrow, or every second furrow, according as it is thought the ground requires it. *Allan MacDougall to Coll Livingstone, 20 January 1838*

CHAPTER THREE

... no stones are to be put into a drain until he [Coll] satisfies himself that it has been properly cut and that after the stones have been put in, that no drain is to be covered over until he is satisfied that it has been properly filled vzt that there is a proper run at the bottom for the water, & that the stones employed to fill the drain are not too large, & he is to consider every stone above 2 ½ in diameter as too large. *Allan MacDougall to the Rev Gregor McGregor, 9 January 1840*

I hope the tenants will attend before filling up their drains to place a thin layer of turf above the stones this prevents the earth getting down amongst the stones and choking the drains. *Allan MacDougall to Coll Livingstone, 15 January 1840*

Digging these drains was very heavy work for the tenants, especially as it had to be completed in the winter before sowing time in spring. In many areas of the island, the topsoil is shallow, overlying compacted gravel and stone that would have had to be broken up by pick. They also had to maintain the open ditches that intercepted the water from above their land, and ensure that existing drains were kept clear. Large quantities of clean stone had to be carted from the shore, and sieved to the correct size. On at least one of the farms, the tenants had other problems:

I thought Myles & Duncan Black would themselves see that it is impossible to say what allowance ought to be made them for work only part finished and you did quite right in telling them first to finish the drains at least the part cut through rock and they may then be estimated. *Allan MacDougall to Alexander Livingstone, 11 November 1844*

Nevertheless, they did persist, under encouragement and criticism, and some did benefit significantly from their work:

- 1846 June 22 By allowance for 95 roods drains at 2/- entered in rent book £9.10.0
- 1848 December 18th By allowance for 64 roods drains at 2/- £6.8.0
- 1852 June 23 By dyke and drains £12.8.6
- [Total] £28.6.6

Extract from Miles Black's passbook in a letter from Allan MacDougall to John McColl, 22 December 1853

Enclosure and Planting

There was little rough grazing beyond the head dykes on much of the island and, since the Baleveolan estate was divided into farms before improved rotations brought pasture into the arable area, most of the livestock would have been sent to the estate common grazing for the duration of the crop growing season. In addition to the drystone dykes separating the new holdings, each would have had at least one enclosed field next to the dwelling house for the return of the livestock in the winter. As with the traditional wintertown of the old multiple tenancies, this secured all of the winter manure for the following crop.

With a view to the need for a set of enclosed fields on each holding if a six course rotation was to be adopted (see below), MacDougall encouraged enclosure, but wanted the tenants to use the new dykes to protect new tree planting, for shelter:

> In laying off the dykes your brother Hugh Carmichael & Dond McCorqudale have to build I hope there is

space left for a little planting. *Allan MacDougall to Coll Livingstone, 15 January 1840*

... if in dyke building they remove rocks from their fields so much the better. Any who wish to plant for shelter I will supply the trees if they promise to keep them enclosed from cattle & sheep. *Allan MacDougall to Coll Livingstone, 20 January 1838*

As an incentive, the estate met the cost of the planting but it was made clear that damage to the young trees caused by straying livestock would not be tolerated. The legislation of the time was very severe, even allowing for transportation of serial offenders.

I hope you will not fail to intimate to the tenants all I have said to you about their cattle or sheep trespassing within the wood enclosures, as in the event of damage being done I am resolved they shall pay a legal penalty. *Allan MacDougall to Alexander Livingstone, 14 March 1845*

The Rob Roy steamer would take 6000 forest plants this day from Glasgow for you and I daresay D Rankin will be with you on Thursday to plant them. ... You can tell Rankin that I am not for his leaving the island until he sees all his planting out of damage from Cattle and sheep. *Allan MacDougall to Alexander Livingstone, 1 April 1845*

MacDougall laid down very clear specifications for the new dykes (Plate 6) but, as for drainage, he was clear that, wherever possible, the work should be done by the tenants, to alleviate their arrears:

I have letters from Dugald Carmichael and the McColls offering to build the dyke required to enclose the planting they both offered to do it for 2/6 per rood, the McColls do not specify the height, D. Carmichael says 3 & ½ feet high with a flat stone cap. I have written them both that I want a dyke 4 feet high with a flat stone cap and proportional thickness at top and bottom, and to be finished on or before the 20th of August next, and that each of the tenants is to build that portion of the dyke that passes their lands. *Allan MacDougall to Alexander Livingstone, 26 April 1845*

Rotations

Drainage and dyking work was paid for by the estate by the reduction of arrears due, but in his attempts to bring his tenants into line with the improved Lowland practice of crop rotation, the factor was employing a different strategy: securing future rents by increasing yields, and reducing the risks of low income, by diversification. The tenants were to adopt the rotations but the estate was to meet the extra costs, with a view to recovering these over a longer period. Although the adoption of the potato in the latter part of the eighteenth century had brought some variation, cereals ('white crops') remained the primary crops on Lismore farms, with alternation between the short-season bere barley (prized for distilling) and oats, grown at a relatively low level of fertility, with limited input of manure. With generations of experience behind them, the Baleveolan tenants were not inclined to change. Although they were assured that farm incomes could be higher and more stable, they were inclined to adhere to a system that ensured 'some yield every year'.

In 1838, MacDougall first proposed that all of the tenants should adopt a standard six course rotation: Year 1 – cereal (normally bere) undersown with grasses and clover; Years 2 to 4 – hay and grazing; Year 5 – cereal (normally oats); Year 6 – green crop (potatoes, turnips).

> I have yours of the 17th. I now enclose you a copy of the Rotations of Cropping I sent your father. You will observe that every tenants possession must be in six divisions. Those tenants who began the system laid down for 1838 should next spring be sowing oats in the same field that carried that crop in that year. You will see that I do not allow two white crops in succession and that the land must ly two years in pasture after hay. Every intelligent farmer know such a system as I lay down is more profitable for him than the old mode which scourged the land and those tenants who do not choose to adopt the system I lay down must just leave the lands. *Allan MacDougall to Alexander Livingstone, 20 November 1843*

This was a revolutionary change to the pattern of farming but it had several potential benefits for the Lismore farmer. The inclusion of pasture improved soil tilth, suppressed perennial weeds, and increased the soil fertility directly though fixation of nitrogen by clover and indirectly through enhancement in the quantity and quality of the manure from grazing livestock. Perhaps more importantly, the fact that only half of the land had to be ploughed each spring reduced the annual energy input (human and draught) and the risks associated with a late wet Spring. Higher quality grazing and more secure winter feeding (hay and turnips) offered the prospect of much higher incomes from more, bigger and healthier cattle and sheep; but, of course, the tenants had to ensure that their livestock, now grazing on the arable land in the growing season, were controlled by adequate fencing or walling round each of the six divisions to keep them out of the cereals, potatoes and turnips. Overall, the diversification of farming brought in by the new rotation promised greater stability in farm incomes since, for example, a poor cereal harvest could be compensated for by income from livestock.

The changes involved significant investment on the part of the estate. For example, the estate paid around £12 each year to supply and transport grass and clover seed:

> I have yours of the 24th and have purchased and dispatched the clover & ryegrass seed which you will let the tenants understand I send upon the express condition that they conform to the rotation of croping I have laid down and I will thank you to be prepared to inform me who do not adopt and keep the rule I have made. *Allan MacDougall to Coll Livingstone, 27 March 1840*

Achieving this revolution on Baleveolan estate was proving difficult. Some of the tenants were totally resistant and, as late as 1844, were offering 'to pay up their rent and arrears, rather that adopt a proper rotation of cropping' (*MacDougall to Alexander Livingstone, 28 May*). Evidence presented to the Napier Commissioners shows that, forty years later, Lismore tenants were still complaining about estate regulations to prevent two cereal crops in succession. The ground officers were kept busy trying to police the new rules:

> I have not got a note from you of the names of the tenants who have been ploughing a part of their young grass. I also want to have the names of all tenants who are taking two white crops in succession, if any have

done so. Those who continue to transgress the rules I have already so often laid down shall be no longer tenants under my charge. *Allan MacDougall to John MacColl, 29 March 1847*

By 1844, MacDougall was acting to deal with one of the technical problems that arose out of the new rotations. As elsewhere in Scotland, the phosphate supply by the soil proved to be insufficient for the turnip crop. In some areas, the solution was bone meal, but he opted for the guano now being imported from Peru:

I find the guano only left Glasgow yesterday. I hope it may not be carried to Inverness. Be so good as send me a sample of the guano that I may satisfy myself as to the quality of the article furnished by the Messrs Downie. ... If the weather has been as dry with you as it has been here for the last month, it is perhaps as well that the turnip seed sowing has been delayed by the non arrival of the guano. *Allan MacDougall to Alexander Livingstone, 28 May 1844*

He was also keen to ensure that the 'ecological benefits' of the new rotations, including the conservation manures and of mineral nutrients, were fully exploited. For example:

I have a letter from McCorqudale (to whom I wrote that I would have to prosecute him for mismanaging the lands), that he wants a house [byre] for his cattle to enable him to keep them upon the Baleveolan lands. He is to build the house at his own cost, and I wish you to point out a stance for it. I have written him that he must consume the manure he makes, and the straw, hay & turnips he grows upon the lands, and I beg you will see that he does so hereafter. *Allan MacDougall to Alexander Livingstone, 13 July 1844*

and towards the end of his time as factor, he was recommending further diversification of the cropping to include mangels, carrots, parsnips and beet to reduce reliance on the potato.

Other Inducements

In 1841, following the lead of the Highland and Agricultural Society, and local agricultural societies, MacDougall resolved to reward the most cooperative tenants financially and in kind, as an encouragement to the others. He proposed to give free seed for the best kept fields, and:

> for the best 1 year old quey [heifer] at the 1 May rent (1842) I will give £1.1 and the best 1 year old stot [bullock] on the 1 May next I will give £1.1 and the second best quey I will give half a guinea, & the second best stot the same money. The quey or stot will be considered one year old even tho calved after this date but they must be bred by a tenant from a cow belonging to himself and in his own possession. *Allan MacDougall to Coll Livingstone, 1 May 1841*

He must have thought that this strategy had borne fruit because, in 1847, he repeated the premiums on offer for the best crops:

> I hope the tenants are doing all that men can do, to put their land in good order. I am going to give a prize to the three tenants who upon the 1 July next have

their lands and crops in best order. *Allan MacDougall to John MacColl, 29 March 1847*

Allan MacDougall and the Potato Famine

By the autumn of 1846, the full severity of the potato disease epidemic was apparent, with the crop a total loss on Lismore. Although in poor health, living at Dunollie, MacDougall reacted quickly to the needs of the Baleveolan community. On 12 October he wrote to John McColl, offering to contribute £5 for the purchase of fishing hooks and long lines for tenants and cottars who were already experiencing food shortages: 'let me know how you think I can best bestow the money in the way of giving work & food'. It is significant that, for once, MacDougall showed concern for the cottars. In the event, the sea proved a partial saviour:

> The herring fishing for the last three years has been a failure, but during the last fortnight a large shoal has been passing the island; the poor were at first unprepared for such abundance, but soon procured the necessary articles from Oban, and they have since been very successful. *Captain Pole to Sir E P Coffin, 3 October 1846.*

According to the parish minister, Rev. Gregor MacGregor:

> The poor would derive great advantage from encouragement as fishermen. Lines for cod fishing and nets for mackarel [sic] fishing are much required by many of the poor. If £2 worth of lines etc were given to about 30 families it would set them up for the next spring fishing, so that they would get on through the next summer. *Pole to Coffin, 3 October 1846*

In 1847, MacDougall was providing practical advice and help to the tenants to adapt to the inability to grow potatoes:

> As to the ground where potatoes should be this year, each tenant must sow half the ground with turnip seed. I would advise every tenant to plough immediately the ground he had his diseased crop of potatoes on last year that the air & particularly the frost, may destroy the rotten matter while in the ground. *Allan MacDougall to John MacColl, 3 February 1847*

> When you see the tenants you will say to them from me in reply to their letter, that I cannot supply them with seed & that therefore they must supply themselves with oats and barley, and as to the potatoes I do not think there will be any seed for sale so far at least as I can learn. If Government should send seed of any kind for sale to this country, I will see that they get it upon as favourable terms as others. *Allan MacDougall to John MacColl, 27 February 1847*

There was a perception that the tenants, at least, on Lismore were not in a serious predicament:

> The Government Agent here [Oban] has intimated to me, that upon my furnishing him with the name of the tenant, property, and quantity of seed, corn, or barley, etc, which a tenant may be purchasing at any port, say Glasgow etc a government steamer will be prepared to take delivery of it there, and deliver it carriage free at any port desired say Port Appin etc. You will understand from the above, that all the government mean to do is <u>to save the tenant the water carriage</u> of the seed. This

offer will I daresay be of consequence to tenants in the Outer Isles, but to places where steamers now call twice or thrice a week it will be of little use. *Allan MacDougall to John MacColl, 4 March 1847*

It seems that the tenants adapted quickly to the new circumstances because blight is scarcely mentioned in MacDougall's correspondence with John McColl after 1846, apart from the offer of resistant seed potatoes in late summer 1848, and the encouragement to grow alternative 'green crops' in 1854. In fact, the position of the Baleveolan tenants actually *improved* during the famine years, as shown by the statements of rents and arrears for Martinmas 1845 and 1847. In 1845, all of the tenants paid their rent in full, with Dugald McCorquodale the limeburner paying off £5 of his arrears in cash. By 1847, the tenants were still able to pay in full, and eight out of twelve had reduced their arrears. The total of arrears in 1845 was £420 but, over two years, this had fallen to £339 (reduction of 20%, Table 3.1), principally owing to allowances for Improvements (see Miles Black's payments for draining above).

Of the cottars, only one elderly woman required emergency support by the parish in 1846, although there were three more estate paupers on the poor list by 1847. Compared with communities elsewhere on the island (Chapter Five), the people on Baleveolan estate were relatively unaffected by the famine.

Table 3.1 Rent Arrears on the Baleveolan Estate, 1845 and 1847

Balimakillichan	Half year rent	Arrears 1845	Arrears 1847
Hugh Carmichael	10 12 6	57 8 8½	40 5 8½
Duncan Livingston	13 12	33 14 6	8 19 3
Dugald McCorqudale	15 15	39 0 3	38 4 9
Donald M Black	15 14	38 5	42 19
D & J McColl	16 10	13	19 5
Dugald McCorqudale	15 7 6	33 10	15 7 6
D & D Carmichael	13	17 12	14 7
Baleveolan			
J&A Buchanan	25 10 0	72 6 4½	61 12 0
D&D Black	26 10 0	53 6 0	45 18 0
Miles Black	14 2 0	30 16 4½	21 6 4½
John McKellach	28	31 0 9	31 0 9
Dugald McIntyre	16		
Totals	£210 13s 0d	£419 19s 11½d	£338 15s 4d

CHAPTER THREE

The Improvements by 1857

The factor experienced a great deal of frustration in his attempts to bring about the changes that he thought necessary for the stewardship of the estate. In the 1840s, he was discouraged by the lack of progress in working off arrears but chose to continue this policy (even though he reveals in a letter in the 1850s that he had been 'reflected upon for letting the tenants remain in arrears' – presumably by the Lockes).

In spite of the continued opposition offered by the tenants, a great deal had changed by the time that he ceased to be factor in 1857. Substantial progress had been made in drainage and enclosure, and it had become normal to include turnips and pasture on the arable land. By the 1850s, he had moved on to try to upgrade the tenants' buildings:

> I will thank you to let me know how many of the tenants have availed themselves of my proposal as to the improvement of their homes. You need not do this however before the 10th of June. *Allan MacDougall to John MacColl, 29 May 1854*

However, his final letter leaves the impression that he realised that there was still much to do:

> I have your favour of the 6th May. I am happy to receive the thanks of the tenants. To make my satisfaction perfect, let me hear, that all are ploughing & cleaning their Lismore land, deeply, and with great care, and that after sowing the seed, they thin out, and clean and stir the soil, with equal care. That they preserve their manure with great care, and laid it in sufficient quantities upon the turnip land. He who ploughs the ground sufficiently

often, gives it several harrowings, cleans it well as above, and dungs it well deserves, & will have the best return.
Allan MacDougall to John MacColl, 9 May 1857

In the same letter, he took the opportunity to reflect on the difficulties of promoting intensive livestock on the island, producing finished carcasses for the butcher:

I went into Oban yesterday to purchase some butcher meat. I found the only mutton for sale was killed in Glasgow, & sent to Oban to sell, & was selling from 6½d to 7d the lb. I was ashamed to find, that the tenants in the District of Lorn, could not themselves keep Oban in eatable mutton. What right has a tenant in Lorn, to complain of the times, when mutton is selling at his door for 7d per lb. There are as good sheep produced in Lorn as in Lanarkshire or the Lothians, and I know from 30 years experience, that the soil of Lorn, is as good for turnips as other, and the <u>climate better</u>. Whenever the Baleveolan tenants will secure the planting agt. sheep they may keep them. You know what I have already said on this subject.

Allan MacDougall as an Evicting Factor

There was an unspoken agreement between MacDougall and the tenants that he had inherited that they would remain in possession as long as they paid their rent and obeyed the instructions issued by him; and that normally the eldest son would inherit the tenancy. Although they do not appear to have had written leases, their financial dealings with the estate were done formally through passbooks. The situation had changed by 1845, when the negotiations for the vacant farm of Portcastle showed that the estate was moving towards a more standard written lease for nineteen years – the duration normally regarded as long enough for the tenant to benefit from any improvements he may have made:

> If you will offer £35 for the lands and agree to conform to the rules of the property, (and I never suggest one which I do not know to be as much for the tenants interest as the landlords, as I consider them one and the same) I will give you these lands for any length of lease you think proper not exceeding 19 years, and will also allow you a sum equal to a years rent for improvements in draining etc. when made by my consent, to my satisfaction, & that they are estimated by two persons mutually chosen as worth that sum according to the usual price paid for such work in the district.
> *Allan MacDougall to Duncan Carmichael, Craignich, 16 January 1845*

Arrears of rent were a chronic problem and the ground officer correspondence over 24 years charts MacDougall's attempts to recover them in the long term, while remaining patient with, and at times supportive of, the sitting tenants. There were exceptions, however, and these cases reveal the limits to his tolerance.

Hugh Carmichael in Creckanbreck
In 1831, Hugh Carmichael, the thirty year old son of John Carmichael, tenant in Balnagown on Lismore, was selected by John MacDougall in place of Duncan McKeich who had been evicted from Creckanbreck. By 1840, he was in arrears of rent, although not as seriously as the other tenants, but he was proving to be a thorn in the flesh of the factor:

> I would ask Hugh how it happens that from first to last he has given me more trouble than all the rest of the tenants. He seems a well meaning creature, but I fear he much neglects his own labours and interest and he has now more than once done his promise. *Allan MacDougall to the Rev. Gregor MacGregor, 28 January 1840*

The problem seems to have involved irregularities in the sale of his crops, but he was also reluctant to play his part in improvements:

> Say to Hugh Carmichael that I suspect he will have to prepare to remove himself from the lands he occupies as he is neither draining or otherwise finishing the improvements pointed out to him and not getting out of debt to the Landlord. *Allan MacDougall to Alexander Livingstone, 20 Nov 1843*

Surprisingly, the factor tolerated his lack of cooperation until the 1850s, when Carmichael had to go:

> I am of the opinion I expressed to you, Hugh Carmichael having had so many opportunities & years, to do better, his stock must now be sold, so you can speak to the auctioneer, hold the sale, and place the bills in Mr Gregorsons bank for me. *Allan MacDougall to John McColl, 9 May 1857*

By 1861, John Keith, who had been away from Lismore on Bute for many years, had succeeded as the farmer of fifty acres of Creckanbreck, and Hugh Carmichael was listed as a quarryman living away from the Baleveolan estate at Point where he died in 1885.

CHAPTER THREE

The MacCorquodales in Balimakillichan

Dugald, eldest son of Donald and Sarah MacCorquodale, tenants in Balimakillichan, rented a smallholding on the township in the 1830s, although remaining in the family home. He was a troublesome crofter, falling into arrears and breaking the estate regulations by 'consuming crop off the estate', although, in 1844, he proposed to solve the problem by building a byre on one of the Baleveolan farms where he could feed his cattle. It is almost certain that he was the D. MacCorquodale who acted, unsatisfactorily, as the estate lime burner. In 1847, MacDougall was in need of lime and found it difficult to establish whether any had been burnt on the island that year.

In view of this history, the factor was placed in a difficult position in 1845 when Donald MacCorquodale died. Although it was not uncommon on Lismore for a widow and her family to be evicted from a tenancy, irrespective of whether there was an adult son ready to succeed, this was not the practice on Baleveolan estate. Dugald would have expected to succeed his father, but there were family problems:

> I have today a visit from the widow, and a son of the late Donald McCorqudale, who informs me that the son Dugald, to whom I proposed to give charge of the possession, agrees with no member of the family, and that the daughter has been obliged to leave the house owing to his treatment of her, and that the brother Donald will not obey him, Dugald. The lad who came here says that he is willing to live with Dugald, if he will consent. To this arrangement I see no objection whatever. You can tell Dugald, that I think it does not look very well, my hearing from so many members of his family, that they cannot live with him. I wish you

would take the trouble to try and bring them to an agreement, and let me know the result. If they cannot agree amongst themselves I will have to take possession of the place for the landowner, & get quit of the whole of them. You can read them what I say, and I will be glad to hear what suggestion you offer, or if Dugald and the lad who came here today are willing to live together, and keep their mother and the brother Donald.
Allan MacDougall to Alexander Livingstone, 10 December 1845

Dugald was obviously a difficult character and it may be that these were the MacCorquodales who had recently 'disgraced themselves' and 'affronted' Ann Campbell Locke when they were over working at Druimavuic. His brother Donald appears to have been inadequate in some way as he is listed in 1861 as a homeless pauper. The factor's solution was to allow the widow, Sarah MacCorquodale, to retain the tenancy, with the support of her grown up sons (Alexander, aged 30 and Hugh, aged 26 in 1851), a daughter (Effy, aged 28) and a granddaughter. Dugald (aged 43 in 1851) moved out to marry and, for the next thirty years he was a landless cottar/labourer on the estate. By December 1856, Alexander was neglecting the land and, under threat of eviction, was conspiring with his neighbour, Donald Carmichael, and others to sell his stacks of grain before they could be disposed of by the landlord (the crime of spuilzie). They might have succeeded but for the vigilance of John MacDugald, the weaver, who alerted the authorities to their activities. Although the family 'entreated me [Allan MacDougall] in tears to give them a further trial', the MacCorquodales were evicted and had gone from Balimakillichan by the 1861 census.

CHAPTER THREE

Duncan Carmichael in Portcastle

The events surrounding the eviction of Duncan Carmichael, and the consequences for his young family were altogether more unpleasant. The census records indicate that, in 1841, he was a sixty five-year old widower with three daughters (aged 25, 15 and 5) and two sons (aged 15 and 12). His farm itself was difficult, much of it low-lying and wet or steep and rocky, he was in arrears of rent, and he was clearly failing to meet the demands of the factor for Improvements:

> I wish you to visit Duncan Carmichael, he is just now the tenant most in arrear, and who has done the least portion of the improvements long ago pointed out to him, having only done in Jany 1843, 24 roods of drains. I want to know how much he has since done, and what he is just now about. I wrote him about his great arrears & little improvement, and that he had yet to send me £7 10 of the sum he ought to have paid at Marts. Let me know what he says in answer to my letter of 11th July. I am very much afraid I will have to sequestrate his subject, in justice to the Landlord, unless I find he makes rapid changes for the better. *Allan MacDougall to Alexander Livingstone, 18 January 1844*

By midsummer the factor was issuing letters of removal, arranging to sell Carmichael's stock, and moving to evict:

> I see Duncan Carmichael must give up his possession. He has not paid the half of his Whity rent & if he cannot do better now he will never be able. To save his subject the charges of a sequestration let him <u>date subscribe before two witnesses and address to me</u> the enclosed letter. If it is not returned to me within 10

days I will order a sequestration. *Allan MacDougall to Alexander Livingstone, 9 July 1844*

However, by November, Carmichael, aged around seventy, had died. The following spring, with the new tenant about to take possession of Portcastle, Carmichael's sons were facing life without parents or home. Dugald wrote to the factor for help:

I beg leave to state that I am the son of the late Duncan Carmichael who had possession of Portcastle & that a younger brother a boy is with me here as yet. I beg you will order to us a little house which is here beside the dwelling house of the farm or otherwise any where you see proper on the property, but this little house would be preferable to us, and will not be any thing agt. the incoming tenant, and on your recd. at your convenience beg to know how matters stand between us, and whether myself and brother get that little house or any other on the property. *Dugald Carmichael to Allan MacDougall, March 1845*

but all that MacDougall would offer was employment at Druimavuic later in the year. No mention is made of Carmichael's three daughters Chirsty (aged 29), Janet (aged 19) and Cathrine (aged 9). Meanwhile Duncan and John McColl, who had been tenants on Portcharron township, had moved to Portcastle and were able to marry in their thirties (1848 and 1849) and start their own families.

CHAPTER THREE

The Baleveolan Estate Cottars

If the factor was seen to be patient with recalcitrant tenants he was impatient with the cottars, viewing them as a burden on the estate. Had he been resident on the island, he might have realised their value to a community that was distant from the services provided by villages and towns. Their rents were low but they were liable to be called upon at any time to do work on the estate (building walls and mending roads) or to travel over to Druimavuic to provide labour to the Lockes:

> Those who come to work I can give the use of the Barn and a place for cooking and they will have meal and potatoes if you can send them but they must bring their own blankets as I cannot furnish them and they will bring spades pickaxes (etc) as I mean to employ them in ditching and fencing the wood. *Allan MacDougall to Coll Livingstone, 8 August 1833*

With the economy of the estate being undermined by the increasing indebtedness of the tenants, MacDougall lost patience with the cottars, writing to Coll Livingstone for a full list so that he could move to evict them all by Whitsunday 1838:

> It is as well that you inform them that I am going to remove them that they may consider where they are to go. *Allan MacDougall to Coll Livingstone, 20 July 1838*

It is not surprising that this turned out to be an empty threat since some of the cottars, for example Mary Stewart (merchant) and John McDugald (weaver), were highly valued members of the community and there were other vulnerable paupers. It is possible that the parish minister, the Rev. Gregor MacGregor, intervened because the next surviving letter from the factor on the subject of the cottars was addressed to him, two years later:

> Please tell Coll to direct the tenants to pay their meal to Mr Cumstie Oban as usual. I wish him also to make out & send me a complete list of all the cottars upon the lands, & to mark those you think ought to have their houses gratis. I am accountable for all they should pay while they remain upon the lands. *Allan MacDougall to the Rev. Gregor MacGregor, 9 January 1840*

Whether with the blessing of the minister or not, by three weeks later, MacDougall had decided to remove all but five households (the MacColl weavers, Angus Graham and the widows McIntyre and Stewart):

> As to the cottars they would not be admonished in any way ... They would not work off their rent – they paid no attention to threats to remove them. They were at length warned to remove. This produced a half years rent from some, but it did not pay the expence of the warning, and I have never been benefited by that most expensive mode of upending them. So go they all must, and they have generally 4 or 5 years rent at least in their pockets which will carry them to the next person that feels disposed to speculate upon the prospect of getting rent or work from them. Let Coll tell them that I will be trifled with no longer, and will not now take their rent. *Allan MacDougall to the Rev. Gregor MacGregor, 28 January 1840*

CHAPTER THREE

In February 1840, Coll Livingstone was instructed to ensure that the others had removed by Whitsunday, when their houses would be 'taken down' and he was to be offered a bonus for each cottar successfully removed:

> I will be inclined to give Coll a premium for every cottar he removes, and you will be so good as desire him intimate to the tenants that I shall hereafter expect to find that no one places a cottar in a house upon the property without my knowledge or consulting. *Allan MacDougall to the Rev. Gregor MacGregor, 25 February 1840*

Whatever the actions taken, the factor's policy, to do away with cottars, did not prosper:

> There are many more cottars upon the lands already than ought to be, and I shall never consent to their increase, but would be very much obliged to you to put me on a way to diminish the number; indeed some have got houses I don't know how, as there seems to be more cottars upon the lands than there were 10 years ago, altho I have never consented to an addition to their number. *Allan MacDougall to Alexander Livingstone, 3 June 1845*

In the 1830/1 rental there were nine cottar families on the estate and these had increased to ten by 1841 and eleven by 1861, although the household of John MacDugald was the only one to continue uninterrupted over the years from the attempted mass eviction.

Allan MacDougall as Factor of Baleveolan Estate

Allan MacDougall wished, above all, to be a good steward of the Baleveolan estate on behalf of his sister and her son Donald Campbell, and he was acutely aware that failure on the part of the tenants would reflect badly on him:

> I hope I may be able to tell the young Laird that they are the best tenants in the country. *Allan MacDougall to Coll Livingstone, 22 June 1833*

> Tell Coll that he will neither do me nor the tenants nor the land justice if he overlooks work which in its execution does not satisfy his own mind & believes will satisfy me without faithfully informing. My perfect reliance upon his sense of justice was my reason for laying out so much money but which I am satisfied will benefit ultimately both Landlord and tenants if the work is faithfully executed. *Allan MacDougall to the Rev. Gregor MacGregor, 27 February 1840*

> You have been before told by me how often I have been reflected upon for letting the tenants remain in arrears. I expect the tenants will give me the satisfaction, and real happiness it will be to me, if I can shew Mr Campbell lands and houses in good order, a good stock, a clean and promising crop, and his rent, and that portion of arrears demitted at this term. *Allan MacDougall to John MacColl, 29 May 1854*

His correspondence and his reading show him to have been genuinely interested and knowledgeable in the developing technology of agriculture, and he was aware of the political aspects, writing to Alexander Livingstone in 1844 about the potential impacts of the repeal of the Corn Laws on unimproved farms. All of the evidence points to a great enthusiasm, and impatience, to introduce new ideas and increase the potential yields and incomes from the estate. However, during much of his factorship he was resident in Edinburgh and had to try to bring about change through the estate ground officers, with some involvement of the parish minister.

Setting aside his prejudice against the landless cottars, there is no doubt that he had the good of the tenants at heart. From a farming family in the West Highlands, he had an understanding of their background and culture, and during the years of the potato famine he showed real and practical concern for both tenants and cottars. The tenants, for their part, were deeply conservative and, remembering the history of the evictions around 1800, must have viewed the Druimavuic Lockes and Donald Campbell as uninterested but demanding landlords.

MacDougall seems to have worked well with the Livingstone ground officers, and had a particularly good relationship with Alexander. Up to around 1850, some progress was made on estate improvements, with the seriously underperforming tenants removed, albeit after several years of warning. Although there is evidence that the young laird still supported the policy of setting improvements against arrears:

> When I got Captain Campbell's permission to lay out the arrears on his property for the benefit of the tenant I came under an obligation – to him to see a full half years rent paid by each tenant at the two annual collections. *Draft letter Allan MacDougall to Miles Black, 20 December 1856*

he must have felt that his uncle was ineffectual, allowing arrears to continue and improvements to stall. Events were to show that MacDougall, in poor health, was losing control. The attempted spuilzie of the MacCorquodale corn stacks, with the help of another Balimakillichan tenant, indicates a contemptuous attitude to the factor; and it is difficult to believe that John MacColl, the ground officer living on the adjacent farm, was unaware of events.

However, the final straw must have been the duplicitous behaviour of the Buchanan brothers. John and Archibald Buchanan had one of the larger farms on the Baleveolan side of the estate, around forty acres, and, although they were in arrears like all of the other tenants, they co-operated in the improvement programme, reporting seventy to eighty roods (around twenty acres) of draining in 1847. With indebtedness mounting, they had their first threat of eviction in 1849, but they were allowed to remain because of the perceived difficulty of securing new tenants, and the estate overlooked the fact that they had not delivered their meal rent:

> Since 1850 I have spoken to the Buchanans about their meal rent but they always answered they could not pay it on account of the potato disease, their losses by it pressing so heavily upon them. *Allan MacDougall to Edmund Baxter, 7 October 1856*

In contrast to their earlier behaviour, the Buchanans now began to neglect their land, including failure to keep their drains cleared:

> I gave you several warnings early this spring & I have since I became factor on the Baliveolan property always warned you through the [ground officer] to sow grass

seeds [i.e. undersown cereal] where you had turnips or potatoes the previous year ... but I see you have disregarded all the warnings I gave you this spring as you have formerly done. I also before you had planted potatoes this spring cautioned you agst planting them & as I found you have since been doing, in land full of the sorts of the worst weeds & in a more foul state [than] in any part of the kingdom. For many years when calling upon you to pay some portion of your arrears you pled poverty and the expence of bringing up your family. I now see however sufft evidence to satisfy me that your means and substance are by no means limiting as you have represented them to me at every succeeding collections many years past. *Draft letter Allan MacDougall to J & A Buchanan 1855*

The factor's suspicions were shortly to be confirmed. The Buchanans were, in fact investing their resources on another estate on the island, and it was left to Charles Baxter, on 8 December 1856, to issue a summons for the recovery of the combined rents and arrears owed by the Buchanans, amounting to the enormous sum of £132 17s 6d. It is difficult to believe that the ground officer was unaware of these developments and it seems reasonable to conclude that his working relationship with the factor had failed. Some resolution of the Buchanans' affairs must have been achieved, because the 1861 census places John Buchanan (aged 70) at Baleveolan, farming 60 acres, and his brother John (aged 71) farming fifty acres in the adjacent Killean township (Appendix 9).

The conclusion must be that, however effective Allan MacDougall may have been in the earlier years of his factorship, his weak control of events in the later years allowed some of the tenants a very free rein. However, as far as the *community* of the estate was concerned, his policies over the twenty four years resulted in the retention of a high proportion of the population (120 in 1861 compared with 155 in 1841; Chapter Six), and the continuation of arable farming at a time when the drive elsewhere was towards conversion of the land to extensive sheepwalks. Of the eleven tenant families on the estate in 1834, at least five were still in possession in 1861 (Appendix 2). In contrast to James Cheyne, who appears to have been motivated to find global solutions to 'The Highland Problem' (notably capital works and emigration; Chapters Four and Five), Allan MacDougall focussed on the land and its people.

Chapter Four
James Auchinleck Cheyne

There are striking parallels between the lives of Allan MacDougall and James Cheyne. Born only three years apart in Edinburgh, they both had very adventurous brothers, but were apprenticed to the law in the capital, joining the ranks of the Writers to the Signet in their twenties. They must have been at least acquaintances in the small legal community of the city, and they were both elected to the Highland and Agricultural Society. However, these were relatively superficial coincidences. The men differed markedly in background and outlook, with a significant divide between the Lowland bourgeois Cheynes and the Highland grandees from Dunollie. They did, however, share an enthusiasm for religion: Cheyne maintained his family's adherence to the Episcopal Church and eventually bequeathed £100 to the British & Foreign Missions; £100 to the Society for the Promotion of Christian Knowledge; £60 to the Scottish Episcopal Church Society; and £100 'for the promotion of the publication of select religious works in a cheap form'.

We know a great deal more about MacDougall because of the obsessive preservation of family and business correspondence at Dunollie, but it is probably safe to conclude that these two men could not have been more different in personality. Cheyne was a confident, energetic man, twice married, with children, whereas MacDougall was a lifelong bachelor and hypochrondriac. They definitely had different relationships with money.

Lawyer and Accountant

James Auchinleck Cheyne, known as the infamous clearer of people from Lismore, was born on 16 April 1795 into a family that had been prominent Episcopalians and Jacobites in Aberdeenshire but were now members of the comfortable middle class of Edinburgh. His father, Ninian Richard Cheyne, a prosperous bookseller and burgess in the city, married twice. With Mary Low he had a daughter Susan and a son George (born 1788), who reached the rank of captain in the navy, seeing active service in the Napoleonic Wars, and finally retired to New Brunswick. With his second wife, Jane, heir to the Auchinlecks of Woodcockdale, modest landowners near Linlithgow, he had a family of four surviving children: Jane, Isabella, James Auchinleck, and Ninian Richard (born 1798). Ninian qualified in medicine and sought his fortune in South America, where he became the personal physician and surgeon to General Simon Bolivar, the liberator of Venezuela, Colombia, Ecuador, Peru and Bolivia. We know that James kept in contact with Ninian from the Trust Deed of 1842 and, in her will, his wife Frances Cheyne bequeathed the substantial sum of £3,000 to 'my dear niece, Amelia Frances Cheyne, eldest daughter of Dr Richard Cheyne of Bogota'.

After school and an apprenticeship in the law, he achieved the status of Writer to the Signet by 1818. However he had

CHAPTER FOUR

ambitions to qualify in the emerging profession of accountancy, and continued as an apprentice for a further two years, gaining recognition as an accountant in 1820. Before the establishment of the first ever society of chartered accountants in Edinburgh in 1854, the right to practice was gained by experience, under the supervision of the legal profession; and a reputation for competence was an important factor. With both qualifications he was equipped to play an active part in the expanding commercial life of the capital.

Shortly afterwards, he entered into an accountancy partnership with John McKean W.S., who had served his apprenticeship in the same legal firm. Cheyne and McKean worked together in conveyancing, offering property for sale from 1822 in the Edinburgh Advertiser and the Glasgow Herald. In relation to one unfortunate property deal in 1824, involving a Miss I Brown from Edinburgh, they were eventually found by the House of Lords to have been negligent. In spite of this, their collaboration was a thorough success commercially: on Cheyne's death, his inventory included seventeen properties in the New Town of Edinburgh owned jointly with the late McKean. The sasine records show that he was dealing in property up to the last year of his life.

In 1821, James married John's sister, Margaret Blair McKean, daughter of the teacher of writing and arithmetic at the High School of Edinburgh. They had five children: Margaret Dorothea (1822), Jane Auchinleck (1823), Elizabeth (1825), Jemima (1827) and James Auchinleck (1829). Margaret died in 1832, and, in 1834, he married Miss Frances Charlton Sprot, the twenty two-year old 'daughter of the late James Sprot Esquire of the Honourable East India Company's civil service, Chittagong in the Presidency of Bengal East Indies'. In fact, Frances Sprot came from a prosperous Edinburgh family of tanners who diversified into wider legal and commercial activities in the 19th century. Her cousin, Thomas Sprot W.S. (1800-1880), a business associate of James Cheyne, sharing his involvement in railways and in the Highland and Agricultural Society, acted as her agent after her husband's death in 1853. In addition to acquiring her substantial inheritance (which included 30,000 Bengal rupees), Cheyne, as elder son of Jane, was also the heir to the Auchinleck family, including the estates of Woodcockdale and Oxendean in Berwickshire. He was beginning to make his fortune.

Cheyne quickly gained a foothold in the commercial world of the capital, becoming, in 1825, one of the founding directors of the new National Bank of Scotland (which eventually became part of the Royal Bank of Scotland). The following year he was employed by the bank to wind up the Fife Banking Company, which had failed owing to poor management and fraud. Around the same time he began a lifelong interest in the potential of the expanding railway network, providing his professional support to the proposed 'Edinburgh Leith Glasgow Paisley Ardrossan and Troon [Railway] Company'. In the 1830s, he was a major shareholder in the Stirling Railway and the Edinburgh & Glasgow Railway, and he was a director of the Scottish Grand Junction Railway Company formed in 1846 to build a line from Ardlui to Oban. This last (unsuccessful) project was at the centre of his proposals for the relief of distress during the Highland Potato Famine (Chapter Five). Possibly the most important evidence of his growing reputation was his appointment in 1830, by the Lords of Council and Session, to act for the crown as factor for 'the mansion house and lands of Kellie' in Fife, on the extinction of the line of the Earls of Kellie. This role continued at least until 1835.

James Cheyne was a very busy young man (thirty-five in 1830) but there were other opportunities to be exploited. Edinburgh was fast becoming a major centre for life insurance and, with his competence in both law and accountancy, he was thoroughly equipped to play an important part, at first for the Scottish Widows Fund. From 1831 to 1837, he was manager of the Standard Life Assurance Company, with an office at 21 South St Andrew Street in the city. His brother-in-law John McKean took a parallel course, acting as manager of the Scottish Widows Fund and Life Assurance until his death in 1839. Cheyne, did, however, find time for other lucrative activities. In 1833, following the abolition of slavery throughout the British Empire, he acted to claim compensation for the freeing of 140 slaves from the Tobago sugar plantations of Charles Wightman of Dunbar. In 1836 he was listed as a land tax commissioner for the shires of Linlithgow and Fife; although the duties were unpaid, this helped to maintain his profile in government circles.

On the death in 1836 of Admiral John Maitland, one of Nelson's commanders, Cheyne was in a position to buy his estate of Kilmaron in Fife, with its gracious mansion house designed by James Gillespie Graham. According to the official history of the Standard Life Assurance Assurance Company:

> During the autumn of 1837 James Cheyne indicated that he wished to resign as manager to devote more time to his many other business interests including banking, the Edinburgh & Glasgow Railway Co, property in Edinburgh and the Kilmaron Castle estate near Cupar. The directors, reluctant to lose his influential connections which extended to the great London financial houses, offered him the post of actuary with responsibility for overseeing the compilation of tables of rates, the annual balance sheet and the quinquennial valuations.

The fact that the company was unwilling to lose his accounting and actuarial experience, dispels any doubts there might be about Cheyne's business competence. He was clearly a leader in the commercial world, and not only in Edinburgh. In the next five years he organised a fundamental review of the terms of business of the company, including improvements in the basic statistical approach to life insurance, switching 'from the out-of-date Northampton mortality tables to the more accurate Carlisle tables drawn up by Joshua Milne, the actuary of Sun Life, in 1815.'

Accountants and the 'Highland Problem'

At first sight, it is difficult to understand why Cheyne did not settle down with his new wife to enjoy his grand estate and mansion house in Fife, while keeping active as an actuary, tax commissioner and railway enthusiast. He had no direct links with the Highlands and Islands, apart from membership of the Highland and Agricultural Society from 1825, and yet he appears to have changed tack in the 1840s, concentrating his energies on Lismore. The explanation must lie in the company he kept, their opinions, and what they were doing in these years.

Cheyne belonged to an elite group of men who were building the reputation of Edinburgh as a world-class centre for accounting. They were playing an important part in fostering modern capitalism, not only in the expanding worlds of trade and manufacture but also in insurance and the management of risk. It was the misfortune of communities in the Highlands and Islands to come under the control of men imbued with a moral code that gave the highest place to financial probity, over and above all other considerations.

The financial troubles of traditional landowners described in Chapter Two continued into the 1830s and 1840s, exacerbated by the failure of the kelp industry, poor harvests, a recession in the cattle trade, and the associated chronic arrears of rent. In some years, particularly during the late 1830s and after 1845, tenants and cottars were unable to feed themselves let alone pay rent, and yet the populations to the north and west of Argyll continued to rise. As estate after estate owner filed for bankruptcy, their assets were placed under trust:

> The obligation [of the trustees] was to treat the property as an asset, to run it efficiently and, if possible, to bring it to a more profitable condition so that, if unentailed, it could be sold in whole or in part to reduce the debts which were attached to it. Under such a régime, social considerations not only became a decidedly secondary consideration but in law had no relevance whatsoever.

Ominously,
> Where [a] property was administered under a judicial trust, the trustee was not obliged to utilise estate resources for the relief of the local poor (Walker 2003).

In the search for men with the competence and experience to act as trustees, the authorities looked no further than the Edinburgh accountants.

James Brown (1786-1864) was the leading Edinburgh accountant of his day, and president of the new Institute of Accountants from its establishment in 1853. From the 1830s, the practice of Brown and Pearson was kept busy dealing with sequestrated estates, earning very substantial fees. They included the failing Barcaldine estates, and the firm eventually sold the Lismore properties to their fellow accountant, James Cheyne. Brown's most controversial activities were on Islay,

Skye and Uist in the late 1840s. As trustee for Walter F Campbell's estate on Islay, where the potato famine had rendered up to 5,000 destitute, Brown pursued rents relentlessly, and carried out widespread evictions. Later, from 1850, when factoring Lord MacDonald's estates on Skye and Uist, and overseeing some of the most extensive and violent clearances of the period, he opposed the idea of subsidising the emigration of tenants, at least partly because it ruled out any future reclamation of arrears. The many cottars were not seen to be the responsibility of the estate; rather they were 'burdens', making it more difficult to find buyers. By 1856, parts of the estates had been sold and the remainder returned to Lord MacDonald.

As a founding director of the National Bank of Scotland, Cheyne worked closely with its manager Patrick Borthwick, and he took Borthwicks's son Archibald (1811-1863) into his practice as an apprentice. In due course, Archibald qualified as an accountant, and worked in the Standard Life Company under Cheyne as its Secretary from 1832 to 1834. Later, he became an expert in bankruptcy, and was appointed trustee of Maclaine of Lochbuy's estate on Mull in the 1840s. In the words of Walker (2003):

> Borthwick's trusteeship of Lochbuy constitutes one of the many episodes of unpublicized eviction which have yet to be comprehensively studied by historians.

As many as 300 people were evicted by due legal process, the estate was reorganised into larger units and, on a sound financial foundation, it reverted to the family in 1856.

These are only two of the Edinburgh accountants who were applying strict capitalist principles to the resolution of financial problems in the area. Both were close colleagues of James

Cheyne. They were able to apply these principles because they belonged to a class, many of whom considered Highlanders to be at the least a lower form of life, and certainly a different race from the energetic men from the Lowlands of Scotland and England. In the 1840s and 1850s, the Edinburgh-based Scotsman newspaper was particularly strident in criticising charitable support to the lazy Celts, who should be encouraged to emigrate. An extreme version of this attitude, held even by Treasury officials overseeing relief efforts during the potato famine, was expressed by James Bruce, after a tour of the Highlands in 1847:

> In the inns of the Highlands, the Saxon language – the language of civilisation – is keeping its own with the Celtic and the latter is happily doomed to be supplanted by the former ... morally and intellectually the Highlanders are an inferior race to the Lowland Saxon.

Walker (2003) concluded 'that accountants were insulated from feelings of remorse by adhering to prevailing assumptions about the inferiority of Highlanders and Gaelic civilisation, and the superiority of their own ideologies.' It is ironic that modern studies of the genetics of the people in the British Isles have failed to provide a basis for these deeply ingrained prejudices.

James Cheyne, therefore, was embedded in a professional and social culture that perceived the Highlands and Islands to be an area ripe for the application of organisation and discipline. Some of his colleagues appear to have had a near-evangelical fervour in the application of capitalist principles, irrespective of the human cost. He, himself, had had experience as factor for the Kellie estate and, during his years with Standard Life, he had been directly involved with a series of failures of Highland landlords. These included MacNeil of Barra (1836), and Campbell of Lochnell, for whose estate he was appointed rent collector in 1837. The urge to take part in dealing with the 'Highland Problem' may have been irresistible to someone used to meeting challenges. However, he did approach it in a different way, becoming a resident owner rather than a trustee or factor. A letter between two senior civil servants who were involved in the famine relief exercise of 1846 gives some clues to the man and his motivation:

> At the entrance to the harbour [Oban], I met him [Cheyne] coming over in his own boat, and having accordingly had a long conversation with him here, which has consumed too much of the morning to leave me time to visit the island ... He appears to be what had been described to me, a well-informed and clear-sighted man, with very rational views of the measures adapted to meet the present emergency with the best effect. *Sir E. Coffin to Mr G Trevelyan, 28 September, 1846*

Later Years

The sasine records show that, by 1842, James Cheyne had bought the lands of Achanard, Fiart and Craignich on Lismore from Charles Campbell of Combie, and followed this up in 1845 by acquiring Kilcheran, Achnacroish, Killean, Baligrundle, Tirlaggan and Portcharron from James Brown and Charles Pearson, the trustees for the creditors of Sir Duncan Campbell of Barcaldine. However, in his trust deed of 1842 he refers to ownership of Achanard, Fiart, Craignich *and Kilcheran*. He must have acquired Kilcheran at a very early stage in the disposal of the Barcaldine estate but delayed registering his ownership for three years. All of these farming townships were adjacent, apart from Portcharron, giving him control of nearly half of the island (Fig. 5.2). How he managed this estate is the subject of Chapter Five.

Unlike all the other landowners from time immemorial, Cheyne actually lived on the island, at least for part of the year. Moving the United Secession (later United Presbyterian) Church from its base in the former Catholic Seminary to Baligrundle, he took over the house at Kilcheran. At the 1851 census, the household included himself (described as 55, landowner and a JP in Berwickshire), his wife Frances (39, born in India), his son James (21, unmarried) and a staff of three (footman, cook and housemaid). He seems to have settled into island life, acting as convenor of a committee supervising the repairs to Lismore Kirk in 1848 – clearly the Rev. Gregor MacGregor did not have any qualms about his dealings with his tenants; on the contrary, MacGregor himself became a tenant of Cheyne, taking over the cleared township of Portcharron around 1850. In his new role as Highland laird, Cheyne posed as an authority on Highland cattle prices in Blackwoods Magazine in 1850.

There are few other traces of his life on the island, although Alexander Carmichael records that, at some point in the 1840s, in the process of improving his estate, Cheyne apparently caused offence by transporting two cartloads of human bones from a cave near Achnacroish (Uamh Dhùn Fraoin) to the seminary burial ground at Kilcheran. At his death, his stable of horses sold for £1,368 (around £130,000 today), indicating an expensive taste in horseflesh, presumably not plough teams. At the same time, he was associating with the highest in the land, in movements to deal with the potato famine, and the threats posed by the repeal of the Corn Laws (Chapter Five).

Cheyne did not enjoy his island life for long. He died on

21 June 1853, aged fifty eight, leaving a very substantial fortune, including 'moveable' assets (cash, stocks and shares, insurance policies, furniture etc.) to the value of £18,995 (£1.8m today). This included the 'winding up dividend on sixty shares in the Scottish Grand Junction Railway'. In addition, his capital assets included his three estates (Woodcockdale, Kilmaron and Lismore) and twenty five properties in the New Town of Edinburgh (seventeen jointly with his late brother-in-law).

Cheyne had made provision for his family in 1842 in the form of a Trust, with three aims: to pay his debts and funeral expenses at his death; to meet the requirements of the contract of marriage with his second wife in 1834; and to divide the residue of his estate into five parts with his son receiving two parts and his three daughters receiving one each. The marriage contract ensured an income for life of £500 a year (around £43,000 today) for Frances Cheyne; at a realistic interest rate of 5%, this would have required the trust to maintain £10,000 capital (around £860,000 today). As well as this regular income, she was to have other financial benefits, including the proceeds of life insurances, and the right to any of his possessions. A major fraction of his fortune was, therefore, to be devoted to his widow, and her stepson was to receive less than half of the residue. It seems likely, from the family history, that these terms were the cause of the rift between father and son, who, aged twenty-three, emigrated permanently to New Zealand in 1852.

In spite of the care that James senior had exercised in preparing the trust deed, the years after his death were marked by a series of legal wrangles. James junior succeeded in having himself legally registered as his father's heir in 1854 but this does not seem to have had any effect on the events, which dragged on until the end of the 1850s. Progress was not helped by the fact that the trust deed specified that all legacies were to be withheld until three years after his death.

Three of the nominated trustees, William Thomas Thomson, manager of the Standard Life Assurance Company; Archibald Borthwick, accountant; and James Rolland W.S. did move very quickly to sell Cheyne's landed estates (as they were empowered to do under the terms of the trust) but failed to sell the Lismore property. In paying Frances Cheyne's annual allowance, they deducted income tax, with the result that she took them to court – and lost, clearly not well advised by her cousin Thomas Sprot. Meanwhile, the Marquess of Breadalbane reported that James Cheyne had not registered his purchase of the former Glenure lands (Achnacroish, Tirlaggan, Killean, Baligrundle and Portcharron) with him as feudal superior. Claiming that Cheyne had not established his 'entry' to this part of his estate, in 1857, he also took the trustees to court for £11 4s feu duty, £100 costs, and the right to all the rents collected since 1845. Other legal problems included the fact that the Lismore property had been registered as security for the government drainage loan (Chapter Five).

Out of this extraordinary muddle, Frances Cheyne emerged as the owner of the Lismore lands by around 1860. According to Frank Auchinlech Cheyne, who met the Cheyne family historian in 1934 in New Zealand, 'his father would never mention his family, giving as a reason that his own father, James Auchinleck Cheyne, a W.S., had married a second time, and had left all his property to his second wife'. Ultimately, the only benefit James junior enjoyed from his father's estate seems to have been an annuity (the interest on £2,000) at her death from his stepmother, out of her extensive fortune (her will lists legacies to the extent of nearly £20,000, equivalent to around £2m today).

Chapter Five
The Lismore Clearances

Unlike Baleveolan, which had been run as a single estate from the early 18th century, James Cheyne's Lismore estate was assembled in the 1840s from townships with different histories of ownership. It differed, too, in including three settlements that were potential nuclei for village development: Kilcheran, with its inn, sheltered port and lime kilns; Achnacroish, the eventual ferry port; and Killean, with its concentration of skilled workers and paupers.

The Townships

The Combie Lands

The townships of Achanard, Fiart, Craignich and Kilcheran (Fig. 5.1) were part of the two thirds of Lismore that came into the possession of Colin Campbell, Earl of Argyll in 1470. By 1751 (Table 1.1), the four-merk land of Achanard and the six-merk land of Fiart were owned by John Campbell of Combie, a successful cattle breeder and dealer, who took his name from a small estate, Claycombie, just to the east of Oban. The Combies were a junior branch of the Campbells of Clenamachrie, who had been tacksmen for Barcaldine on Lismore. They extended their island holding by acquiring the 4-merk land of Craignich (owned by Coll McDougall in 1751; Table 1.1).

Achanard, at the southern end of the island, is upland, exposed, with steep slopes and shallow soils (Plate 8); marginal for crops, its rent in 1751 was surprisingly high at £11 3s 6d. Fiart, although dissected by limestone ridges, contains some of the best (potential) arable land on the island, level and sheltered from the west (Plate 9); it was rented at £22 3s 10d in 1751. According to William Roy's Military Map of 1747, the principal settlement was adjacent to the mill at Miller's Port, but a smaller grouping, partly associated with a ferry to Mull and later with supplying the lighthouse on Eilean Musdile, lay near the southern tip of the island at Point of Fiart (Dalnarrow). However, by 1815, the joint tenancies had been broken up and the land had been divided into separate holdings. The quality of the land of Craignich, stretching over an undulating landscape from Kilcheran Loch to the south side of Sailean bay, is more varied, with a rent of £22 2s 2d in 1751. The traditional focus for settlement appears to have been near where the boundaries of modern Craignich 5, 7 and 8 converge (Fig. 6.1) but, by 1836 at the latest, the township had also been subdivided into individual holdings.

Under the Combies, Fiart and Craignich carried sizeable communities of indigenous islanders (>110 people; Table 5.1, Appendices 3,4) but there were signs of decline before they passed into the ownership of James Cheyne. There was a tradition of emigration to North America from the south end of the island: Blacks from Fiart were on the *Jupiter* of Larne that sailed from Appin to North Carolina in 1775 and several

CHAPTER FIVE

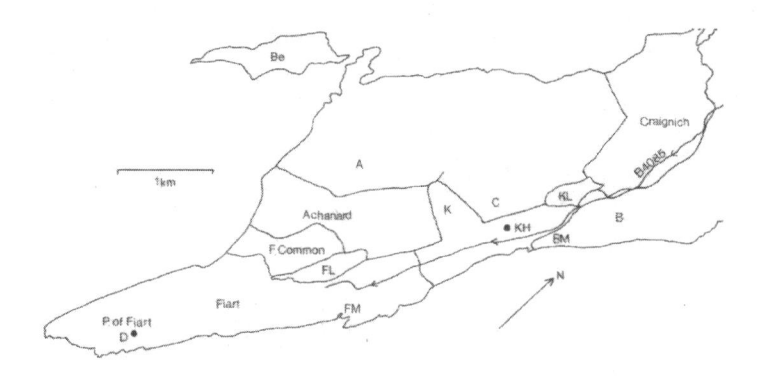

Fig. 5.1 Campbell of Combie's Lands on Lismore 1840 (Fiart, Achanard & Craignich)

(A Achinduin; B Baligrundle; BM Baligrundle Mill; Be Bernera; C Cloichlea; D Dalnarrow; FM Fiart Mill; FL Fiart Loch; K Kilcheran; KH Kilcheran House; KL Kilcheran Loch)

Achanard and Fiart families settled in Canada after the Napoleonic War. The 1834 church 'list of communicants being male heads of families' had six in Fiart, including Duncan Black the miller, and three in Point of Fiart. Five of the nine families were Blacks, indicating a tight kinship group, but the list must have underestimated the number of households since female heads were ignored. At the 1841 census (Appendix 3), there were five tenants, one of whom was a teenage boy living with his widowed mother and younger siblings, and three cottar households headed by women. The eight Fiart households made up a population of around forty, there were no tradesmen within the township, and the mill seems to have been abandoned around 1835 (no trace of the miller in the communicant list). The fact that Fiart and 'Pointfiart' were able to provide twenty one potential militiamen (aged 18 to 45) in 1805 is a clear indication of the population decline by 1841.

Table 5.1 The Demography of the Cheyne Estate, 1841-1881
(H = households; P = people; T = Tenants)

	Fiart	Kilcheran	Craignich	Baligrundle	Achnacroish with Newfield	Tirlaggan	Killean	Portcharron with Taylochan	Total	Rest of Lismore
1841										
H	8	19	14	10	6	10	24	7	98	
P	42	101	69	44	32	39	112	40	479	669
T	6	3	6	5	4	6	7	2	39	
1851										
H	9	12	13	7	5	6	24	5	81	
P	34	52	55	30	32	18	89	28	338	672
T	3	1	6	1	2	1	6	0	20	
1861										
H	3	9	12	1	10	10	23	4	72	
P	6	28	54	2	26	33	91	17	257	608
T	0	0	7	0	4	1	6	0	18	

CHAPTER FIVE

	Fiart	Kilcheran	Craignich	Baligrundle	Achnacroish with Newfield	Tirlaggan	Killean	Portcharron with Taylochan	Total	Rest of Lismore
1871										
H	2	5	1	1	10	4	26	8	57	
P	4	15	3	9	41	23	78	18	191	529
T	0	0	0	1	2	0	5	0	8	
1881										
H	2	3	1	2	11	5	18	8	50	
P	5	14	6	7	30	21	63	22	168	453
T	0	0	0	0	2	2	6	0	10	

The list of eight male communicants in Craignich in 1834 also underestimated the community. The 1836 estate plan of the township lists 8 tenants with holdings varying from three to forty acres (Appendix 4) and, in 1841, there were six tenants but a higher population of cottars than in Fiart (eight households, five of which were headed by women). As in Fiart, there were no specialist craftsmen. The population of the township in 1841 was around seventy – Blacks, MacCorquodales, Carmichaels, MacColls, MacGlassens and Kieths (McKeich, later almost invariably spelled Keith). Five out of the six tenant families had been resident in the township for at least a decade, but probably several generations.

In contrast, the more marginal Achanard had an unsettled history. Realising that the township lands were most suited to livestock production, with the potential for higher rent, John Campbell's son David had the land divided up into grass parks by drystone dykes, and removed most of the people because there was no longer a need for a large work force. By 1789, John McKillop may have been the only remaining tenant and he was about to be evicted:

> The bearer John M'Killop who and his predecessors has been always kindly men and followers of the family of Dunstaffnage, is at present a tenant with Combie at Achnard, but as the greatest part of the farm is now inclosed and divided into grass inclosures, he is under the necessity of turning away most of his tenants. I therefore beg leave to request you will be so good as let the bearer have half a merk of Achindown, which I suppose is the twelfth part, he will agree to pay what augmentation or input you get from others. Your compliance will much oblige. *John M'Killop to Sir Donald Campbell of Dunstaffnage, 7 January 1789*

CHAPTER FIVE

In the event, he did not get land at Achinduin, but moved to Kilcheran.

For the next twenty years, there were no more than two tenants on the township, although it did provide seven potential militiamen in 1805. However, the parish baptism records show that other families began to move back before 1810, from the surrounding townships of Fiart and Achinduin. Some of these would have been cottars, driven to seek uncultivated land in an overpopulated island. The estate survey of 1815 recognised four holdings on Achanard (of 84, 63, 48 and 20 acres, predominantly pasture) and several small arable fields had been opened up on the more sheltered east side.

The fact that the incoming cottar families and their successors were able to stay for the next thirty years was probably because the Combie finances were beginning to fail, and the estate was poorly managed by David's son Charles, whose focus was on the development of Oban. Baptism records show that between 1810 and 1840, there were normally six or seven families of Blacks, Campbells, Carmichaels, Kieths and McDonalds living on Achanard but there was a great deal of turnover, with families shuttling between the township and Fiart, Achinduin, Kilcheran and Craignich. However, the last recorded birth in the township was in 1838, and by 1841, the people had gone, leaving only one inhabited house, where a shepherd, Archibald Black, lived with his mother, brother and a seaman lodger. Three families had moved to tenancies in Fiart, Kilcheran and Craignich (Appendix 13) and six cottar families in Kilcheran in 1841 had come from Fiart or Achanard (Appendix 15). Although the ruins at Achanard (Plate 8) show that the living conditions for the cottars were very basic, more than fifty five children were born in the township over the forty years from 1800 to 1840. Some of them would seek a new life in the New World.

By the time that James Cheyne became owner of these three townships, one (Achanard) had been cleared and the population of a second (Fiart) was in decline. This seems to conflict with the excellent reputation as a landowner that Charles Campbell of Combie attracted in evidence presented to the Napier Commission (see below). Cheyne had settled to buy Charles Campbell's property on Lismore for £16,500 as early as 1838, but the transfer was delayed until 1842 by the legal process of overturning the entail. It is just possible, therefore, that Cheyne was already directing the management of the townships in 1838, in the expectation of the eventual purchase. Whether this is true or not, the Combies must be held responsible for two successive clearances of Achanard.

The Barcaldine Lands

The three-merk land of Kilcheran, originally part of the Argyll portion, was owned by Niel Campbell of Dunstaffnage in 1751 but, towards the end of the century, the family was in financial difficulties. The township, with a substantial new house, was sold for £5,000 in 1803 to the Roman Catholic Church in Scotland, as a more accessible site for its Highland seminary than Morvern. Kilcheran prospered under the management of Bishop John Chisholm, who promoted the economic development of the township, for example, by building new limekilns near the shore. The seminary lasted only twenty six years on Lismore, moving to the mainland and eventually to a permanent site at Blairs in Aberdeenshire. By 1833, Kilcheran had been sold to Sir Duncan Campbell of Barcaldine. The 1841 census (Appendix 5) describes an active and balanced community of 100 people in twenty one households, centred on the port, including four tenants, several tradesmen (lime burner, quarrier, (boat) carpenter, wright, weaver, publican running an inn, preacher, and general labourers) and a household of sailors. As the port nearest to Oban, it could well have developed into the ferry terminal for the island; in fact, it was the base for the Oban/Lismore/Mull packet operated by Donald Black (Donald the Dancer/Dòmhnall an Dansair – celebrated in the popular song and dance tune; Appendix 15) in the middle of the century.

Five other island townships (Balgrundle, Achnacroish, Tirlaggan, Killean and Portcharron), originally owned by the Lords of Glenorchy, had been transferred to their factors in Lorn, the Campbells of Barcaldine, by the 1730s. Patrick Campbell of Barcaldine, in turn, gave these lands to his son, Colin Campbell of Glenure – the Red Fox of the Appin murder. In the complex weaving of fortunes, Colin's brother Duncan inherited his property after the murder in 1752, and prospered, whereas the senior line (the Barcaldines) went into liquidation, surrendering their property and title to Duncan. Thus it was that Sir Duncan Campbell of Glenure and Barcaldine, the hero of Talavera, owned these five townships as well as Kilcheran in 1840. His finances, stretched to breaking by his ambitious building projects, failed in due course. After his death in 1842, the estate was administered by the leading accountancy firm of Brown and Pearson as trustees, who appear to have transferred Kilcheran immediately to Cheyne, and the remaining townships to him by September 1845.

In contrast to the insecurity on Achanard and Fiart, the farming community of the six merk land of Baligrundle and Tirewin (Plate 11), including the Kilcheran Islands, had been remarkably stable (Appendix 6). Donald MacColl (aged 50) had operated the mill powered by the outflow of Kilcheran Loch since 1815, and Dugald McColl (aged 60), Dugald Carmichael (aged 50) and Archibald McColl (aged 75) had been tenants over the same period, seeing their rents rise by fifteen per cent from 1824. Allan Black had succeeded his father Duncan, but James Carmichael, who farmed jointly with his brother Dugald at least until 1830, had left the island and died in Glasgow in 1871. In 1841, these farming families were associated with five households of cottars including labourers, a tailor and a school teacher. Until recently, the community had also included Hugh Carmichael (brother of Dugald and James) and his wife Betty, the parents-to-be of Alexander Carmichael, the renowned folklorist (Appendix 13).

This stability did not last long beyond the 1841 census. The tenants were ageing, and the death, in 1843, of Archibald MacColl, the senior tenant (paying a rent £120 out of the total of £424, averaging £1 12s per acre), precipitated a crisis on the island. It was not uncommon for a widow to be evicted under these circumstances, even though she had a son who could follow his father. Archibald's twenty seven-year old son Malcolm appears to have resisted, with violence, the attempt of the authorities to deliver a notice to quit – the crime of deforcement – and, in a subsequent riot at Achnacroish, a crowd of fifty or sixty islanders liberated MacColl from arrest, and sent the police packing. Two months later, on 27 September, the procurator fiscal crossed to the island with a strong team of officers and arrested three ringleaders but not the original deforcer. In December 1843, at Inveraray Sheriff Court, they were sentenced to sixty days imprisonment but, since they had already exceeded that period in detention awaiting trial, they were released. The islanders' actions had protected Malcolm MacColl, who disappeared from the scene, later emigrating to Canada. These events, after the death of Duncan Campbell in 1842, were at the hands of the estate trustees, Brown & Pearson, who, no doubt, saw the benefit of vacant possession, in attracting a buyer for the estate. They showed no loyalty to the MacColl family, even though the late Archibald had served as ground officer for the township.

With their Bronze Age cairns, two Iron Age duns and a Gaelic/Norse name, the productive lands of Baligrundle had provided homesteads for farmers over several thousand years. This continuity was about to be broken.

In 1841 Achnacroish (with Newfield) and the four merk land of Tirlaggan were smaller communities mainly occupied by tenants (four in Achnacroish with two cottar households; five in Tirlaggan with a crofter and four cottar households); the total population of the two townships was seventy one (Appendices 7,8). According to the 1751 valuation roll, they were very much inferior to Fiart and Craignich (Achnacroish rent £8 13s 7d; Tirlaggan £5 5s 3d). There is no mention of the former mill at Achnacroish, and no indication of the future importance of the township as a focus for settlement. By 1851 the two main holdings on the townships were in Tirlaggan (35-40 acres) and Newfield (around 25 acres).

The land of Killean (Plate 15) was also considered to be inferior (£8 13s 7d rent in 1751) but, traditionally, it had housed a high population of landless craftsmen and paupers. In 1841 (Appendix 9) there were 112 inhabitants, seven tenants, and seventeen cottar households: blacksmith, lime burner, shoemaker, two tailors, weaver and seaman. Most of the tenants were really crofters, with holdings from three to seventeen acres, and one small farm of twenty eight acres. Unlike some other townships, there was a considerable range of family names, some from the mainland: Buchanan, Black, Carmichael, Cunningham, MacCallum, MacColl, MacCorquodale, MacDonald, MacIntyre, MacLachlan, MacKeich. At the time, Killean and Kilcheran were the two main centres for services on the island.

Separate from the other original Glenure lands and lying between the townships of Baleveolan and Balimakillichan, the twenty-shilling land of Portcharron (Plate 12) had a population of forty in 1841 made up of two tenant and five cottar households. Hugh and Betty Carmichael farmed the land at Taylochan next to Clachan, and here Alexander Carmichael the folklorist was born in 1832. It was one of the least valuable townships on Lismore in 1751 (£6 16s 8d), difficult to cultivate and most suited to permanent grass.

Together, the lands that James Cheyne purchased from the Barcaldine trustees included the highly productive Baligrundle (1830 rent of £424 equivalent to around £35,000 in 2012); two townships with very strong communities of cottars (Kilcheran and Killean); and three other townships with mixed potential for arable and grassland farming. This purchase brought his landholding on the island to around 2,300 acres (920 ha) in total, equivalent to nearly half of the island, and certainly including more than half of its potential arable land (Fig. 5.2).

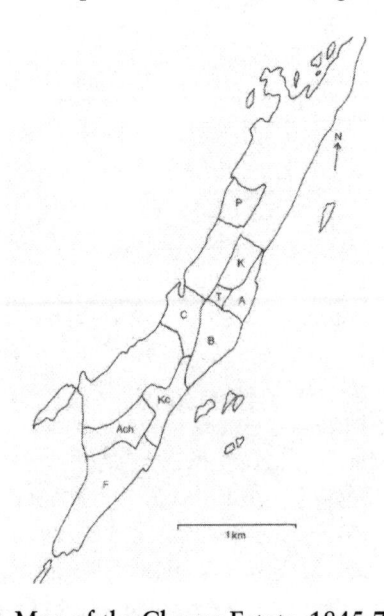

Fig. 5.2 Sketch Map of the Cheyne Estate, 1845-74
(A Achnacroish; Ach Achanard; B Baligrundle; C Craignich; F Fiart; K Killean; Kc Kilcheran; P Portcharron; T Tirlaggan)

CHAPTER FIVE

The People
(Table 5.1; Appendices 3-10)

Nearly 500 people lived on the townships that came into the possession of Cheyne in the 1840s (Appendices 3-10). The number of households in the southern townships had already declined before the transfer to Cheyne, and landless families, in particular, were on the move, with concentrations on three townships. Before any allowance is made for underestimation in lists of communicants (female heads of household; families adhering to the Secession/United Presbyterian Church), the number of households in Killean rose between 1834 and 1841 from twenty one to twenty four, in Kilcheran from nine to twenty one, and in Craignich from eight to fourteen. Eight of the twenty one families in Kilcheran in 1841 had until recently lived elsewhere on the island (Appendices 13, 15).

The population was made up of three main groups of people: tenants and crofters; active cottars (skilled workmen, craftsmen, sailors, fishermen, merchants and labourers) largely without land but who could earn a reasonable living as long as they had their health and a place to live and work; and the poor (widows and the elderly, sick, infirm and disabled, particularly those lacking family support). These groups were not fixed, because some tenants and tradesmen ended their lives as paupers when they could no longer farm, practice their trade or do general labouring work. For example, Myles Kieth, successively tenant in Kilcheran and Craignich, died a pauper in Killean (Appendix 13); Duncan MacCorquodale, handloom weaver in Portcharron, continued to make his living through the famine years but, aged 80, had joined the poor list by 1855. Some of the cottars with parcels of potato land were indistinguishable from crofters.

The 1841 census gives a misleading picture of the state of the poor, listing only five paupers on the island, supported by the parish, and all of them born in Ireland. This does not square with the parish records, which show that, in the first forty years of the century, there were normally between twenty and thirty people receiving 'relief' from the parish; it is also not consistent with the evidence presented to representatives of the Poor Law Inquiry on the island on 16 August 1843.

The parish minister, Rev. Gregor MacGregor, was either absent from the island or declined to meet the visiting officials, although he completed their questionnaire. However, the Rev. William Wood of the 'United Church's Station in Lismore' (at Kilcheran the forerunner of the United Presbyterian Church at Baligrundle) was able to summarise the position, which was far from satisfactory, even before the potato famine:

> The aid which the poor of his congregation get from the parish is very small; but there is no distinction made between the poor of his congregation and the poor of the establishment. The poor live chiefly by the assistance of their friends. He means to have a collection in the course of a fortnight for a few of the poor in his neighbourhood who are very needy, without distinction as to what congregation they belong. He has not yet been long enough in the parish to form a correct opinion of the propriety or impropriety of raising funds for the maintenance of the poor by a legal assessment. That very few of the poor go about begging in his part of the parish. There are a great many poor people on the island. He cannot say correctly how they come through. Some of them raise potatoes on bits of ground, and some of them catch fish, and some make a little by raising potatoes and selling them at Oban.

CHAPTER FIVE

The testimony of two tenants on the island underlined the gulf that existed between the tenant class and the poor:

Mr Donald M'Coll, Achnacrush. Has lived all his life in Lismore. He knows a great number of the poor in the parish. What they get from the [kirk] session is not at all sufficient to maintain them. Some of them get only 3s once or twice a year. They are chiefly maintained by going through the parish to farmer's houses, which they do once a quarter, and receive meal, potatoes, and anything else the farmer can spare for them. This is the way in which they are supported. The most of the people who go around in this way are women; there are very few men begging. He cannot estimate what they may get by begging. Their houses are very poor. Their bedding is very poor, but they generally have bed-clothes. He thinks they are not very badly off, but some of them are very poor. The tenants provide them with thatch for their houses. The women are often very badly off for shoes and clothing, and particularly for covering for their heads. He thinks an assessment [of landowners and tenants] would be very much against the parish, because the lands are high rented, and the tenants many of them poor.

Mr James M'Nicol, residing at Kilchearn. Is an elder of the parish of Lismore. Has only been appointed elder within this short time, and he is not acquainted minutely with the allowances given to the poor, but he knows that they are very small. Their collections are sometimes not more than 2s or 1s 6d upon a Sunday. The poor are supported by begging. Some of them get potatoes, and some meal and some milk, from the farmers. Their means of living are very precarious indeed. They are very ill-off for body-clothes. He has not been in many of their houses, but they have a very poor appearance. He cannot speak as to their bedding and bed-clothes; but their appearance altogether looks destitute. He is very doubtful about the propriety of raising an assessment for the poor, for although they are poor they are contented, and the tenantry could very ill bear an assessment, for they are poor themselves. There are a number of small tenants in the parish. Very few tenants pay more than from 30*l* to 50*l* rent, so far as he can judge, and there are a number who pay very small rents. He is not aware there are any so small as 7*l* or 10*l* rents. There are a few cottars, having a cow's grass, but he does not know their number.

By visiting eight households on the island, the commissioners gained an accurate view of the miserable living conditions of those living in poverty (Appendix 11).

The questionnaire responses by the parish minister, and the parish records, indicate that paupers were paid out of church collections, fees for the proclamation of banns, the hire of the parish mortcloth (to cover the coffin during funerals), and the occasional fines (usually 10/- or £1, but it is not known what serious offence Carmichael in Cloichlea committed to justify £5). There were no regular contributions to the poor by the landowners of the parish, although there was one major benefactress in Appin. No 'relief' was given in the parish to 'able-bodied men on account of want of employment, or of temporary sickness'; to 'able-bodied widows with only one child, or to able-bodied single women, on account of want of employment, or of temporary sickness'; to 'single women, mothers of illegitimate children'; or to 'wives deserted by their husbands'.

The islanders had been deeply affected by the 1838 famine, during which some had needed food relief, distributed by the Rev. Gregor MacGregor, and the landless families were the most at risk. These vulnerable people, up to 600 of whom, across the island, relied on their potato patches for much of their food, were about to feel the full impact of the potato famine. Surprisingly, the parish poor records do not show an increase in dependence in the 1830s, during the first period of famine, but they do show a marked decline in givings. For example, in 1840,

Income	Amount	Expenditure	Amount
Weekly collections	£4 16 4½	Precentor's fee	£1 10 0
Proclamation of banns	18 6	Bellman's fee	£1
Total	£5 14 10½	Divided among poor	£2 5 0
		(23 receiving 2/- each)	

Two shillings was much less than the support given in earlier years (rarely less than 4/- and up to 7/6 in 1817) and certainly less than the standard 10/- paid in Appin.

Clearance and Famine on Lismore: Evidence to the Napier Commissioners

On Monday 13 August 1883, Lord Napier and four of his commissioners assembled in the Baptist chapel at Bachuil (Plate

13) to hear what the people of Lismore had to say. Their arduous journey round the Highlands and Islands, as well as the Northern Isles, was the Whitehall government's response to twenty years of discontent and civil disobedience, centred on Ross, Skye and Lewis, arising out of the miserable living and working conditions of the crofting communities. Gladstone's Liberal government, which was also faced with similar issues in Ireland, made inspired choices in the men they chose to consult the people. The chairman was a very senior Scottish diplomat with wide experience, including a spell as Viceroy of India. Three members, native Highlanders and fluent in Gaelic, were well aware of how things stood in the area. Alexander Nicolson, Sheriff of Kircudbright (a native of Skye), and Donald MacKinnon, Professor of Celtic at Edinburgh University (a native of Colonsay) had both been active in promoting school education in the Highlands; and Charles Fraser Mackintosh, although a landowner, had been tireless in supporting the crofting cause. The Liberal MP for the Inverness from 1874 to 1885, he subsequently held the seat for the Crofters' Party. The landed interest was represented by Sir Kenneth Mackenzie of Gairloch but Sir Donald Cameron of Lochiel, the Tory member for Inverness-shire was absent on the day. The notebooks of Alexander Carmichael, the Lismore-born folklorist, indicate that he was an observer of the proceedings, and he provided a commentary on farming practice to the commission in November 1883.

In preparation for the meeting, the Lismore crofters and others had met at least twice to nominate delegates to speak to the commissioners. Much of their evidence would have been in Gaelic, translated for the final report; some of the difficulties in interpreting Duncan MacDonald's evidence may be the result of poor translation. In the presence of a sympathetic audience for the first time, and assured that they would not

CHAPTER FIVE

be penalised by factor or landowner, ten crofters and farmers and the Baligarve public schoolmaster gave very full, and at times passionate, accounts of their many grievances over the years (high rents, unfair payments for the depreciation of property, and the eviction of widows). Under the circumstances, it is not surprising that some of the issues were oversimplified. As far as Alexander Buchanan was concerned 'the factors are the greatest evil in the country' even though his father, a tenant on Baleveolan, had been treated with great leniency by Allan MacDougall in the 1850s (Chapter 3). Charles Campbell of Combie was remembered as 'a laird who was an object of praise for his conduct towards the tenantry and the poor' even though his family was responsible for two clearance episodes on Achanard, and the lack of control of their finances resulted in the sale of their Lismore estate to James Cheyne.

The private and estate papers of Combie and Cheyne covering this period are not available for study and, despite extensive trawling of the papers of local estates, there is very little documentary evidence of the events on Lismore in the 1840s and 1850s. As a result, the testimonies of Duncan MacDonald and Alexander Buchanan to the Napier Commission, the only published accounts of the Cheyne clearances more than 30 years before, have come to be regarded as authoritative.

In his evidence, Duncan MacDonald (73) was described as a crofter in Port Ramsay, but he was also a carpenter, conducting a boatbuilding and repair business with his stepson (Plate 14). In supporting the fleet of sailing smacks in the port, he was following his father, Niel MacDonald, who had built small clinker-built dinghies at Kilcheran:

My father and brother and myself were boat builders – building boats for those who required them, bringing sea-ware ashore, and other things. We built boats for the district around. Latterly, nobody upon the estate required a boat. *Napier Report paragraph 36851*

The MacDonalds had not been tenants in Kilcheran, although Duncan's testimony indicates that they had access to some land for grazing:

> We had about that time four sheep, and under one of the conditions [of the estate] we were deprived of them; and then we were not allowed to keep a pig, and things of that kind which contributed to pay our rents. *Napier Report paragraph 36860*

They had not been evicted:

> I was not sent off, I had to flee away. The very customers to whom we supplied boats were not allowed to come and purchase boats from us. *Napier Report paragraph 36864*

Because of his knowledge of the events thirty year before on Cheyne's estate, MacDonald had been selected as a delegate to the hearing. Under questioning by Mackenzie of Gairloch, he gave the following testimony:

> ... When [the laird] died the estate was bought by another [Cheyne] who promised well, but he remained a good proprietor only a very short time. He deprived us of our peat ground. Then, it appeared, it was his intention to put stock of his own upon the whole estate. The property consisted of six or seven townships. There have been over 400 or 500 souls there, and over the

whole tract now there are only three shepherds and a manager. He exacted some conditions – I do not know properly what they were – from his tenantry. There was a field of ryegrass, green, and he was sending us away one after the other, and he himself gathering stock which he placed upon every place as it became vacant. I don't know how many years he insisted upon grass being in those places, instead of its being arable. When he got the whole place under grass instead of under crops, then he stocked it all, and the people were all away by that time. Those who had the means to take them to America went there, and some went to the large towns. The poorest became labourers to him at 1s. a day for the men, and 6d. for the women, and they were paid each Saturday by a sort of meal. If they would not go to work for him on these terms, he threatened to pull down the houses of the poor people about their ears. I didn't mean a different quality of meal when I said 'a sort of meal'. It was oatmeal; only one year when there was a want of oatmeal, he got barley meal and ground it down. *Napier Report paragraph 36849*

What year was that? – About thirty or thirty two years ago. *Napier Report paragraph 36850*

Was that the time of the potato disease? – Yes. I have seen some of these people who formerly had crops and cattle, and butter and cheese, and milk afterwards, in those years, going with their barley scone to a good well which was beside us when we were building, and take their meal – barley and water – and it grieved me sorely. *Napier Report paragraph 36851*

[Cheyne] died leaving the place all under stock of his own. *Napier Report paragraph 36854*

Did Mr Cheyne give you the grass seed to lay down in pasture, or did you buy the grass seed for yourselves? – I believe he commenced by giving them the seed grass. He gave them seed grass in the first years whatever, so far as I can remember. *Napier Report paragraph 36871*

Did he pay you or make any allowance to you in your rent for the sheep he grazed upon your grass? – Well, you know he was sending them away, and then he was putting stock upon the ground. *Napier Report paragraph 36872*

Do you know how long it is since he first began to send them away? – It is my opinion that he began to send some of them away before the potato disease, but I cannot speak with certainty. I believe the clearing was going on thirty years ago. *Napier Report paragraph 36873*

Under questioning from Fraser-Mackintosh:

What was the name of the town you were in yourself? – Kilchairan village. *Napier Report paragraph 36856*

Can you give the names of the different towns that were cleared? – Yes ... Run-na-Fiart [Point of Fiart] and Fiart itself; Achananad, Baligrundle, Creaganaich, Gortcharrain [Portcharron], Achanacroigh – but I think that last place has still people on one half of it; and Killean. *Napier Report paragraph 36857*

CHAPTER FIVE

Did Mr Cheyne raise the rents before he turned the people out? – I cannot say. It was this stocking of the land which was laid out in grass that was injuring us. *Napier Report paragraph 36858*

He compelled you to leave out a certain quantity in grass and put stock on it, and thereby impoverished you? – He compelled us to leave out a certain portion of the croft in grass each year. He himself put stock upon it, and so the arable ground of our croft was continually reduced, and then he sent us away. I am not aware that he raised the rent. *Napier Report paragraph 36859*

Was that the policy pursued by Mr Cheyne – first to impoverish the people, and then to turn them out on the world? – That was it. *Napier Report paragraph 36861*

Did Mr Cheyne's action give a great blow to the population, from which they have never recovered? – I can say those magnificent dales, once cultivated, are now covered over with useless weeds and moss, as if the land itself were to say, 'I shall return to my original state'. *Napier Report paragraph 36866*

Under questioning by the Chairman:

You mentioned the names of a number of townships that have been cleared in Mr Cheyne's time. Can you give us any idea of the number of families that were in them at the time? – I might give a pretty close guess. The place was allotted out into crofts of such a size

> that each tenant kept four milk cows – six and eight was the average. *Napier Report paragraph 36868*

> Did Mr Cheyne's clearances begin before the potato famine? – Yes. *Napier Report paragraph 36869*

> Are there any crofts left upon the ... estate now? How many are there in Achnacroish? – There is the one-half of Achnacroish and also Killean in the hands of small tenants. I cannot say how many there are in Killean. Some of the crofts have been made larger upon these places. *Napier Report paragraph 36870*

> When Mr Cheyne grazed his stock upon the ground which he had made them turn into pasture, did he graze his stock on their pasture the whole year, or for only part of a year? – It was left under grass for two or three grass crops, which were taken off it. It was cut, and I believe these belonged to the tenants; but it was after that that it was thrown out into pasture, and he was putting stock upon it, as he was bringing the stock into the country. *Napier Report paragraphs 36874-5*

Duncan MacDonald was followed by Alexander Buchanan, unmarried son of John Buchanan, a long-standing tenant on Baleveolan estate, who had farmed 45-60 acres until his death in 1874 at the age of eighty six. Alexander had then been obliged to leave Baleveolan and is recorded as a sixty-year old quarryman lodging in Tirlaggan in the 1881 census. The Report describes him as a labourer, Killean (aged 60). He was asked to provide information on the Cheyne clearances although he had no relevant, direct experience. Under questioning from the chairman and Fraser-Mackintosh, he explained that:

CHAPTER FIVE

The last witness did not explain exactly about the grass. When Mr Cheyne commenced to remove the tenants, he made them lay out a piece of arable land for a year under grass, what the tenant should have had under cultivation; and he made the tenant sow this piece every year with rye grass; and after he got the whole arable land under rye grass he sent the tenant about his business, and took all to himself for stock. That was the reason for making them sow it under grass, that he might send the tenant about his business and take the croft to himself; and he did so until he had the whole estate cleared except a part of Auchnacroish and Killean. *Napier Report paragraph 36876*

Did he make them also pay the full rent? – Yes, the full rent. *Napier Report paragraph 36877*

Did the tenants get a crop of hay? – I cannot say for that. *Napier Report paragraph 36878*

He made the tenants prepare the ground for the sheep farm? – Yes, and sow it down with grass. *Napier Report paragraph 36879*

And sent them away? – Yes, one by one, until he had the whole estate to himself. *Napier Report paragraph 36880*

Did he begin this process before the potato famine? – I believe he did. I think the potato disease commenced about 1848 or 1849. *Napier Report paragraph 36881*

1846, was it not? – There might have been symptoms of it then. *Napier Report paragraph 36882*

Are you one of the tenants? – No; I [was] on the estate of Captain Campbell [of Baleveolan]. *Napier Report paragraph 36883*

You were never upon his land? – No, but I recollect it. *Napier Report paragraph 36885*

Do you recollect what he did creating a great deal of sensation at the time? – Yes, when I was young the population in Lismore was 1800. The parish schoolmaster we had told me, a year or two before he died, that when he came to Lismore [1816] the population was, I think, 1650, and now it is not much more than 637. *Napier Report paragraph 36886*

Under questioning by Professor MacKinnon:

Are you able to say how many years were allowed the tenant in Mr Cheyne's time to convert his croft from an arable croft suitable for himself to a grazing croft suitable for Mr Cheyne? – Maybe two years, until he got the ground in order for himself. *Napier Report paragraph 36895*

Was the preparation going on at the tenant's expense? – At the tenant's expense. *Napier Report paragraph 36896*

For the good of Mr Cheyne? – Yes, and sometimes he sent the tenant away and took hold of everything. I had an uncle who had a croft, and he might be £10 or £15 in arrears. He was getting old and of a religious disposition, and Mr Cheyne was always bothering him for arrears, and he sent horses and cattle to Mr Cheyne, and he never got a farthing back, although they would have brought a good deal more than the amount of his debt. *Napier Report paragraph 36897*

Was it a general rule that Mr Cheyne himself took the stock of those who went away? – I could not say; but he took the stock of those who were in arrears. *Napier Report paragraph 36898*

And those who were not in arrear [sic] he allowed to make market where they could? – Yes, I believe so. *Napier Report paragraph 36899*

Are any of those who were in that estate still in Lismore? – Yes, but I cannot say whether any one of them is to speak today. Some may have gone to America, but not very many, I think. *Napier Report paragraph 36900*

Do their relatives at home ever hear how they are prospering? – They are doing pretty well, I believe. *Napier Report paragraph 36901*

And what became of those who went to the large towns? – They are working away as best they can – some are doing well, and some indifferently... *Napier Report paragraph 36902*

According to MacDonald and Buchanan's accounts of the Cheyne clearances, the new owner of the nine townships started the process of converting the arable land to permanent grazing immediately, before the start of the famine in 1845/6. The tenants were required to sow a proportion of their ploughland, possibly one third, to ryegrass each year so that the conversion would be complete in three years. They were then evicted from their holding and left the island, or became penniless labourers. The whole area, with the exception of Killean and part of Achnacroish, was then turned into a sheepwalk. The delegates also gave hints about the limited support given to destitute victims of the potato famine. As there were no challenges to their testimonies, it is likely that this was the accepted position in the 1880s.

There are some difficulties, however, with the evidence. Neither witness had first- hand experience of the transactions between Cheyne and his tenants, and they could not answer basic questions such as the rent arrangements, the fate of tenants' livestock, who paid for the establishment of the grassland, and whether the tenants took the crop for their own use during the conversion. If the interviews had taken place a decade before, there were several former tenants on the island (Appendix 13) who could have provided exact information.

MacDonald compared Cheyne very unfavourably with Combie but, in the 1840s, his family were living in (and were obliged to leave) Kilcheran, which had actually been part of the estate of Duncan Campbell of Barcaldine and never owned by Combie. Although Barcaldine had owned more than half of the new estate, he was not mentioned. Duncan MacDonald was actually referring to earlier times when his family had been resident successively in Point of Fiart and Achanard, from which they moved on to Kilcheran some time after 1836 (Appendix 15).

There are also problems with the timetable for the events, which they place before the potato famine (1845 onwards).

Since Cheyne did not buy most of the Barcaldine estate until 1845, and there were still three tenants in place in Fiart as late as 1851, this evidence can refer only to Kilcheran (acquired by 1842). Of the other Combie townships bought before the potato famine, Achanard was already a sheepwalk, and Craignich was not cleared until the 1860s, in the second wave of clearance long after Cheyne's death (see below). Interpretation is also hampered by the confusion between crofts and farms, although the inquiry was supposed to concentrate upon crofts. MacDonald describes the Cheyne tenants as crofters with a few cattle but many of the holdings on the new estate could only be called farms. For example, the Baligrundle rental for five tenants was £424, with Archibald MacColl paying £120 (Lord Napier recommended protection for crofters paying an annual rent of up to £6 but the resulting Crofters Act of 1886 set the 'threshold' at £30).

James Cheyne and Lismore (1842-1853): documentary evidence
The Treasury Correspondence, 1846

Kilcheran House had been occupied by the United Secession Church, but Cheyne must have moved them on quickly to their new site on Baligrundle as he is recorded as resident by September 1846, when the full implications of the potato famine were unfolding. There is an almost complete lack of estate documents (rentals, letters to ground officers etc.) from this time, but official correspondence provides unique insight into his attitudes and actions, as well as the conditions on Lismore.

Realising the need for good information on the spread of the potato blight epidemic and its impact on Highland communities, Sir Charles Trevelyan, a senior civil servant at HM

Treasury, dispatched the ominously named Sir Edward Pine Coffin and Captain Pole to the West Highlands in autumn 1846. Coffin met Cheyne at Oban on 28 September, 1846 and, in his very full report to Trevelyan, noted that Cheyne was on his way to a 'county meeting' called at Inveraray to discuss 'the measures adapted to meet the present emergency'. As far as Cheyne was concerned this would result in an application to the government for:

> ... assistance, in some shape, towards carrying into execution the railway from hence [Oban] to Glasgow, for which an Act was obtained in the last session of Parliament

which would provide

> ... general relief throughout the Highlands under the impending calamity. In point of extent, he states that it would furnish employment for at least the greater portion of the otherwise idle labourers throughout the islands, as well as on the coast of the main land; and he expresses his belief, with apparently sound reasons for it, that it would, from the situation of the work, be divested of all the objections which restrain the Highlander from seeking occupation at points more remote from his home, and under circumstances less akin to his habits. But the consideration on which he lays the principal stress is, that it would be a remunerative work, tending to provide future as well as present employment for the people, and serving to supersede the necessity of having recourse to unproductive modes of employing the people for subsistence, which must eventually bring on the result so universally

dreaded in Scotland, compulsory assessment for the support of the able-bodied.

Coffin took the opportunity of making Cheyne aware of the Treasury view that there would be no possibility of government support for such a project:

> ... I have accordingly taken pains to make Mr Cheyne aware of the utter improbability of such interposition [of Government], in reference both to general principle, and to the practical decision of the Government in other cases of the kind.

> He is too well informed a man to be insensible of the force of both these obstacles to success in the proposed object, but he nevertheless expresses his confidence that the matter can be placed on such a footing, by a proper mode of proceeding on the part of those interested, that all objections may be overcome; and as it is not my business, nor do I feel myself competent to examine the grounds of his confidence, I have contented myself with reiterating the reasons which I have for entertaining an opposite opinion, and with cautioning him and the other proprietors against relying upon so doubtful a resource as the intervention of the Government in aid of their railway project, and neglecting, in the mean time, such other modes of relief as may really lie within their reach.

Nevertheless, Cheyne had decided to go with Lords Breadalbane and Lorne to lobby the Prime Minister, Lord John Russell, for support for the project. Meanwhile he was

> ... *prepared to give full employment to all who want it on his own property* [original italics in the printed document]. With respect to the conditions of the remaining part of the [Lismore] population, living on the land of various non-resident proprietors, he speaks more doubtfully, and he adds, that the grain crops, though good and well-saved, will not suffice for the subsistence of those living on the island without importation.

While Coffin was taking stock of developments on Mull and Tiree, Captain Pole was delegated to visit Lismore. The full text of his report is at Appendix 13. His summary of the situation on the island was:

> The potato crop is wholly gone.
> About 400 of the poor will shortly be destitute.
> No means of employment are available for the poor.
> At present no scheme is on foot by the upper classes to avert famine, or procure employment for the poor.

Later in the month, Coffin summed up the situation in a letter to Trevelyan, including his judgement of the conditions on Lismore:

> Captain Pole has given me very full reports of his proceedings at Lismore and Islay ... The general result of his inquiries as to the condition and prospects of the people, is similar to that in other quarters: that their potatoes are wholly lost, – that these are the chief means of subsistence in ordinary seasons, – and that they have now little other resource to look to but such employment as may be specially provided for them. I have

CHAPTER FIVE

before noticed Mr Cheyne's assurance that he would find work for all resident on his land; but it does not appear that any steps to this effect have yet been taken by him, or the non-resident proprietors of Lismore; and want is expected to become severe by the end of this month. The island produces a sufficiency of food to replace the potatoes; but without work and wages the poor will have no power of obtaining it.

The proceedings of the Inveraray meeting are, however, of a still more practical and reasonable character throughout, and I enclose a copy of them, in case they should not yet have reached you. I think I can trace in them something of the effect of my conversation with Mr Cheyne. *2 letters, Sir E Coffin to C. Trevelyan, 7 October 1846*

Out of the official prolixity of this correspondence, several important themes emerge. Although we know from the Napier Commission evidence that Cheyne did eventually provide employment and food payments to the needy, he was clearly not in a hurry to do so in autumn 1846, by which time many cottars would have realised that they would have nothing to eat over the winter. Meanwhile, in spite of Cheyne's claims to the contrary, Allan MacDougall was, in October 1846, providing support to the Baleveolan community in the form of fishing tackle.

Cheyne was more interested in a major capital investment – a new railway linking Glasgow and Oban (The Scottish Grand Junction Railway) – that would provide paid work for destitute men (the 'idle labourers') so that they could support their families. This was the railway age, and he was collaborating with enthusiasts that were the highest in the land, but the official line was that government would not provide any financial support for the development of infrastructure. In the event, the necessary finance did not materialise. The Callander to Oban Railway Company was not formed until 1864, and it took another sixteen years before the rails reached Oban.

The correspondence also refers to a major change in the arrangements to support the poor. As noted above, 'relief' in many parts of Scotland, including Lismore, had been based on voluntary giving during the church service on Sundays, and by local benefactors, with some income from marriage fees, the hire of mortcloths, and fines exacted from offenders. Drawing on the findings of the Poor Law Inquiry of 1843, and influenced by the fact that the Disruption of the Church of Scotland had undermined the financial viability of parishes, The Poor Law (Scotland) Act 1845 established standard practice across the country. Support was to be organised by parochial boards, which had new powers to raise taxes on property, and the responsibility to employ a local Inspector of the Poor. A national Board of Supervision based in Edinburgh was responsible for ensuring that the system was working.

The new Lismore and Appin parochial board met first on 16 September 1845. It confirmed half yearly payments of 2 to 5/- per pauper (a significant improvement on the miserable 2/- for the Lismore poor in 1840) but set the rates at £1 to £3 per annum for 1846, following national guidelines. The cost of these payments were to be met by taxation, based on property values, with equal contributions by landowners and occupiers. It was calculated that a fund of £350 for the joint parish would be sufficient for 1846, but, as the effects of the famine took hold, the costs rose sharply to £420 for 1847 and £650 for 1848. On Lismore alone, the poor list rose from twenty seven in 1845 to around forty between 1847 and 1855; twenty two people required emergency 'relief' in the crisis year of 1846; and, by 1855, individual payments had risen to as much as £8. Captain Pole's conversation with the Baligrundle schoolmaster indicated that these very new arrangements had not been well received by landowners and tenants on Lismore, when they themselves were facing serious problems. By November 1846, ten island tenants had failed to make full payment.

Cheyne and the Public Money Drainage Act (1846)
The Corn Laws, which effectively banned the import of grain until a price threshold had been passed, were introduced around the end of the Napoleonic War with the intention of stabilising prices and protecting farmers' incomes. For the next thirty years, their repeal was the subject of intense political debate but, by the 1840s, cheap food for the cities had become more important than the protection of farmers and the 'free-traders' prevailed. Robert Peel's government announced in January 1846 that the legislation would be withdrawn over three years, but it acted to gain the support of the farming community by introducing the Public Money Drainage Act. £4m was set aside by government to provide loans to landowners for agricultural improvements, primarily drainage, on the security of their estates. This was the Act that Captain Pole referred to in his discussion with Rev. Gregor McGregor in October 1846 (Appendix 12).

This legislation, applying to the whole of the United Kingdom, was very popular amongst Scottish landowners who succeeded in monopolising half of the funds, which were exhausted by 1854. This was at least partly because officials dealing with relief of the potato famine recommended landowners to use the funds to provide work for their 'idle labourers'. However, it was not sufficient to stifle the discontent of the 'protectionists', who feared that the rise of free trade, and unrestricted imports of a range of agricultural products, would destroy the livelihoods of farmers. A mass protest (The Great Protection Meeting) was held in London in May 1850 and James Cheyne, an active member of the Scottish Protective Association, was one of five Scots to sign the petition handed in to 10 Downing Street. He was quoted, in the published account of the events, as an authority on the steep fall in prices of cattle in the West Highlands, and he warned of

> ... the tide of emigration setting in among the respectable class of farmers, who can take some capital with them. Free-trade prices and poor-rates will soon, in the Highlands and Islands, as in Ireland, compel the most substantial and industrious of the farmers to fly to other lands, if they would avoid the final evaporation of their substance, and their ultimate degradation to the pauper list. *Blackwoods Magazine 67, 239-40, 1850*

His solution was to encourage his tenants to:

> abandon their prejudice, or their partiality, as you may please to term it, for the pure West Highlander, and to adopt the Ayrshire, or a cross from it, according to circumstances; and to kill their produce, as calves, at whatever price they may get for them, and turn their attention to make the most of the dairy produce.

In spite of his stance as a protectionist, Cheyne was one of the first to exploit the potential of the government loans. His application for £2000 'for the Drainage of the Lands hereinafter specified: Feyard, Auchanard, Kilcheran, Craiganish, Firlagan, Ballegundle, Killean and Portharran. United Parishes of Lismore and Appin', was posted in the Edinburgh Gazette on 10 February 1847. The sasine records show that a Certificate of Advance of £191, the first part of a total of £2000, was issued by the Enclosure Commissioners of England and Wales [sic] on 11 December 1848. Advertisments for the sale of the estate in the 1850s indicate that the loan had been thoroughly exploited in draining substantial areas. There is no evidence that Allan MacDougall applied for a government loan, but a handwritten note on the back of a copy of the rental of Baleveolan (Martinmas 1845) reads: 'Mr Cheyne wishes [the] march [dyke] between his lands and Mr Campbells repaired more especially the march between Portcharron & Balimakillichan. He also wishes to drain the wet parts of Baliveolan Killean and Tirlagan at the mutual expense of Campbell and himself. He has the way to do this in another farm.'

It is unlikely that MacDougall would have cooperated in this way because his outlook was diametrically opposed to that of Cheyne. On Baleveolan, the agricultural improvements were carried out by the tenants, and the work was financed by the writing off of arrears. The landlord gained by the enhancement of his capital asset, and the tenant gained by the increased yield that resulted from improvement. Cheyne, by contrast, raised finance externally by taking a government loan and then employed labourers, who had no stake in the future, to do the work. The tenants played no part in the enterprise, and the landlord could look to higher income from increased rents.

The Lismore Clearances: Testimony of the Census Returns
The Tenants (Table 5.1; Appendices 13-15)

The census records for Lismore confirm that there was a major loss of population from the townships making up Cheyne's estate between 1841 and 1861. Total numbers fell from 479 to 257, a reduction of nearly half over twenty years. Out of the original nine townships, by 1861 there were no tenants living on five (Achanard, Fiart, Kilcheran, Baligrundle and Portcharron), where there had been sixteen tenants in 1841. By any measure, this was a serious demographic change, but there are difficulties in reconciling these data with the testimonies delivered to the Napier Commission. For example, there were actually *more* tenants on Craignich in 1861 (i.e. after the death of James Cheyne), and a stable number of tenants on Achnacroish and Killean.

The census figures are not entirely helpful in charting the populations on Lismore. The 1841 results lack details of family relationships and, in early June, a proportion of the population would have been off the island, doing seasonal work on the land, at the fisheries, and, increasingly, at sea (see Fig, 5.3). The lack of death records before 1855, when compulsory national recording began, means that it can be difficult to trace the life histories of some elderly people. There is also the problem of a limited number of personal- and family-names. Nevertheless, a clearer picture emerges if the census records are supplemented with births, marriages and deaths (parish records to 1854, official records from 1855) and information from the Lismore emigration register (identifying emigrants by reliable data from Lismore *and* where they settled). In general, it has proved easier to trace tenants than cottars, and men than their widows (see below).

These records do not support the idea that most of Cheyne's tenants were bundled off the island at an early date, in the 1840s. Of the thirty nine farming or crofting families on the eight townships in 1841, at least thirty two (the original tenants or their sons) were still living on the island in 1851, although not all had retained tenancies. Charting the lives of the twenty

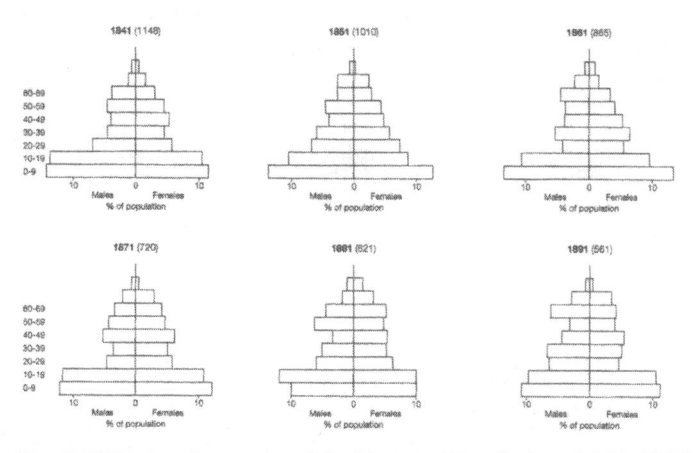

Fig. 5.3 The Age Structure of the Lismore Population, 1841-1891

two heads of families (i.e. including sons succeeding their father) on the townships that were effectively cleared by 1861 (Fiart, Kilcheran, Baligrundle, Tirlaggan and Portcharron; Appendix 13):

> 3 had died (without sons succeeding on the island)
> 8 had moved to tenancies on other parts of Cheyne's estate (Craignich, Killean), although, by 1861, several were landless (but still on the island)
> 3 had moved to tenancies on other estates on the island
> 4 were landless cottars on the island by 1851
> 1 had moved to work in the central belt
> 3 had emigrated to Canada

In 1861, eight years after the death of James Cheyne, the families of more than half of the original tenants were still living on Lismore, but this was possible only because of the loss of tenants elsewhere. For example, of the seven listed in Killean in 1841 (Appendix 9), five had died without a successor, one was succeeded by a widow and one family remained in Killean but without land (Appendix 13).

The inventory of James Cheyne's estate (1853) lists his remaining tenants, allowing a clear division of the clearance events on Lismore into two phases: phase one (in Cheyne's lifetime, to 1853) involved the removal of tenants from Fiart, Kilcheran, Baligrundle, Tirlaggan and Portcharron, with substantial losses of population on Kilcheran and Killean; and phase two (in the lifetime of his wife) involved the complete clearance of Craignich and the departure of most of the remaining population on Kilcheran (Table 5.1). The story of these movements, as the proprietors moved them across the chessboard of the estate, can be understood only by considering each township in turn.

The First Wave of Clearance
Kilcheran, Fiart and Baligrundle

Taking full ownership of his estate by 1845, James Cheyne concentrated his attention on these three townships. Kilcheran was the 'home farm' of the estate, surrounding the 'big house' (Plate 10) and steading, but, by 1851, the principal tenant James McNicol, who had given evidence to the poor law inquiry in 1843, had gone. He had been replaced by James Law, but as an employed grieve, with a team of three young ploughmen enlisted from the adjacent townships on the island. The use of the term 'ploughman' here and elsewhere in the 1851 census itself signals a change from the generalist approach to farming.

Law, from Fife, was no doubt hired as an industrious, English-speaking 'Saxon' from Cheyne's Kilmaron estate. Kilcheran was to become the operational centre for the whole estate, and by 1861, it had a resident manager (J H J Stewart, 'farmer of 1,200 acres, from Dumfriesshire' in 1861). Of the other three tenants in 1841, Donald Carmichael (aged 20) and John McColl (aged 48) emigrated to North America, and Myles Kieth (aged 60) had, by 1851, moved to a twenty acre holding on Craignich.

To the south, the township of Fiart, was destined to be almost completely cleared to make way for sheep. By 1861, it had two shepherd households only. The main phase of the clearance took place between 1851 and 1853 (as attested by the lists of tenants in Cheyne's inventory following his death in 1853). The youngest, Myles Black (aged 15, farming with his widowed mothers in 1841) had already left by 1851; he can be traced to Old Monkland, Lanarkshire, by his death in an accident in 1863. Of the other four tenants, two were moved to crofts (15-17 acres) in Killean, which were still in the possession of the families in 1861 (see Appendix 14 for a detailed account of the Black families); and two were moved to holdings on Craignich.

The changes on Baligrundle appear to follow more closely the pattern described by Duncan MacDonald in 1883, in rapidity and completeness. Although Cheyne did not acquire the township until 1845, all of the tenants had departed by 1851. Archibald MacColl's holding, which featured in the deforcement, was already vacant in 1843, and the township miller left the estate to take up a twenty five acre tenancy elsewhere on the island (Achuran). Of the other three tenants, Dugald McColl emigrated to Ontario, Canada, Allan Black moved to Kilcheran where he ended his working life as a shepherd (see Appendix 14), and Dugald Carmichael (uncle of the folklorist) died a landless pauper in Achnacroish. By 1851, the community included a shepherd, a new miller, and three families of labourers, presumably completing the work financed by the Drainage Act loan.

Of the six tenants in Tirlaggan in 1841, two had died by 1851, two had moved to holdings in Craignich and two of the families were still on the island but landless. They were replaced by a single family of MacCorquodales farming forty acres in 1851 and thirty five in 1861 (Appendices 8,13). By 1871 there were no tenants on the township.

The two tenants of Portcharron in 1841 had left by 1851 to take up tenancies on neighbouring estates (Appendix 13). The township, adjacent to the parish manse, became a sheepwalk let to Rev. Gregor MacGregor. One of the wool producers approached by Allan MacDougall in 1859, he paid a rent of £18 6s, but had already run up arrears of £21 2s 6d by 1853.

The Second Wave of Clearance

The conversion of Achanard, Fiart, much of Kilcheran, and Baligrundle into a continuous sheepwalk was complete by the time of James Cheyne's death in 1853, but the next phase of clearance, concentrating on Craignich, did not start until the next decade. The township had supported six or seven tenant families, but there was a considerable turnover of people (Appendices 4, 13); the impression is that the Cheynes used it as a holding place for displaced tenants on their way to becoming landless cottars.

Of the six 1841 tenants, the families of James Campbell (originally from Achanard) and John Black continued at least to 1861 and the McGlassans/Grays to 1851 after which they moved on to Killean as cottars. By 1851, the MacCorquodales had moved to a Cheyne tenancy in the adjacent Tirlaggan township and Hugh Carmichael had died. This left room for Sarah Black and her son Archibald who moved in from Tirlaggan, in the opposite direction to the MacCorquodales;

for Myles Keith who had been dislodged from Kilcheran; and for William Black and John Campbell from Fiart. Over twenty years, tenants had been moved to Craignich from Achanard, Tirlaggan, Kilcheran and Fiart.

In the early 1860s, all of the tenants and cottars (54 people, 12 households) left Craignich (Appendix 13). None of them received land elsewhere, although at least four of the tenants remained on the island. In 1871 there was a single household of three:

Dugald Black	Head	Unmarried	29	Shepherd
John	Brother	Unmarried	17	Ship smith
Donald McDonald	Nephew		6	born in Glasgow

The Townships not Cleared of Tenants

Although the two remaining townships (Achnacroish and Killean) did not suffer complete clearance of tenants during the Cheyne years, they experienced considerable uncertainty and turnover. Indeed, Hugh Buchanan was the only tenant across the whole estate who retained his tenancy until 1871, eventually retiring to his daughter's home in Baleveolan in his '80s. Of the three others on Achnacroish in 1841, Donald and Alexander MacColl emigrated to Ontario, and John McIntyre had a temporary holding in Craignich in the 1850s. They were replaced by Archibald Campbell, who was also an innkeeper and spirits dealer up to the 1870s and, in Newfield, by Duncan Black. Black was the son of Duncan Black, tenant in Craignich in 1841. By 1861 he was back farming eighteen acres in Craignich but, after the clearance there, he was listed as a general servant at Achuran in 1871. A fresh tenant occupied Newfield up to the 1880s.

There were seven crofters on Killean in 1841. Five died in the 1840s without leaving successors, one widow retained her croft, and another stayed on as a labourer (Appendix 13). Four new crofters in 1851 included tenants moved in from Craignich and Fiart and, 1861, there were more: Donald Black the roadman now had five acres, another tenant's son from Fiart had arrived, and Archibald Buchanan, formerly a tenant on Baleveolan, now had the largest holding in the township (fifty acres). At any time over twenty years there had been six or seven tenants, but none of the original 1841 families still had land. This was effectively a clearance, although not for sheep.

Three Tenant Families (Appendix 14)

Concentration on tenants and their heirs conceals the full impact on the wider family. The three case histories in Appendix 14 show that the clearance events of the 1840s and 1850s had major long-term effects on their families. Niel Black represents the group of tenants who were moved from their native township to a croft elsewhere on the estate. His son Hugh succeeded him at Killean but lost the croft in the 1860s and was obliged to earn his living at sea, later as a carpenter in Achnacroish in the 1880s. Unmarried, he lived on to the age of eighty five in Achnacroish. Of his siblings: Niel died young; Mary left home early but married an estate employee and remained on Lismore; Christina left the island, marrying a sailor in Govan and dying in Glasgow; Dorothy went into service on the mainland but returned to the island in her fifties to look after her brother; Isabella married a sailor and remained on Lismore; and Archibald, listed as a ploughman in 1861 and Catherine, disappear from the records. Meanwhile, John Black, who lived in his brother Niel's household in Fiart, held

CHAPTER FIVE

on as a cottar there in 1851 (needing emergency parochial support in 1846), but his family appear to have left for Glasgow, returning as paupers to the island by 1871.

Allan Black, successor to a family that had been tenants in Baligrundle for generations, represents those who lost their land immediately. The children of Allan Black's first marriage moved away in their late 'teens or early twenties to Glasgow or into service locally. With the loss of his tenancy he would not have been able to support a large family, although he later became a wage earner as a shepherd on the Cheyne estate. The return of a grandchild from Glasgow in 1861 is a recurring familiar theme amongst Lismore families, although few of these children remained on the island. The later history of the Black family is difficult to trace because of their common names but, in spite of their large family of children, Allan and his wife were left on their own for the parish to support in their old age.

Hugh Carmichael represents the small group of tenants who left the Cheyne estate to take up tenancies elsewhere on Lismore. Moving from life as a cottar in Baligrundle to a tenancy on Cheyne's land in Portcharron and then transferring to the adjacent township of Kilandrist, Hugh avoided the fate of his brother Dugald (Baligrundle tenant) who was cleared and died a landless pauper in Achnacroish. His landlord (Airds) did sell up in 1853, but Hugh, old and blind, was still in possession in 1861. However, all of his surviving children left the island. Catherine emigrated to Ontario in 1857. Mary married Duncan Carmichael from Balimakillichan and, before 1841, they had moved to Greenock, where Duncan worked in a 'sugar house'. They provided a home for Alexander when he was at school in Greenock. In the '50s, Mary moved back to Lismore to care for her parents, but followed her sister to Ontario in 1871 after Hugh died. Alexander eventually settled in Edinburgh, after a career as an exciseman in England, Ireland and the Western Isles.

Each of these tenant families, with deep roots on Lismore, eventually lost their landholding on the island. Some of the children of the first generation succeeded in maintaining a life on the island but the majority left, principally for Glasgow and elsewhere in the central belt. Only the Carmichael daughters had the resources to emigrate to Canada.

The Cottars

Life had become even more difficult for the landless cottars, who had been severely affected by the potato famine of the 1840s; nearly all of the forty two paupers on the parish list in 1851 were from cottar families. They had been part of the community of each township, providing services and skills as well as labour at peak times of sowing and harvest. Many were substantial families, pillars of the parish church. Clearance for sheep had a disastrous effect on their lives: there was no longer a need for their labour and the people that they had supported as weavers, tailors, shoemakers, merchants and publican had gone. As the century progressed, the livelihoods of craftsmen were also being undermined by the availability of cheap manufactured goods, and the demand for labour for lime quarrying and burning did not increase until the expansion at Sailean in the 1860s. On the other hand, the number of paid employees on the Cheyne estate, mainly shepherds, did rise to six by 1861.

However, probably the greatest threat to their survival on the island was lack of housing; tenants moving within the Cheyne estate would expect a house and steading, however basic, to be provided but, unless a cottar's skills were in demand, it was unlikely that any landlord would provide

PLATE 1. Idealised image of mixed farming in the lowlands of Scotland, showing a fully enclosed arable landscape with grassland and livestock production as integral components of the rotation. Autumn, Kinnordy by James McIntosh Patrick.
© The artist's estate/The Bridgeman Art Library

PLATE 2. Part of the original Baleveolan Estate. The southern fields of Balimakillichan.

PLATE 3. Portcastle Farm, with traces of rig and furrow in the foreground.

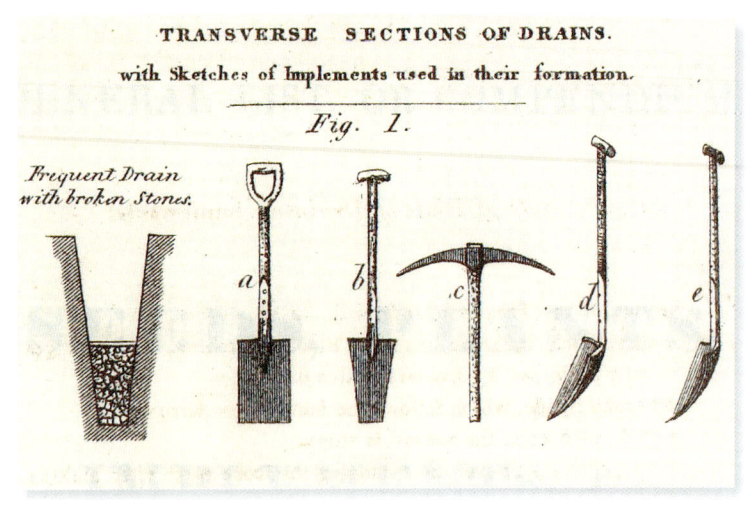

PLATE 4. Illustration from James Smith of Deanston's pamphlet 'Remarks on thorough draining and deep ploughing'.
W. Drummond & Sons, Stirling 1831.

PLATE 5. Rev. Gregor MacGregor, parish minister of Lismore, 1836-1885.

PLATE 6. Drystone dyke on Baleveolan estate built in the 1840s.

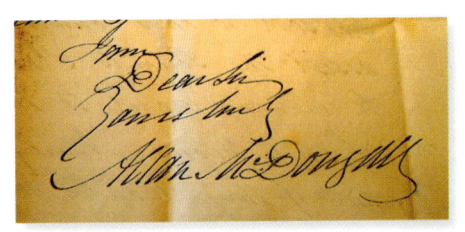

PLATE 7. Signatures of Allan MacDougall (a) and James Cheyne (b) from business correspondence.

PLATE 8. The abandoned township of Achanard, reproduced by permission of John Raymond

PLATE 9. Fields on Fiart township.

PLATE 10. Kilcheran House in 1970. © Crown Copyright:
RCAHMS. Licensor www.rcahms.gov.uk

PLATE 11. Baligrundle township from above Baligrundle 2 farmhouse.

PLATE 12. The abandoned township of Portcharron.

PLATE 13. Bachuil, where the Napier Commission met in the Baptist Chapel in 1883 (undated early aerial photograph from the Lismore Museum Archive).

PLATE 14. Duncan MacDonald's sawpit at Port Ramsay.

PLATE 15. Cottar houses with mortared walls and gable hearths at Killean.

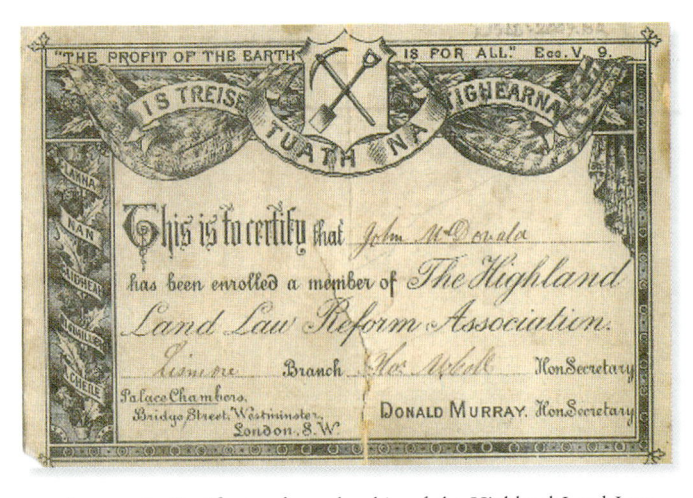

PLATE 16. Certificate of membership of the Highland Land Law Reform Association for John McDonald, Lismore, 1880s (from the Lismore Museum archive).

accommodation or allow them to build for themselves. Just how stark the problem could be is shown by the application to the parochial board in September 1847 by Mary Black, widow of John Black, tailor in Killean, which stated that 'her family are merely sheltered in the ruins of the house lately occupied by them'. In his testimony to the Napier Commission in 1883, Hugh Cameron, cottar in Killean, reported that Mrs Cheyne had built four houses for the poor but later decided that they were too good for paupers and, instead, rented them out. His view is supported by the valuation of 1865/6, which lists several houses in Killean that were let to cottars at rents from £6 to £10, but no rent-free property. Allan MacDougall's attitude to cottars (Chapter Three) is probably a fair guide to the opinions of island landlords. For many cottars, there was only one course of action: the migration of the entire family, not just the younger members.

The story of the one-hundred strong community in Kilcheran (Appendix 15) shows the vulnerability of the landless families. Even before the arrival of James Cheyne, the population was insecure, with six households having recently arrived from Achanard or Fiart; these were mainly headed by men described as labourers or by widows. Between 1845 and 1851, under Cheyne's management, eleven cottar families (out of a total of twenty one households) left Kilcheran. This first wave of migration removed nearly all of the independent skilled workers, resulting in the abandonment of the lime kilns (the limeburner departing to Sheep Island), the closure of the inn (the publican leaving Lismore), and the removal of the wright to Craignich. In his evidence to the Napier Commission, Duncan MacDonald explained that his family had had to leave Kilcheran because there was no longer any need for boats in the community. He and his brother Donald were fortunate that their woodworking skills were in demand, allowing them to settle at the north end of Lismore (Appendix 15). The Kilcheran weaver had left by 1861, also finding a croft at Port Ramsay.

Five cottar households were headed by women without husbands in 1841 and there were two further widows by 1851. All of these families had left Kilcheran by 1861 but only four widows were able to transfer to other townships in the estate. The other three either had died or left the island by 1851.

Overall, in 1841 there were sixty cottar households across the nine townships on the Cheyne estate, and there were still sixty in 1851, but the number had fallen to 46 by 1861. As these included original tenant families that had become landless (Appendix 13), the corresponding number would be no more than forty. By 1871, there were forty two cottar households, of which ten were headed by paupers.

Piecing Together the Puzzle: What the Cheynes did to Lismore

By 1842 and 1845, James Cheyne had finalised his purchases of land on Lismore from estates that were in financial difficulties. The Combies had been in trouble for decades, and Charles Campbell had been trying to sell Achanard, Fiart and Craignich for several years, prevented only by the terms of an entail. Ever since his return from the wars, Sir Duncan Campbell of Barcaldine had been warned by his advisors about his reckless spending, and this culminated in the collapse of the family fortunes by his death in 1842. Neither family would have been interested in investment on their island properties and, in fact, the Barcaldine estate increased their rents by fifteen per cent in 1824.

Across the island, farmers and cottars were just recovering from the poor harvests and hunger of the late 1830s, and arrears were widespread. To make matters worse, shortly after

Cheyne moved to Lismore, events were overtaken by the potato famine and the resulting miseries for everyone, but the cottar population in particular. In short, he acquired an estate of neglected land, burdened with rent arrears, supporting a community of tenants and cottars struggling to overcome an unparalleled series of misfortunes and threats to their health and livelihood. As it stood, it was hardly a good investment.

From his experience of owning Kilmaron, Woodcockdale and Oxendean, Cheyne would have had a vision of his Lismore estate with the big house at its focus, a smart steading, and a home farm managed by a team of paid staff. His ambitions would have included a planned landscape round the house, in the fashion of the times, with plantings of native and more exotic trees. There would be no place for a crowded cottar town in the plan. He would also be following current agricultural practice in converting most of the rest of his property into a sheepwalk, particularly in view of the fact that wool prices were still buoyant but arable agriculture was in recession.

To achieve the first part of his vision, he had to shift most of the people from the immediate surroundings of his house at Kilcheran and replace them with estate staff. This he achieved very quickly in the 1840s: only six of the twenty one households in 1841 survived to 1851. The principal tenant on Kilcheran died in this period and, of the other three, two chose to emigrate to North America (possibly aware that the tenancies on offer would be inferior to their existing land) and one transferred to Craignich (Appendix 13). Under his direction, the land was now to be managed by a grieve from the Lowlands with a team of ploughmen. In place of the innkeeper and tradesmen (limeworkers, boat carpenters, wright), Cheyne brought in Donald Black to be the estate boatman, and two island labourers were selected to be trained as shepherd and forester.

Meanwhile, he was initiating the changes needed to prepare for his sheepwalk, including moving the tenants on, and converting their cropland to high-quality grazing. There is no evidence that the previous owners had provided written tacks for their tenants; this was certainly not the case on Baleveolan in the 1840s. Appendix 13 shows that most of the tenants on Fiart, Baligrundle and Craignich were from families that had been in place for most of the century, and probably for several generations. The unwritten agreement between these tenants and the landlord would have been that they would remain in place, from year to year, as long as they paid their rent and observed estate regulations. The fact that Niel Black, William Black and John Campbell could be in debt to the extent of £45 to £70 in 1853 (Appendix 13) shows that Fiart tenants must have been seriously in arrears in the 1840s, and vulnerable to eviction.

As a lawyer in the public eye, Cheyne would have wanted to be seen to be acting within the law. In this period, the legal business of Argyll was processed through sheriff courts in Inveraray, Tobermory and Fort William. The surviving court records are not complete but there is no evidence from the Minute or Rolls Books for this period of any actions by James Cheyne. In particular, there are no processes for removal in the records of the Fort William Sheriff Court, which dealt with the north of Argyll (e.g. appeals by paupers in Appin). Even though the tenants were seriously in arrears, and therefore vulnerable, it seems that he did not move formally to evict.

Starting with the townships of Fiart, Kilcheran and Baligrundle, he must have required them to move elsewhere on his estate, mainly to where deaths had provided vacancies. Of the five tenants on Fiart, four moved to Killean or Craignich, and only one left the island. The migration to new tenancies took up to a decade (completed between 1851 and 1853), a longer period of transition from ploughland to grass than that featuring in the Napier evidence.

The transition on Baligrundle was more abrupt, completed between 1845 and 1851 and none of the tenants retained land on the estate. A substantial part of the township was already vacant with the death of Archibald McColl, father of the deforcer. One tenant moved out to Achuran on Lismore, one emigrated to Ontario, and two became landless (one joining Cheyne's payroll in Kilcheran). Unlike his actions in Kilcheran, Cheyne seems to have left the cottars here and in Fiart in place, although they dispersed in the 1850s (Table 5.1). In the same period, Tirlaggan and Portcharron were rationalised to a single tenant.

This first wave of clearance was over by the time of Cheyne's death in 1853. The people were not burned out of their houses or driven to eke out a living on the shore; indeed a high proportion of the tenant families continued to live on Lismore. However, the human cost should not be underestimated. Tenants on Fiart and Baligrundle, from families that had held their land for generations, were moved like 'pawns' around the island, mainly filling tenancies that had arisen out of the death of small tenants in Craignich and Killean. Within another decade, most of them would be landless. The livelihoods of craftsmen were undermined, and many of the more vulnerable cottars (unskilled labourers and widows) disappeared from the island. All of this was happening at the height of the potato famine, which must have damaged the health of the poorest people and may have contributed to the early death of several of the householders in Appendices 13 and 15. With his drive to use his lands efficiently, Cheyne would probably have considered this degree of human suffering to be acceptable, and that migration in search of work was a logical solution to the perceived overpopulation of the island.

The long term impact of these years was on the young, who had no stake in an island where the numbers of tenancies were reducing, the demand for services was declining and there were few alternative sources of income. Human fertility was high; for example, Duncan McColl, tenant in Tirlaggan, had nine living children aged fifteen to thirty one at the time of his death in 1855 (Appendix 13). The biographies of Lismore tenants and cottars (Appendices 13-15) give long lists of children, but many of the survivors disappeared from the island as young adults to find work on the mainland. A survey of the 1851 census found 324 families or individuals born on Lismore but living elsewhere in Scotland; 103 of these were in Glasgow, 101 elsewhere in Argyll (excluding Oban), twenty two in Dumbartonshire, eighteen in Renfrewshire, sixteen in Oban, thirteen in Greenock/Gourock, and ten in Bute. They were mostly house, farm or general servants. Few islanders had the resources to emigrate abroad.

By the time of Cheyne's death, on 29 August 1853, his son had left to settle in New Zealand, and his wife showed little interest in his Lismore project, shortly moving back to Edinburgh. Once the legal wrangling over Cheyne's Trust was concluded, Mrs Cheyne assumed the ownership around 1860. Around this time, David Paterson and his sons, farmers based in Dumfriesshire, but not resident on Lismore, were engaged as overall managers and, by 1861, John Hope Johnstone Stewart from Dumfriesshire (a 'gentleman' in his death record), had been installed at Kilcheran, as the 'farmer of 1200 acres'.

These were the years of the second wave of clearance on Lismore. On the night of 7 April 1861 there were twelve households on Craignich, including seven tenants. These were people who had been brought together from all over the Cheyne estate (Appendices 4,13). Later in the same year, the entire township was let to Lachlan Smith at a rent of £232.

CHAPTER FIVE

At the 1871 census there was only one household of three headed by an unmarried shepherd; a community of more than fifty people had been dispersed, possibly in the space of a few months. Although, following the earlier pattern, members of at least nine of these families were still resident on Lismore, all of the tenants lost a stake in the land. Only one, Archibald Campbell, who had farmed the biggest holding on Craignich (fifty acres), was retained as an estate employee, becoming the ground officer in Tirlaggan.

Between 1851 and 1871, the population of the other parts of the estate continued to fall (Table 5.1), but the sharpest decline was in Kilcheran, where there were only fifteen inhabitants in 1871, out of the original 100 thirty years earlier. The community had dwindled to six households: farm manager, ploughman, ferryman and three elderly cottars.

In view of the heavy burden of arrears of the remaining tenants across the estate in 1853 (£901), and the advice (entered on Cheyne's inventory) that it was unlikely that more than half could be recovered, it is surprising that all of the tenants and cottars had not been evicted out of hand by Archibald Borthwick, acting as trustee. It may have been that he prepared the way for the second wave of clearance, but Frances Cheyne cannot avoid the responsibility for the removals. By letting the township at £232, compared with the £256 due from the seven tenants, she was opting for a lower but more reliable income. At her death, the entire estate was sold to the Duke of Argyll in 1874.

Chapter Six

How Lismore Lost its People – and Held on to Some of Them

Emigration

The exodus of people from Lismore began in the second half of the eighteenth century, long before the Cheyne clearances. Because they prospered in the new world, we know something of the history of a group of islanders, Carmichaels and Blacks, who had the ambition and resources to emigrate to the Carolinas, the main destination of Highlanders at that time. Early emigrants prepared the way for other members of the families, and the total number of people leaving Lismore at this time cannot have been less than fifty.

After the end of the Napoleonic War, there was a renewed movement of people across the Atlantic. One large family of Blacks left Point of Fiart/Achanard for Quebec in 1817 but the preferred destination was Cape Breton Island in Nova

Scotia. Archibald Black from Achanard was able to buy his new farm there by 1823, and in his letters home to the island in the 1840s, Duncan MacDonald was describing a network of Lismore families (Blacks, Buchanans, Grahams, McColls, McDonalds), farmers and craftsmen, which must have represented a substantial number of original emigrants. However, less demanding areas were opening up, and the focus was now on the rich arable lands in Ontario, west of Toronto. All of the five Cheyne tenants, four of them McColls, who decided to seek new lives abroad, settled in and around Elgin County, where some of their descendants live to the present day. They were followed by many others in the next generation, including the sisters of Alexander Carmichael (Appendix 13).

Apart from the determined attempt by Duncan Campbell of Glenure to set up a linen industry in the 1760s and 1770s, and small-scale kelp production by Campbell of Airds in the 1790s, the absentee landlords of Lismore had little interest in establishing alternative forms of employment. Indeed, there is evidence of actual hostility to the cottar craftsmen, tradesmen and labourers, who were seen as a burden on estates. Young islanders had little choice but to seek work elsewhere, either permanently or in seasonal activities (fishing, agricultural work including harvesting, general labouring and domestic service). Their need for work coincided with expanding opportunities offered by the industrial revolution in the central belt, particularly Glasgow, Dumbarton, Paisley and Greenock. In the 1840s, population pressures, compounded by the hunger experienced by the cottar community in the later 1830s, were primary factors in the migration of people from the island. Fig. 5.3 confirms that a significant number of young male islanders were absent in spring 1841.

It is not possible to quantify the number of people who left the island by emigration and migration before the clearance period but, in contrast to areas to the north and west where the population continued to grow well into the century, Argyll communities began to decline in the 1820s. The first full census for Lismore (1831) did not provide lists of inhabitants but the global figure (1497) is a fair estimate of its peak population (Fig. 6.1).

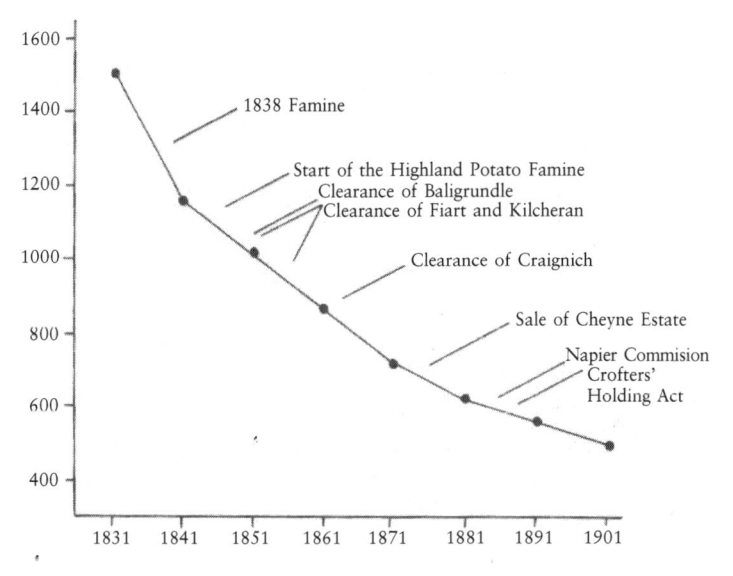

Fig. 6.1 Population Changes (Census data) on Lismore and Associated Events 1831-1901

Famine

Around the time that James Cheyne died (1853), the effects of the Highland Potato Famine were beginning to recede. In the autumn of 1846, the Rev. Gregor MacGregor had predicted that 400 people would shortly become destitute because they were entirely dependent upon the potato. In the event, only twenty two people required emergency 'relief' and the poor list rose only to forty in the 1850s, although it is not known how many people actually died or left the island as a direct result of hunger. The parochial board arrived just in time to give support to the most needy in the community (principally the elderly, the blind and the mentally ill).

The minister's pessimism arose, presumably, out of his experience of distributing food aid in 1838, when all crops had been affected. In the event, the Report of the Destitution Committee of the Free Church of Scotland, which took early responsibility for relief across the Highlands and Islands, gave details of food supplies to Mull and Ardnamurchan, but not to Lismore. Indeed, in December 1846, Captain Pole reported that a boat carrying meal for sale from Lismore, had arrived in Loch Moidart. It seems that a combination of good fishing and locally-organised relief, including 'food for work' on Cheyne's estate, carried the island through the crisis. On Baleveolan estate, the introduction of rotations, introducing 'green crops' other than the potato, may well have played a role in maintaining food supplies; and payments for improvements eased the burden of debt, as least among the tenants.

In trying to detect the effects of the two famines on population numbers, it is important not to place too much reliance on early census figures. In particular, it is likely that the 1841 population (Fig.5.3) is an underestimate, possibly by as many as 100 because of seasonal migration. Nevertheless, Fig. 6.1 does not provide evidence of an extreme loss of people (due to mortality or migration), particularly if the curve is corrected for this underestimate. Rather than increasing mortality, the famines of 1838 and from 1846 must have caused a loss of confidence and morale, at a time when there were other threats to island livelihoods. This may explain why a community that had shown very strong resistance to external authority, does not have a record of opposing the clearance activities of the Cheynes.

The Cheyne Clearances

Of the original thirty nine tenants on Cheyne's estate, three had died, but at least thirty two (tenants or sons) were still living on Lismore in 1851, not all of whom had retained a landholding. By 1861 most of the survivors, or their family successors, were still on the island; and even some of the Craignich tenants, cleared out completely in the 1860s, were able to stay on. In spite of this, the rate of decline of the population of the Cheyne estate was much higher than the rest of the island. Between 1841 and 1861 (first wave of clearance) the losses were 222 (46%) compared with 61 (9%) and between 1861 and 1871 (second wave) 66 (26%) compared with 79 (13%) (Table 5.1).

This shows that, although the tenant class remained largely in place, even if landless, the victims of the Cheyne clearances were the younger generation and the cottars. The family structure of islanders (Appendices 13-15) reveals a sustained level of fertility, but a high proportion of their surviving children left home as soon as they could be economically independent, predominantly for the central belt. There was some scope for small-scale fishing (ten men identified as fishermen on the island in 1851) but, apart from the lime industry and the coastal trade, which took off in the 1860s (employing six and sixteen respectively in 1871), there was little alternative employment on the island. This trend is shown clearly in the population structure for 1861 (Fig. 5.3), where the 20-29 age class is strongly under-represented, particularly for men. Another aspect of the trend is the number of young children born in Glasgow, Greenock of Dumbarton who were sent back to their grandparents on Lismore between 1861 and 1891; there were probably several reasons for this (both parents working, illegitimacy, seeking better health and schooling) but few of these children remained on the island for long. There is, therefore, clear evidence that the Cheynes, husband and wife, caused a disproportionate loss of population from Lismore in the years from 1845 to 1865. It seems that the demonization of James Cheyne in local oral tradition is justified, but the idea that the *tenants* were the main victims (rather than the cottars and the younger generation in general) cannot be supported.

Population Decline Across Lismore

The population of the island fell sharply between 1841 (before the potato famine) and 1861 (net loss of 283 people; Tables 5.1, 6.1; Fig. 6.1). The clearance of Cheyne's townships and the subsequent departure of younger family members and cottar families represented three quarters of these losses, with a net loss of only sixty-one people from the rest of the island. Although allowance must be made for a small amount of relocation from the cleared townships to other parts of the island, these figures indicate that clearance (more specifically the lack of opportunities for housing and work for cottars and young people in the nine townships) was the major factor driving people from the island in these decades rather that any *direct* effects of the potato famine.

CHAPTER SIX

Table 6.1 The Demography of Lismore, 1841-1881

Area	Population		
	1841	1861	1881
Lismore	1148	865 (-25%)	621 (-28%)
Cheyne's Townships	479	257 (-46%)	168 (-36%)
Baleveolan Estate	157	122 (-22%)	77 (-37%)
Rest of Lismore	512	486 (-5%)	376 (-23%)

However, rapid decline continued between 1861 and 1881, with a net loss of a further quarter of the population of the island (244 people; Table 6.1; Fig. 6.1). As a result of the Craignich clearance in the early 1860s, Cheyne's former estate contributed around a third of this total but the (uncleared) remainder of the island had a net loss of 155 people, showing that migration for work, mostly to the central belt, had become the dominant reason for leaving. This conclusion is supported by the age structures of the island, which show marked depressions in the proportions of people of working age, especially between 1861 and 1881 (Fig. 5.3). The island population became skewed, with some families consisting of grandparents and grandchildren. In the words of the devout and doleful John McDougall, weaver in Balimakillichan: 'Death is very busy in Lismore this year [1881]. The most of the island is old people.'

Although the farms on Baleveolan estate were not cleared, and continued to be managed for mixed farming (arable and grassland), the losses of population there were greater than other uncleared parts of the island (Table 6.1). By 1861, only four years after Allan MacDougall relinquished his role as factor, the number of tenants had fallen from fifteen to ten

(Table 6.2), and the size of holdings had increased. For example, John Buchanan had twenty acres on Baleveolan in 1851, increasing to forty eight acres in 1861; the two Black crofts of seventeen and a half acres were reunited so that Peter McDougall, an incomer from the mainland, had forty acres in 1861. Rationalisation continued in the 1860s and 1870s, resulting in only six tenants in 1881. On Balimakillichan (including Creckanbreck and Portcastle), John Livingstone retained his family croft of around twenty acres, but the rest of the township was split between two new tenants: James Black (twenty five acres) and Donald Buchanan, an incomer from Craignish on the mainland, who had eighty acres. On Baleveolan township, the Buchanan farm had actually reduced to twenty acres, the MacDougalls had forty acres, and the twenty six-year old Dugald McIntyre, based on Sailean, had 160 acres.

Table 6.2 The Demography of Baleveolan Estate, 1841-1881

Year	Population	Households	Tenant households	Cottar households
1841	157	29	13	16
1851	137	26	15	11
1861	122	22	10	12
1871	101	18	5	13
1881	77	18	6	12

Surprisingly, although the number of cottar households on Baleveolan estate fell from sixteen in 1841, it then remained unchanged at eleven to thirteen from 1851 to 1881 (Table 6.2). The status of cottars appears to have been better than during Allan MacDougall's factorship: the Napier Commission record shows that Donald Carmichael, labourer, newly removed from Park was able to find a cottar house on Balimakillichan in 1882/3. As elsewhere, household size had decreased, with younger islanders emigrating for work. The cottar population of sixty three in 1841, had fallen to thirty six in 1881, of whom only twenty (56%) were of 'working age' (15-65). John McDougall (77) living alone with his wife Catherine (71) was the sole survivor of the once-thriving wool weaving community on Baleveolan estate. Their six surviving children had all left the island and their eldest, John, emigrated to Minnesota in the 1870s.

Village Development

The clearance of Achanard, Fiart, Kilcheran, Baligrundle and Craignich changed the social structure of Lismore in another, important way. For at least two hundred years, and probably much longer, up to the end of the eighteenth century, there had been no resident landowner on the island. One result of this had been the lack of any attempt to concentrate island services (mill, ferry, inn, shop, blacksmith, carpentry, weaving, cobbling etc.) in a nucleated village centre near to (but not *too* near) the laird's house. This could have changed, with the arrival of Bishop Chisholm and his seminary at Kilcheran in 1803. With the need to provide economic support for his work, he established new lime kilns on the shore, providing local employment. Although his time on the island was relatively short, the community in the township prospered in the early decades of the nineteenth century.

A decade after the seminary closed (1841) there were 100 people in Kilcheran, including tenants, and cottars employed in quarrying, lime burning, boat building and carpentry, engineering (wright work), weaving, and crewing boats, as well as general labouring (Table 5.3). Kilcheran was well on its way to becoming a ferry port, with the associated services, including an inn. Indeed Donald Black (*An Dainsair*) did operate an Oban to Mull packet from Kilcheran in mid-century. However, with the decline in the demand for services and for agricultural work in an area cleared for sheep, the Kilcheran community declined quickly and, by 1881, there were only three households: the estate manager, the family of a farm worker from Appin, and Donald Black the ferryman, now retired. To the south there were only two shepherd households in Fiart. The centre of gravity of the island had moved north.

Table 6.3 Cottar Communities, 1841-1881

1841 – 1881	Population Numbers				
	1841	1851	1861	1871	1881
Kilcheran	100	58	28	15	14
Achnacroish with Newfield	32	44	26	41	31
Killean	112	89	91	78	63
Tirlaggan	40	18	33	23	21

The population of Killean in 1841 (112) was actually greater than in Kilcheran, with households headed by crofters, a blacksmith, shoemaker, two tailors, weaver, limeburner and sailor (Table 6.3). As part of the Cheyne estate it became, increasingly, a 'repository' for tenants and cottars moved out of the cleared townships. In spite of this continued immigration, the community decreased by around half over the forty years to 1881, and there was a concentration of paupers and retired servants and labourers. Apart from the blacksmith, the skilled craftsmen had gone, although four households were supported by the sea (sailors and fishermen) and one of the crofters was also a road contractor. Clearly, as part of the Cheyne estate, Killean did not develop as a 'service centre' to fill the void created at Kilcheran. The immediately adjacent township of Tirlaggan, also a 'repository' for displaced people, housed several craftsmen at different times but did serve the community with a grocer's shop for most of the forty years. The other merchants in other parts of the island in 1881 were located at Bachuil and the port of Sailean, which supplied most of the island's domestic coal. As elsewhere, the Tirlaggan population fell from forty in 1841 to twenty one (five households) in 1881.

Today, the greatest concentration of housing on Lismore is at Achnacroish, with its school and ferry port, although the church, manse, shop, fire station and heritage centre are scattered elsewhere. The demography of the township (Table 6.3) shows that this concentration did not occur during the Cheyne period: the population fluctuated, but returned to the same level, over the forty years from 1841 to 1881. It was not until the building of the steamer pier by the Duke of Argyll in 1882, that Achnacroish began to be a focus of development but, even by 1901, with a resident piermaster and postmistress, the population remained at thirty. In spite of the regular steamer service, Achnacroish did not develop to fulfil the role of island 'village'.

The Steady Loss: 'Push and Pull'

Reviewing the 19th century (Fig. 6.1) it is clear that, at least up to the 1880s, there was a steady loss of people from the island by emigration abroad and migration to the mainland, whose rate was unaffected by individual events (famine, clearances). It started before 1830 and, after the Cheyne clearances, the haemorrhage of people continued unabated in the 1860s and 1870s. The losses must have seemed more serious to those left behind because the *proportion* of the population leaving was greater. Taking a long view it can be argued that the Cheynes simply brought forward losses of population that were being caused by the forces of modernisation and globalisation.

As elsewhere in the Highlands and Islands and, indeed in poorer areas across Europe, the factors leading to migration were complex: the 'push' of over population, hunger, clearance, and lack of employment was matched by the 'pull' of land without a landlord, the opportunity to earn a steady income, work for the family, and the aspiration for a higher standard of living. Increasing contact with the wider world revealed not only opportunities in the towns and the empire but also the possibility of a better life (modest improvements for cottars such as mortared walls, gable chimneys, and good joinery for draught-proof windows and doors; as well as a more varied diet including modest luxuries such as tea and sugar). Once there were well-established 'colonies' of islanders (in Glasgow, Paisley & Greenock; from the 1820s in Ontario), they contributed to the 'pull', sending encouraging news of changed lives, and providing support on arrival. Another important factor for Lismore was education, particularly by the leading schoolmaster of the day, Samuel McColl, who taught at the parish school from 1809 to 1862. According to Rev. Gregor MacGregor, the young of the island were given a sound grounding in 'Gaelic and English reading, writing, arithmetic, and book-keeping', but 'English Grammar and Latin, and occasionally the elementary parts of mathematics' were also available for the more able academically. Inevitably, outstanding pupils, such as Alexander Carmichael, were 'prepared for export'. However, there is no evidence that, as in Tiree, involvement with dissenting churches played a role in the resolve to migrate; this is a topic for future research.

The full story of the emigrants abroad and migrants to the mainland remains to be told. Inevitably there were many who exchanged a hard life on Lismore for a different but equally hard life in the slums of the industrial towns and cities. Nevertheless, there were others who were well prepared for the change, and prospered. The Lismore Emigrant register has identified at least twenty two families or individuals who emigrated to North America or Australia between 1840 and 1870, but several of these families spent time in the central belt before acquiring the resources and, possibly, the confidence to embark for overseas. The 1851 census found Dugald Carmichael, his wife Sarah Kieth and their adult children at different addresses in Glasgow. Three were visitors at the home of Duncan MacColl from Lismore and the record notes that Dugald (23) and Mary (21) were 'on their way to America'. By 1861 the Carmichael family was settled in Ontario.

Others spent longer in the central belt before emigrating. Duncan & Mary Carmichael married on Lismore, settled in Greenock in the 1840s where he found work in the sugar industry, but were back on Lismore before 1861 to support her aged parents. After their death, the family embarked for Canada in 1871 aboard the *Corinthian*, and settled amongst their kinsfolk in Elgin County, Ontario. Others used Glasgow as a springboard for an assisted passage to Australia.

The life of Archibald McColl (1833-1910), one of the many children of Duncan McColl, crofter in Tirlaggan in 1841 and Craignich in 1851 (Appendix 13), shows the kind of opportunities offered by the central belt to islanders with health, energy and skill. In spite of their modest means and large family, his parents clearly valued education (he was still a 'scholar' aged 17 in 1851, and schooling was also available to his sisters of 11 and 13). After his father died in 1855 he left the island. Lismore men were known for their horsemanship, and by 1861, Archibald was first ploughman on a large farm in Shettleston, then a village outside Glasgow. Around that time, aged twenty six, he married Marion Paterson from Lanarkshire, and they moved into Glasgow where he worked for many years as a carter for a brewing company. At different addresses in the East End of the city they had eight children, the sons finding work in tool making and the daughters in textiles. By 1901, aged sixty seven, his household in Dennistoun included his wife, four unmarried children (aged 16-24, all employed), a widower son (working with his father in the brewery) and three grandchildren (aged 5-12, all at school). Marion MacColl died in 1902 aged sixty-one. Having provided a secure and modestly prosperous life for his family, Archibald himself died, aged seventy five, in 1910.

Meanwhile, some islanders were taking advantage of the commercial opportunities of the city. For example, John McColl (1823-1880), the son of John McColl (joiner) and Bell Black in Craignich was a 'provision dealer' in Anderston from the mid 1850s. He prospered to become a master grocer with two shops in Govan.

The Resettlement of Baligrundle and Craignich

The decline continued into the twentieth century, with numbers down to 400 in 1911 and continuing to fall. The island might well have struggled to maintain its viability had not the Board of Agriculture for Scotland intervened.

George Campbell the 8th Duke of Argyll had reported to the Napier Commission in 1883 that

CHAPTER SIX

> I have no hesitation in saying that my property in Lismore is one of the few cases I know in which consolidation has been carried much too far. But I am not responsible. I purchased the property only a few years ago, and found almost the whole of it under lease to one sheep-farmer, whose ordinary residence and whose largest farms are in the Low Country.

Although many of the islanders, hungry for a landholding that would allow them to earn their living on Lismore, would have agreed, the Duke did not move to divide the estate. The cause was taken up during the parliamentary election of 1885, by Mr MacFarlane, the Liberal candidate for Argyll. In his address to voters in the Baptist Chapel at Bachuil, he made a great deal of the fact that half of the island was a sheepwalk, while so many were landless.

Following the Report of the Napier Commission, the Crofters' Act was passed in 1886, establishing secure tenure for crofters for the first time. On Lismore, one of the first results was a review of the rents on the Argyll and Fell estates in 1892, resulting in considerable reductions for 26 small tenants. However, the Act did nothing to increase the availability of crofts and, in 1893, 26 electors and 35 non-electors petitioned the County Council for land on Lismore, without success. Another petition in 1907, for the break up of Frackersaig on Lismore into smallholdings, failed, probably because the island was not classed as a 'congested area'.

Fresh impetus was provided from 1912, with the establishment of the new Board of Agriculture for Scotland, one of whose remits was land reform. In 1913, with forty-seven applications from the parish of Lismore and Appin for land under the Small Landholders (Scotland) Act 1911, the Board decided to act. John Campbell, the 9th Duke, declined to negotiate about their proposal to break up of part of his Lismore estate into smaller holdings

> His Grace is <u>opposed</u> to the breaking up of useful sized grazing farms such as Craignich and Baligrundle into small holdings as proposed. *Chamberlain, Argyll Estates to the Board, 24 February 1913*

> the landlord thinks it right to record that it is his view the farms are at present being put to their most suitable purpose, which, on a limestone soil like Lismore, is a grazing purpose, and that they are not adapted for division into small holdings. ... he has had no opportunity of considering the proposed new holders. *30 May 1913*

Nevertheless, the Board used its powers to survey the lands, eventually dividing Craignich into nine crofts and Baligrundle into four; by 30 October 1913, the proposal had been approved by the Scottish Land Court, which set fair rents. On 12 November 1913, the Board submitted its list of approved applicants for the new holdings, with the proposed annual rent. They were mature men with some capital in terms of money and/or livestock. All had experience of farm work, and at least half were single, needing land to enable them to marry. The selection criteria were drawn up to ensure that the land would be well managed, and took no account of whether their families had been evicted from the Cheyne estate; but four were grandsons of men who had moved on by the Cheynes: Dugald Campbell (John Campbell in Fiart); Colin Black (Donald Black in Craignich); Dugald Carmichael (Hugh Carmichael in Craignich); and Duncan Campbell (Craignich 9) (Colin Campbell, originally in Achanard) (Appendix 13). Entry was set for Martinmas 1914.

CHAPTER SIX

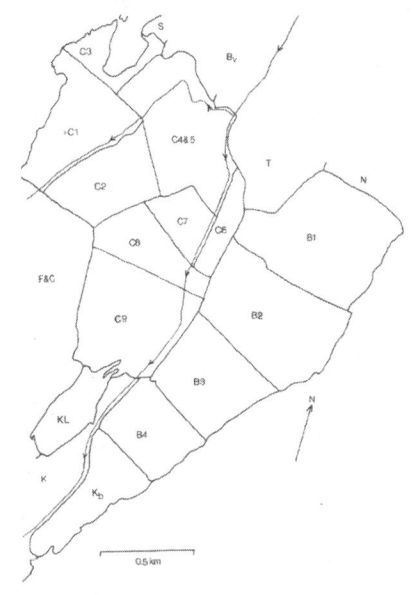

Fig. 6.2 The Division of Baligrundle (B1-4) and Craignich (C1-C9)
(Bv Baleveolan; F&C Frackersaig & Cloichlea; K Kilcheran; KL Kilcheran Loch; Kb part of Baligrundle transferred to Kilcheran by James Cheyne; N Newfield; S Sailean; T Tirlaggan)

By 1915, the new Duke had thirteen new tenants. The original selection for Baligrundle (Fig. 6.2; areas rounded to the nearest acre) had been:

1. Dugald MacGregor, 35, single, with £300 capital. Mason, living at Kilandrist. 90 acres. Rent £40 12s
2. Dugald Campbell, 35, single, with £250 capital. Ploughman, living at Killean. 82 acres. Rent £40 [An outstanding ploughman, medallist and cup-winner]
3. Alexander MacGregor, 36, single, with £200 capital. Ploughman, living at Balure. 54 acres. Rent £26

4. John Black, 55, married with 1 son (7) and 4 daughters (16, 14, 12, 10), with £40 capital, 1 cow and young cattle. Shepherd, living at Kilcheran. 39 acres. Rent £19

In the event, as shown by the rent books for Martinmas 1914, Dugald Campbell got Baligrundle 1 and Alexander MacGregor got Baligrundle 2. Colin Black (64), ploughman in Achuran, with three sons and four daughters, was selected for Baligrundle 3.

The nine holdings on Craignich (Fig. 6.2) were occupied by:

1. Duncan Black, 69, married with 2 sons (22, 29) and 2 daughters (24, 28), with £200 capital, 1 cow and 2 young cattle. Shopkeeper, living in Sailean. 55 acres. Rent £20 15s
2. Duncan Campbell, 45, single, with £80 capital. Sailor living in Sailean. 45 acres. Rent £20 10s
3. Donald Buchanan, 39, single, with £90 capital, 1 cow and 1 heifer. Roadman living in Sailean. 16 acres. Rent £6
4. Dugald Carmichael, Killean. 61 acres. Rent £23 (replacing the 43-year old Hugh Black, ploughman, Port Ramsay, who had originally been selected)
5. Alexander MacGregor, 48, married, with £50 capital and 1 cow. Postman living in Killean. 12 acres. Rent £6 15s
6. Malcolm MacDonald, Achnacroish. 19 acres. Rent £12
7. Norman McLellan, 48, with 1 son (27) and 3 daughters (21, 23, 25), with £50 capital. Sailor living in Achnacroish. 19 acres. Rent £12 [originally from Uist]
8. Hugh McColl, 29, single, with £50 capital, 5 cows and 5 sheep. Postman in Killean. 34 acres. Rent £13
9. Duncan Campbell, 35, single, with £60 capital. Shop assistant living in Baleveolan. 70 acres Rent £24 15s

CHAPTER SIX

All of these original tenants were still in place in 1920, except Hugh McColl who died of tuberculosis in 1917.

The principal difficulty in resettling the townships was the lack of dwelling houses and farm buildings on land that had been a sheepwalk for several decades. The Board agreed to buy the existing buildings and paid the other capital costs (dykes, fences etc.) at a total cost of £1707, based on valuations by the Land Court. The buildings were then sold on to the incoming tenant, who qualified for a government loan on reasonable terms. Any new building would be at the expense of the tenant, again financed by loans arranged by the Board. It was proposed that the tenants of Baligrundle 1 and 2 would share the farm buildings on Baligundle 2, and that there would be a need for new houses on Baligrundle 3 and Craignich 4, 8 and 9. In the event, the register of voters for 1918 shows that new tenants were living on all four Baligrundle holdings and at least four of the Craignich holdings; the others were presumably still farming from their original homes.

The outgoing tenant, John Shankland, whose father had married into the family of Patersons, factors on Lismore for decades, had expected to farm the two townships for several more years. The Shankland family submitted a huge claim for £3505 for 'losses and injury' associated with the resettlement, precipitating a long wrangle with the Board that lasted into 1916. It is more than likely that the cost of the Baligrundle and Craignich resettlement prevented the Board from proceeding to deal with Fiart, which had considerable potential for more intensive occupation.

Chapter Seven
Legacies

As in many parts of the Highlands and Islands, the legacy of the turbulent events of the nineteenth century on Lismore is an empty landscape. Most of the descendants of the bustling community of 1,500 in 1830 are now overseas, in the central belt of Scotland, or have moved on from there to other parts of the UK. Nowadays, there is a steady stream of visitors from Canada, the United States and Australia seeking out their ancestors in the island townships.

Perhaps the only positive result of the Cheyne years on the island is the extensive Kilcheran woodland, started during the 1840s. Otherwise his legacies are the lost village of Kilcheran and the unusual 'empty quarter' of the island where the abandoned houses at Fiart and Dalnarrow (Point of Fiart) testify to the last people to live there up to the 1930s (although Dalnarrow was occupied for lambing to the 1950s). To visitors, the complete absence of trees, resulting from decades of extensive grazing, emphasises the bleakness of the area. In the early twenty first century, with the population edging upwards to 200, ruined houses and cottages are being rebuilt and renovated across Lismore, but the long-term lack of investment in infrastructure (particularly electricity supply) for the south east corner of the island means that it is likely to remain an 'empty quarter'.

There is an island tradition that James Cheyne tried to persuade his fellow landlords on Lismore to clear the whole island for sheep in the 1840s. Faced with the pressures of the time, Allan MacDougall's response was quite different. By acting to help his tenants and cottars through the crisis of 1846, and by his longer-term policy of reducing arrears by paying for improvements, he ensured that the Baleveolan estate continued to be farmed and occupied. Under his factorship, the tenants retained a stake in the future of the townships. Although the estate population halved between 1841 and 1881 and, under new management, the number of tenancies fell from fifteen to six, there was no question of moving to extensive grazing. MacDougall's legacy can be seen today in terms of the high quality drystone dyking and in the well-drained fields, particularly on the better lands of Baleveolan and Balimakillichan. As in Baligrundle and Craignich, most of the holdings are individually owned, some by descendants of nineteenth century tenants, and there are at least six permanent households on the former estate.

The island would have been much emptier had it not been for the actions of the new Board of Agriculture for Scotland in resettling Baligrundle and Craignich in 1915. Under 'right to buy' legislation, all of the holdings are now individually owned and at least nine houses are permanently occupied. In contrast to Fiart, where the land use today is mainly extensive grazing, most of the Baligrundle and Craignich crofts are managed more intensively, including conservation of winter fodder. They provide bases for families finding work on the island and the mainland, and supporting local activities. If the Board had submitted to the opposition of the Duke, the 'empty quarter' would indeed have occupied up to half of the island. The legacy of the Board's action is a healthy population on the townships today.

❊ ❊ ❊

This journey began with Hugh Anderson and *Orain do Lios Mòr*. In the spring of 1901, he wrote to Alexander Carmichael from his ship, the S.S. *Marmion* lying at Falmouth, to describe an intensely emotional return to his native island:

> I walked up to 'Druim na Bithe' to have a look round and after I surveyed with the eye all the surrounding familiar lovely hillocks whereon I often roved in my youthful days. 'Port a charrain', 'Moine nan Corr', 'Cnoc-Aingil' ... After I took these views in, and while looking on, shall I tell you what I was obliged to do? I had to sit down and wet my handkerchief in my tears. 'Baligarve', 'Clachan', the 'Manse', 'Killeondrist' etc etc seemed to make efforts to and say 'are you not sorry for us?' Afterwards I dandered down to the 'Crois' (cemetery) and spent a while among the dead, and after looking & reading, I wrenched myself away, went down to 'Tobar a chlachain' & washed my face. No one knows this ordeal but yourself. *CW MS 527*

Having witnessed the events of the 1840s and 1850s, he was expressing not only nostalgia for his youth but also distress at the haemorrhage of people, and awareness of the damage done to the Gaelic culture of the island. His childhood had been enriched in the ceilidh houses of Baligarve, where his mother and aunt (Janet and Isabella MacGregor) had been leading tradition bearers. Deep feelings persisted for many decades because, in spite of the strong character and independence of the islanders, they were ultimately *powerless* in the face of a battery of challenges: insecure tenure, agricultural depression; famine; the disappearance of the traditional landowners, to be replaced by commercial entrepreneurs; the loss of traditional skills, jobs and markets; the pull of the mainland where there was paid employment and a higher standard of living (albeit, for some, the most degrading living and working conditions); and the opportunities offered by the empire. These were not unique to islanders but the experience of the common people across Scotland.

Anderson did not live to see the resettlement of Baligrundle and Craignich, and subsequent bards have continued to dwell on the sadness of the past. It is regrettable that there is no recognition, let alone celebration, of the contribution of Allan MacDougall or of the astonishing facing down of the Duke of Argyll by the Board of Agriculture on behalf of the land-hungry islanders.

Appendix 1
The Baleveolan Estate Community in the 1830s

(Ages from the 1841 Census; areas from the 1851 census; annual rents from the 1831 rental, checked against the 1844 rental)

Baleveolan Tenants

John McDonald (or McKillaich), 55, his wife Anne (or Agness), 35, his mother, 75, five children between 3 and 11, and a female servant 15. Farming 59 acres. Cash rent £56. John McDonald registered to vote, 1832.

Duncan Black, 75, his wife Anne, 65, two adult sons, their wives, two grandchildren (1 and 3), a herd 10, female servant 15, and a lodger. Farming 35 acres (by 1851, this has been split into two holdings of 17.5 acres for the two sons Donald and Duncan). Cash rent £53. Duncan Black registered to vote, 1832.

John Buchanan, 50, his wife Peggy, 40, and five children between 5 and 14.

Archibald Buchanan, 55, his wife Anne, 40, and six children between 3 and 15.

Together farming 40 acres. Cash rent £51

Myles Black, 50, his wife Mary, 50, one adult son, and two children, 10 and 14

Farming 30 acres. Cash rent £28 4 0

[Myles is the anglicised form of Maoilios = Servant of Jesus]

Baleveolan Cottars

Mary Stewart, 50, merchant, with a household of four, including son John, 20.

John McCorquodale, 40, publican, his wife Janet, 30, and five children between 2 months and 10.

Archibald McCaig, 30, weaver, with a household of 2 (probably his mother and one child, 10).

Duncan McColl, 40, weaver, with four children between 5 and 10.

Archibald McColl, 25, shoemaker, with his wife Bell, 25 and one child, 3.

Hugh Black, 65, his wife Cathrine, 50 (paupers by 1851).

Duncan McIntyre, 65, his wife Anne, 65, two adult sons and one granddaughter aged 1.

Sailean Tenants

Dugald McIntyre, 60, his wife Chirsty, 60, 2 female servants, a lodger and a three year old child (probably a grandchild). Cash rent £33. Dugald McIntyre registered to vote, 1832.

John McIntyre, 25, his wife Cathrine, 20, and two male servants.

Sailean Cottars

Donald McIntyre, 40, carpenter, his wife Anne, 40, and 4 children between 2 and 15

[his workshop was in the great Sailean cave].

Donald McIntyre, 35, and John McKillop, 35, labourer.

Mary Livingstone, 65, independent.

Niel Carmichael, 40, labourer, his wife Anne, 30, and 1 child, aged 1.

Bell McColl, 55, independent.

Balimakillichan Tenants

Duncan Carmichael, 65, one adult daughter, and four children between 5 and 15.

Farming 30 acres at Portcastle. Cash rent £33.

Donald McCorquodale, 65, with his wife Sally or Sarah, 60, three adult children, and two children/grandchildren 2 and 15. Farming 24 acres. Cash rent £31 10 0.

John Black [successor c1840 to Donald Mòr Black], 55, his son Donald, 35 and wife Dorothy, 35, one adult daughter, and 9 children/grandchildren, 1 month and 15. Farming around 30 acres. Cash rent £31 8 0.

Duncan Livingston, 50, his wife Sally, 35, and three children between 9 and 13.

Farming 22 acres in partnership with his brother Coll, Bachuil. Cash rent £27 4 0.

Dugald Carmichael, 55, his wife Cathrine, 50, 2 adult sons, 5 children/grandchildren between 3 and 15. Farming 25 acres (called Tir a'Choirce = Land of corn). Cash rent £26.

Hugh Carmichael, 35, his wife Mary, 30, four children between 9 months and 10, and a herd 14. Farming 30 acres at Creckanbreck. Cash rent £21 5 0.

Balimakillichan Cottars

Gilbert McDonald, 70, his wife Bell, 70, and one adult daughter.

Donald McColl, 45 weaver, his wife Cathrine, 35, and five children between 1 and 14.

John McDugald, 35 weaver, his wife Cathrine, 30, and four children between 1 and 8.

Angus Graham, 60 and his wife Mary, 65.

Total Population of the Estate, c.155.

Appendix 2

The Baleveolan Estate Community at the 1861 Census

(rents from 1858/59 valuation)

Baleveolan Tenants

John Buchanan, 70, 4 adult children and one grandchild, 6. Farming 60 acres (£51).

Peter McDougall, 58, his wife Margaret, 62, two adult children and a herd, 14.
Farming 35 acres (£35).

Miles Black, 74, his son, daughter in law and six grandchildren, 6 months to 12.
Farming 35 acres (£28 12s).

John McDonald or McKellaich, 64, his wife Anne, 57, two adult sons and one son of 14. Farming 50 acres (£55 12s).

Donald McIntyre, 46, his wife Mary, 35, six children between 4 and 14, and one farm servant. Farming 50 acres.

Sailean Tenant

John McIntyre, 49, farmer and lime burner, his wife Cathrine, 45, seven children between 9 months and 18, and three farm servants. (£33)

Baleveolan Cottars

Dugald McCorquodale, 54, labourer, his wife Isabella, 34, and three children between 9 months and 9.

John Carmichael, 32, labourer, his wife Mary, 32, and two children aged 3.

John McCorquodale, 65, mason, his wife Janet, 54, two children, 7 and 18.

John McIntyre, 53, fisherman, and his sister, 40.

Donald McIntyre, 60, labourer, and his wife Cathrine, 46.

Balimakillichan Tenants

Duncan McColl, 59, his wife Mary, 35, three children between 2 and 11, and his brother's family of seven (children aged 1 -11). One shepherd. Farming 28 acres at Portcastle with his brother John (in succession to Duncan Carmichael) (£53).

Duncan Livingstone, 73, his wife Dorothy, 55, one adult son and 2 grandchildren, 4 and 12. Farming 18 acres (£27 4s).

Donald Carmichael (absent at census), 35, his wife Mary, 32, and 4 children aged 1 – 14 at Tir a'Choirce (in succession to his father Dugald, but a pauper by 1871) (£33 8s).

Dugald McColl, 68, his wife Cathrine, 59, one adult son, two grandchildren, 2 and 8, and a boarder. Farming 24 acres (£28).

John Keith, 67, his wife Mary, 63, three adult children and one grandchild, 11 months. Farming 50 acres at Creckanbreck (in succession to Hugh Carmichael) (£40).

Balimakillichan Cottars

John McDougall, 57, weaver, his wife Catherine, 51, and two children, 10 and 13.

John Black, 73, pauper, his wife Jean, 60, and three children, 2-17.

James Graham, 36, labourer and his sister Catherine, 39.

Donald Black, 60, labourer, his wife Dorothy, 60 and one son, 14, in Creckanbreck (£5).

Donald Connell, 77, pauper, with a household of three including 2 children, 9 and 13.

Duncan Carmichael, 30, his wife Janet, 35, and two children, 2 and 8.

Total Population of the Estate, c.120

Appendix 3
The Fiart Community 1841-61

1841 Census (including Point of Fiart)

Tenants

James Black, 60, his wife Catherine, 35, 4 children and a herd.

Janet Black, 50, with 4 children, 8-15. Son Meals (Miles) (15) listed as the tenant.

Niel Black, 50, his wife Mary, 40, his brother John, 40 (co-tenant) and 7 children, 4-20.

William Black, 35, a female servant Sally, 25, 2 children (5) and a herd (12).

John Campbell, 65, his wife Ann, 60, one adult son and 5 children (6-15).

Cottars

Mary Black, 60.

Mary McCorquodale, 50, with one adult daughter and 2 children, 13 and 15.

Mary McLaren, 30 and a child aged 2.

Total Population of the Township in 1841 = 42

1851 Census

Tenants

James Black, 72, and 3 sons, 13-17. Farming 15 acres.

William Black, 45, one adult female servant, and 2 children, 13 and 15. Farming 25 acres.

John Campbell, 73, his wife Ann, 58, with a grown up son and daughter. Farming 25 acres

Cottars

John Black, 63, his adult daughter and 4 grandchildren, 1-6.

Mary Black, 72

Colin Campbell, 28, ploughman, his wife Ann, 29, 2 children, 2 months and a male servant, 14. [Point of Fiart]

John McDonald, 50, Labourer, his wife Ann, 46, and 3 children, 2-14.

Mary McLaren, 43 and her daughter 12.

William McLellan, 22 light-house boatman, with his wife Harriot [sic], 20. [Point of Fiart]

APPENDIX 3

Total Population of the Township in 1851 = 34

1861 Census

No Tenants

Cottars

Peter Kieth, 75, pauper, formerly agricultural labourer, his wife Janet, 60, and his son John, 28, shepherd.

Robert McMorran, 31, shepherd (born Crawford, Lanarkshire), his wife Elizabeth, 25, and a son aged 1.

Total Population of the Township in 1861 = 6

Appendix 4

The Craignich Community 1836-71

1836 Estate Plan (areas rounded)

Mrs Noble's Croft	40 acres
Duncan Black	25
John McKeith	33
Donald McGlashan	22
Donald Black	26
Malcolm McColl	33
Duncan McKeith	33
Donald McColl	19
John Black	3
John McKilloch	19
Total (incl. roads)	259

1841 Census

Tenants

Donald Black, 70, 2 adult sons, a daughter in law, three children, 6 months to 3 and two female servants, 12 and 15.

John Black, 40, his mother and one child aged 8.

James Campbell, 50, his wife Bell, 40, one adult son, and 6 children, 2 months to 15.

Hugh Carmichael, 60, his wife Mary 55, 3 children, 8-15, and a resident family of 3 headed by an agricultural labourer.

John McCorquodale, 65, his wife Cathrine, 3 adult males, one adult female and 2 children, 11 and 13.

John McGlassen, 30, his mother, 2 adult brothers, and 2 servants, 14.

Cottars

Duncan Black, 50, his wife Mary, 40, 2 children, 6 and 10, and a resident male labourer.

Hugh Black, 65, and Anne Black, 70.

Harriat [sic] Cameron, 35, independent, with 3 children, 1 month to 11.

Anne Campbell, 70.

Mary Carmichael, 40 and 3 children, 8-20.

Peter Kieth, 50, his wife Janet, 35, and 4 children, 3-11.

Anne Livingstone, 70 and Cathrine Livingstone, 60.

Christy McColl, 60, independent with her mother.

Total Population of the Township in 1841 = 69

1851 Census

Tenants

Sally Black, 64 and her two sons, 17 and 31. Farming 25 acres.

James Campbell, 70, his wife Bell, 52, 2 adult sons, and 3 children, 9-16. Farming 20 acres.

Donald Gray, 42, his wife Sally, 32, and 3 children, 1-4. Farming 13 acres.

John Gray, 45, his wife Margaret, 35, his mother and 3 children, 2-7. Farming 20 acres.

Myles Keith, 72, his wife Chirsty, 56, one adult son and 2 children, 6 and 8. Farming 20 acres.

Duncan McColl, 58, his wife Mary, 46, and 5 children, 7-17. Farming 12 acres.

Cottars

Mary Black, 60, with her sister (pauper) and one daughter.

Archibald Campbell, 70, with his wife Margaret, 48, adult son and daughter, and 4 children, 5-12.

Margaret Campbell, 58, with one daughter.

Mary Carmichael, 62, Pauper, with 2 adult daughters.

Cathrine Gray, 74, Pauper.

Anne McColl, 58, with one daughter and one grandson.

Cathrine McColl, 58, with one son.

Total Population of the Township in 1851 = 55

1858/59 Valuation

John Campbell	£77 3s
John McIntyre	£60
Duncan Black	£20
Donald McGlashan (Gray)	£22
James Campbell's heirs	£23
William Black	£20
Colin Campbell	£10
Malcolm McColl	£10
John Black	£5

1861 Census

Tenants

Duncan Black, 62, his wife Mary, 44, one adult son, and 6 children, 5-17. Farming 18 acres.

John Black, 63, his wife Anne, 42, and 4 children, 4-12. Crofting 4 acres.

William Black, 60, with his sister. Farming 15 acres.

Niel Buchanan, 40, his wife Janet, 27, and one son, 2. Farming 12 acres.

Archd. Campbell, 44, his wife Ann, 25, his father, 3 children, 1 month to 3, and a servant. Farming 50 acres.

Colin Campbell, 37, his wife Ann, 37, and 6 children, 2-12. Farming 37 acres.

Donald Campbell, 34, his wife Kitty, 31, and one daughter, 2. Farming 15 acres.

Cottars

Mary Black, 34.

Duncan Campbell, 39, labourer, his mother, sister and nephew, 6 months.

Margaret Kieth, 59, and one grandson, 2.

Archd. McColl, 50, labourer, his wife Harriet, 55, and 2 children, 15 and 17.

Malcolm McColl, 60, labourer, his wife Dorothy, 48, and 3 children, 11-15.

Total Population of the Township in 1861 = 54

1861/2 Valuation

Lachlan Smith £232

1867/68 Valuation

Lachlan Smith 11 year lease from 1867 £232

1871 Census

One shepherd, 3 people

Appendix 5
The Kilcheran Community 1841-71

1841 Census

Tenants

Donald Carmichael, 20, listed as the tenant, his mother, 3 children, 1-15, a female servant and a herd, 15.

Myles Kieth, 60, his wife Chirsty, 40, and 3 children, 3-12.

Janet McColl, 40, her mother and 3 children, 7-12. Her husband John was absent.

James McNicol, 61, his wife Mary, 61, 2 adult daughters, 1 adult son, 2 children, 10 and 11, and 5 others including 4 servants.

Cottars

Angus Black, 50, labourer, his wife Eve, 45, and 3 children, 5-10.

Alexander Black, 45, labourer, with a household of 4 including 2 children, 2 and 5.

John Black, 35, publican, his wife Isabella, 25, one child, 1, and a female servant, 12.

Mary Black, 45, and 2 children, 9 and 12.

Archibald Campbell, 50, quarrier, his wife Peggy, 35, 5 children, 6 months to 12.

Margaret Campbell, 45, and a household of 7 including 5 children, 3-14.

Duncan Carmichael, 40, and 2 children, 5 and 9.

John Carmichael, 55, his wife Flory, 60, and one child, 10.

Anne Demster, 30, servant.

Hugh Fletcher, 50, his wife Catherine, 55, and another adult female.

John (Fraser), 30, preacher.

Catherine McColl, 45, with 3 children, 6-15.

Dugald McColl, 30, wright, and a household of 2 including one child, 12.

Alexander McCorquodale, 20, sailor, and Alexander McKinnon, 15, sailor.

John McCorquodale, 50, weaver, his wife Mary, 45, an adult labourer son, and 3 children, 8-14.

Niel McDonald, 50, carpenter, his wife Flory, 50, 2 adult carpenter sons, and 3 children, 10-15.

Malcolm Sinclair, 40, and a household of 3 including a lime burner.

Total Population of Kilcheran in 1841 = 101

1851 Census

Farm Staff

James Law, 47, grieve from Fife, with 3 adult ploughman sons, and a herd, 15.

Tenant

John McColl, 58, his wife Janet, 56, 3 adult sons, one adult daughter, and a grandson, 1 month. Farmer of 30 acres.

Cottars

Allan Black, 55, labourer, his wife Cathrine, 40, and 3 children, 3-14.

Donald Black, 48, boatman, his wife Janet, 35, and one daughter, 6.

Eve Black, 56, and her son, 18.

Duncan Carmichael, 54, store keeper, his wife Cathrine, 33, with 4 children, 3-7 and a servant, 16.

John Carmichael, 70, labourer and his sister, a pauper.

Cathrine Fletcher, 72, her daughter and one grandson, 9.

Jean Kieth, 40, pauper, and 2 daughters, 8 and 12.

John McCorquodale, 65, weaver, his wife Mary, 60, 3 adult sons, 2 adult daughters, and one grandson, 4 months.

Angus McDonald, 42, labourer, his wife Janet, 26, and one son, 1.

Donald McIntyre, 56, carpenter, his wife Ann, 54, and 2 children, 14 and 16.

Total population of Kilcheran in 1851 (excluding James Cheyne and his household) = 52

1861 Census

Farm Staff

J H J Stewart, 37, from Dumfriesshire, farmer of 1200 acres.

Allan Black, 66, shepherd, his wife Catherine, 43, one child, 14, and one grandson, 7.

Niel Carmichael, 65, shepherd, and his wife Ann, 54.

Alexander McGregor, 30, ploughman, his wife Catherine, 30, and 3 children, 6 months to 3.

Cottars

Bell Black, 20, domestic servant, and her sister Nancy, 22, dressmaker.

Donald Black, 58, boatman, his wife Janet, 45, and 3 children, 5-10.

Duncan Carmichael, 66, woodplanter, his wife Cathrine, 46, one adult house carpenter son, and 3 children, 8-13.

John Carmichael, 80, pauper, formerly farmer.

Mary McCorkindale, 53, servant, and one niece, 11.

Total Population of Kilcheran in 1861 = 28

1871 Census

Farm Staff

William Shankland, 27, manager from Dumfriesshire, his wife Sarah, 26, one adult brother and one son, 5.

John Campbell, 24, ploughman, and a household of 3 including a nephew, 8.

Cottars

Allan Black, 74, pauper, and his wife Cathrine, 61.

Donald Black, 68, ferryman, and 3 children, 14-17.

Mary MacGregor, 62, servant.

Total Population of Kilcheran in 1871 = 15

Appendix 6
The Baligrundle Community 1841-61

1841 Census (rent 1830)

Tenants

Allan Black, 40, his wife Mary, 35, and 5 children, 3-12. Rent £48.

Dugald Carmichael, 50, his wife Christian, 50, and one child, 13. Rent £42 5s 6d.

Archibald McColl, 75, his wife Ann, 60, two adult sons, one adult daughter, a servant, 15, and a herd, 12. Rent £120.

Donald McColl, 50, miller, his wife Ann, 30, his sister, 4 children, 1-7, two servants, 14 and 20, and a herd, 14. Rent £51 8s 6d.

Dugald McColl, 60, a housekeeper, an adult son, one child, 10, and a herd, 10. Rent £60.

Cottars

Archibald Black, 35, and a housekeeper.

James Black, 35, labourer.

John Campbell, 35, schoolmaster, a housekeeper and one child, 10.

John McColl, 55, labourer, his wife Mary, 40, and one child, 13.

Peter McLachlan, 35, tailor, his wife Catherine, 35, and one child, 5.

Total Population of Baligrundle in 1841 = 44

1851 Census

Farm Staff

James Black, 45, shepherd, his sister, and three children, 3-18.

Tenant

Malcom McCallum, 40, miller, his wife Chirsty, 36, and two children, 2 and 4.

Cottars

Archibald Black, 44, labourer, his sister, 40, and one child, 7.

James Black, 46, pauper.

Archibald McColl, 41, labourer, his wife Harriot [sic], 47, and four children, 5-15.

John McLachlan, 55, labourer, his wife Flora, 42, and 6 children, 7 months to 16.

Peter McLachlan, 54, tailor, his wife Cathrine, 57, and one child, 16.

Total population of Baligrundle in 1851 = 30

1861 Census

Farm Staff

Hugh McPhail, 47, shepherd, with his sister in law.

Tenants

None

Cottars

None

Total population of Baligrundle in 1861 = 2

Appendix 7
The Achnacroish Community 1841-71

(including Newfield and Taynastaroch)

1841 Census

Tenants

Hugh Buchanan, 45, his wife Kett, 40, and 6 children, 2-12.

Alexander McColl, 35, his wife Mary, 20, one child, 1, and a servant, 15 (Newfield).

Donald McColl, 55, his wife Mary, 38, and 6 children, 2-14.

John McIntyre, 25, with a household of 3.

Cottars

Chirsty Black, 75, with one child, 10.

Dugald McColl, 35, joiner, his wife Betsy, 30, and 4 children, 8 months to 6.

Total Population of Achnacroish in 1841 = 32

1851 Census

Tenants

Duncan Black, 52, farmer of 23 acres, his wife Mary, 33, 7 children, 1-13, a servant, 17, and a lodger (Newfield).

Archibald Campbell, 34, farmer of 10 acres, his mother, 3 siblings, 20-31, and a herd, 11.

Cottars

John Black, 50, labourer, his wife Ann, 37, and 3 children, 2-6 (Taynastaroch).

Duncan McDonald, 42, boat builder, his wife Cathrine, 40, 3 children, 3-6, and an apprentice, 18.

Janet McDonald, 33, sailor's wife, and 3 children, 1 month to 4.

Total population of Achnacroish in 1851 = 32

1861 Census

Tenants

Hugh Buchanan, 69, farmer of 35 acres, his wife Catherine, 66, and one adult son, ploughman.

Donald Black, 29, farmer of 35 acres, his mother and brother.

Archibald Campbell, 45, innkeeper & farmer of 15 acres, his wife Sarah, 26, one child, 1, and a servant, 18.

Hugh Campbell, 32, farmer of 20 acres, with two adult sisters.

Cottars

Janet Black, 44, pauper, formerly servant, with one daughter, 10.

Duncan Buchanan, 77, grocer, and his wife Sarah, 70.

Dugald Carmichael, 84, pauper, formerly tailor, his wife Christina, 70, and one adult daughter.

Catherine McColl, 40, servant, with her mother a pauper.

Peggy McGlashen, 64, pauper, formerly servant.

Donald McIntyre, 63, ship carpenter, master, employing 2, his wife Ann, 62, and an apprentice, 21.

Total population of Achnacroish in 1861 = 26

Population in 1871

2 tenants (26 & 43 acres), 41 people

Appendix 8
The Tirlaggan Community 1841-71

1841 Census

Tenants

Archibald Black, 20, with his mother and one child, 12.

Cathrine McColl, 45, with a household of 5, including 4 children, 3-14.

Dugald McColl, 50, his wife Anne, 45, and 4 children, 6-15.

Dugald McColl, 85, crofter with a household of 2 including one child, 12.

Duncan McColl, 45, his wife Mary, 35, and a household of 7, including 6 children, 2-13.

Hugh McColl, 40, his wife Mary, 30, and 3 children, 2-7.

Cottars

John Black, 60, labourer, his wife Peggy, 40, and one child, 5.

David McColl, 60, cottar, with one child, 15.

Peggy McColl, 70.

Flory McLain, 50, grocer.

Population of Tirlaggan in 1841 = 40

1851 Census

Tenant

Cathrine McCorquodale, 80, and 5 unmarried adults, farming 40 acres.

Cottars

Cathrine Black, 74.

John Carmichael, 55, shoemaker, his wife Effy, 51, and one child, 11.

Cathrine McColl, 71, pauper, and her adult daughter.

Flory McColl, 78.

Hugh McColl, 57, labourer, his wife Mary, 45, and 3 children, 11-16.

Total population of Tirlaggan in 1851 = 18

1861 Census

Farm Staff

James Black, 66, shepherd, his sister and niece, 12.

Tenant

Dugald McCorkindale, 60, farmer of 35 acres, 3 unmarried siblings, and a niece, 14.

Cottars

Sarah Black, 77, retired farmer.

Catherine Carmichael, 36, dairymaid.

John Carmichael, 67, boot & shoemaker, his wife Effy, 65, one pauper daughter and a grandson, 7.

Ann McColl, 44, pauper, formerly servant, her mother and 3 children, 4-13.

Hugh McColl, 69, agricultural labourer, his wife Mary, 56, one adult daughter and one grandson, 1.

Isabella McColl, 36, grocer, her sister and 2 children, 4 and 7.

John McDonald, 65, agricultural labourer, his wife Nancy, 56, and 2 children, 12 and 15.

William Wood, 72, minister of UP Chapel, with one servant.

Total population of Tirlaggan in 1861 = 33

1871 Census

4 households, no tenant, ground officer

Appendix 9
The Killean Community 1841-61

1841 Census

Tenants

Duncan Buchanan, 50, his wife Sarah, 45, and one child, 15.

Archibald McCallum, 45, his wife Cathrine, 40, and 2 children, 5 and 10.

Donald McColl, 50, with a household of 6 including 3 children, 4 months to 12.

Malcom McColl, 65, his wife Mary, 55, and a household of 7 including 5 children, 1-12.

John McIntyre, 60, his wife Isabella, 55, 2 children, 10 and 15 and a pauper.

Malcom McIntyre, 70, with a household of 3, including a servant, 14.

Niel McIntyre, 65, crofter, his wife Janet, 65, and two adult children, 20 and 25.

Cottars

Anne Black, 55, independent.

Donald Black, 35, mariner, with his mother and brother.

John Black, 50, tailor, his wife Mary, 30, and 3 children, 2-8.

Ann Buchanan, 50.

John Carmichael, 45, shoemaker, his wife Effy, 40, and 5 children, 2-12.

John Carmichael, 45, his wife Bell, 40, and 5 children, 4-14.

John Cunningham, 45, smith, his wife Cathrine, 40, and 2 children, 12 and 15.

Duncan McCallum, 50, his wife Bell, 50, and 4 children, 8-20.

Donald McColl, 75, with one adult female.

James McColl, 40, tailor, his wife Effy, 35, 3 children, 1-5, and a servant, 15.

Duncan McCorquodale, 60, weaver, his wife Nelly, 35, and 5 children, 2-15.

Martin McDonald, 60, his wife Peggy, 50, an adult daughter and 2 children, 9 months and 15.

Donald McIntyre, 55, his wife Mary, 45, and 5 children, 4-12.

Gilbert McIntyre, 50, lime burner, with his wife Ann, 56, and one child, 10.

Kett McKeich, 75.

Cathrine McLachlan, 70, independent.

John McLachlan, 70, with a household of 5 including 3 children, 4-15.

Lachlan McLachlan, 50, his wife Mary, 50, and 2 children, 10 and 20.

Total population of Killean in 1841 = 112

1851 Census

Tenants

Niel Black, 73, farmer of 17 acres, his wife Mary, 60, an adult son, and 2 children, 15 and 18.

Jean Carmichael, 43, farmer of 16 acres, and 4 children, 5-15.

James McColl, 50, tailor and crofter of 3 acres, his wife Effy, 47, and 4 children, 1-15.

Malcolm McColl, 50, farmer of 12 acres, his wife Dorothy, 37, and 4 children, 1-8.

Isabella McIntyre, 66, farmer of 28 acres, 2 adult children and a herd, 9.

Niel McIntyre, 80, crofter of 3 acres, with 2 adult children.

Cottars

Anne Black, 75, pauper.

Cathrine Black, 54, pauper.

Donald Black, 41, roadman, his wife Margaret, 46, and 2 daughters, 13 and 14.

Hugh Black, 77, pauper.

Duncan Buchanan, 67, labourer, and his wife Sarah, 57.

Archibald Campbell, 37, shoemaker, his wife Mary, 33, and 2 children, 2 and 8.

John Carmichael, 55, farm labourer, with one son, 13.

Niel Carmichael, 57, labourer, his wife Anne, 41, and 4 children, 6-11.

John Cunningham, 54, blacksmith, his wife Cathrin, 54, 3 adults and one granddaughter, 1 month.

Duncan McCallum, 60, labourer, his wife Isabella, 60, his pauper mother, fisherman son, 18, and granddaughter, 1.

Cathrine McColl, 60, her daughter and 2 grandsons, 5 and 12.

Duncan McColl, 15, scholar with his niece, 9.

Martin McDonald, 73, labourer, 2 adult daughters, and 2 grandsons, 3.

Archibald McIntyre, 37, labourer, his wife Janet, 32, and 3 children, 2-8.

Donald McIntyre, 66, fisherman, his wife Mary, 58, and one adult daughter.

Effy McIntyre, 80, pauper, with her adult niece.

Gilbert McIntyre, 74, and 3 adult children.

John McLachlan, 30, handloom weaver.

Total Population of Killean in 1851 = 89

1861 Census

Tenants

Donald Black, 50, farmer of 5 acres, his wife Peggy, 58, and one adult daughter.

Duncan Black, 29, farmer of 10 acres, with his grandmother, one adult brother, and a nephew.

Hugh Black, 34, farmer of 15 acres, two siblings and 3 children, 9 months – 12.

Archibald Buchanan, 71, farmer of 50 acres, his wife Ann, 64, 3 adult children and one grandson, 8.

Mary Campbell, 36, farmer of 13 acres, with 6 children, 1-11.

Jean Carmichael, 55, occupier of 7 acres, her adult daughters and 2 grandsons, 5 and 7.

Cottars

Archibald Black, 60, agricultural labourer.

James Campbell, 30, boatman, his wife Nancy, 28, 2 children, 1 month and 1, and a servant, 10.

John Carmichael, 70, labourer, and one grandson, 5.

Margret [sic] Cunningham, 30, dressmaker.

Jean Kieth, 55, pauper, formerly servant, 2 daughters, 15 and 20, and one grandson, 4.

Miles Kieth, 79, pauper, formerly farmer, and his wife Christina, 65.

Donald McColl, 30, master smith, his wife Sarah, 30, and 2 children, 4 and 6.

James McColl, 63, tailor, his wife Euphemia, 56, and 2 sons, 12 and 26.

Mary McColl, 56, one daughter and grandson, 7.

Angus McDonald, 36, ploughman, his wife Janet, 32, and 3 children, 2-11.

Peggy McDonald, 79, pauper, formerly ag. labourer, her two pauper daughters, and one grandson, 12.

Cathrine McGlashen, 80, pauper.

Donald McGlashen, 54, sailor, his wife Sarah, 48, and 3 children, 7-14.

John McGlashen, 57, agricultural labourer, his wife Euphemia, 38, and 3 children, 3-10.

Archibald McIntyre, 46, agricultural labourer, his wife Janet, 40, and 3 children, 3-11.

Donald McIntyre, 80, pauper, his wife Mary, 69, 2 daughters and 2 grandsons, 5 months and 8.

Malcom McIntyre, 35, labourer, with 2 siblings.

Total Population of Killean in 1861 = 91

Appendix 10
The Portcharron Community 1841-61

1841 Census

Tenants

Duncan McColl, 30, with his mother, brother and a herd, 14.

Hugh Carmichael, 55, his wife Betty, 50, one adult son, one child, 7, a servant, 15, and 2 lodgers.

Cottars

James Carmichael, 55, his wife Mary, 40, and 5 children, 6 months – 14.

John McLachlen, 70, his wife Cathrine, 65, and a household of 7 including 3 children, 1-6.

Archibald Black, 55, his wife Cathrine, 45, and a household of 3 including one child, 11.

Anne, 60, and Peggy McGlasson, 50, independent, with one child, 1 month.

Hugh McColl, 50, with 4 children, 5-20.

Total Population of Portcharron in 1841 = 40

1851 Census

Tenants

None

Cottars

Archibald Black, 72, pauper, his wife Cathrin, 60, 4 adults and 5 grandchildren, 2 months to 10.

Anne McGlashen, 76, pauper, with her sister and adult nephew.

Cathrin McLachlan, 80, pauper, with one daughter, one granddaughter, 5, and a pauper lodger.

Duncan McCorquodale, 76, handloom weaver, his wife Dorothy, 49, and 3 children, 9-18.

Hugh McColl, 63, 3 daughters, 13-36, and one grandson, 5.

Total Population of Portcharron in 1851 = 28

1861 Census

Cottars

John Cameron, 41, labourer, his wife Cathrine, 41, and 4 children, 4-19.

Dorothy McCorquodale, 55, 2 adult children and one granddaughter, 8.

John McLachlan, 66, labourer, and one son, 11.

Hugh McColl, 72, pauper, with 2 adult daughters and one grandson, 8.

Total Population of Portcharron in 1861 = 16

Appendix 11

Lismore Households Visited by Commissioners of the Poor Law Inquiry in August 1843

Chirsty Black, widow, aged fifty-two. Five children. Eldest working out, and supporting the rest. One little boy in the house, very ill-clothed. Very poor bed, blankets, and a coverlet. House very poor. Little girl, with very little clothing on her. Has no assistance from the session.

Widow Keith, about fifty. Not on the session. House comfortable. Very poor, but cleanly. *Note.* This year the allowances from the session funds in Lismore was from 1s 6d up to 5s.

Widow Solomon M'Coll, aged ninety-three. Got 3s 6d at last division. She is supported by her daughter. House tolerably comfortable for a highland house, but wants a chimney. Has a glazed window. Crockery and dresser very good, and clean. Decent bed. She is the oldest person in the island. A hale old woman.

Ann Livingstone and Kate Livingstone. One upon the borders of eighty, the other sixty. Both are on the poor's list. They had 5s 6d between them. They get assistance from their neighbours. One decent bed, and crockery. Mr Wood sometimes assists them, though they do not belong to his congregation. Eldest can't go out at all; the other goes about and gathers what is needful. They have no near relations.

Widow Carmichael. Has not been out of the house for three years. Has seven children; three at service, and four at home. The son at home does for himself, and helps his mother. One poor bed. Some of them sleep in another house. They got 3s 6d for the whole family. They have a bit of potatoe [sic] ground.

One old man in the parish has been long deranged. He is very poor, and the country support him. One younger man, M'Culloch, came home from Luing last night deranged. He had been hearing some preaching, and got some delusion into his head. He is very violent, and determined to destroy himself.

Mrs Hugh Black. Bed-ridden. Her husband is alive. He was once a farmer. He can do nothing now, but work a little amongst the potatoes. Gets 3s 6d in the year. House very poor but clean. Very little crockery. One decent bed. He has a son who is not able to assist him. The son would work, but cannot find employment. Such people as their son are worse off than those who beg. They have nothing but the potatoes grown on the little bit of ground given them by the farmers. The wife is seventy-five years of age.

Peggy M'Coll, about fifty. Has a small house, rent-free from Mr Sinclair. No glass in the windows. Three sons and a daughter, – two of the sons and the daughter are at service in the low country. They give her a little assistance, but not much. One son herds. Very little work is to be had hereabouts. She has potatoe [sic] ground from the neighbours, for which she pays rent in labour. She wants nothing from the church. She would not take it; she has more spirit than that yet, but she can't tell what she may come to.

Widow Black. Has three children, – eldest seven years old. Her husband died lately. Her father supports her a little. Her rent was 25s when her husband was alive, but her landlord won't be hard upon her for her rent now. She has no assistance from the parish. Good house. Very respectable looking.

Appendix 12

Full Text of the Letter from Captain Pole to Sir Edward Coffin, 3 October, 1846 (Treasury Letters, 1847)

Oban, October 3, 1846

I have the honour to acquaint you that I this day, in pursuance of your orders, visited the Isle of Lismore, and walked over the northernmost half of the island, visiting several of the dwellings of the poor, and conversing with them, whenever we could mutually understand each other. Of the potato crop there is nothing left fit for use; the root is rotting in the ground where it was planted.

The information on which I set the greatest value was obtained from the Rev. Gregor McGregor, who has been 13 years in the island, and was present on the occasion of the great distress in 1838-9; on which occasion he was appointed the distributor of meal to the poor of Lismore, purchased by the money subscribed generally over the kingdom for the relief of the poor in the Highlands.

Lismore is 11 miles long and on average two broad, containing about 14,080 acres; producing corn, barley, turnips and clover. The rental of the island is about £4000. There are four landlords or owners – Mr Cheyne, Campbell of [Lochnell], Campbell of [Baleveolan], and Sir John Campbell of Airds – Mr Cheyne being the only resident proprietor, absent at present in attendance on a meeting at Inveraray respecting the poor.

The population is 1400, less three, by the latest computation. Of these, the Rev. Gregor McGregor considers 700 poor, and 600 entirely dependent, on the potato. There can be little doubt, from the general statement of Mr McGregor, that 400 of the poor in Lismore will very shortly require aid as to food.

There is as much food in the island as would support the people on it, but it is of no more use to the poor than if it did not exist. There are about 500 head of cattle on the island, but not above 200 sheep.

With respect to the employment of the people, Mr McGregor spoke of the Oban and Glasgow Railroad; but upon a calculation which I requested him to make, he found that not above 40 able-bodied labourers fit for such occupation could be turned out of Lismore. The following proposition was then made by Mr McGregor, as to the improvement of estates and the maintenance of the poor:- 'Give me a sum of money; I have a bit of ground worth little at present per acre, and I will put it under crop directly; out of the proceeds I will pay a small interest, 2½ or 3 per cent on the capital expended. I will take out of the proceeds merely the price of the seed, and apply the rest of the proceeds to the payment of the debt.'

I hereupon referred Mr McGregor to the Drainage Act of last Session, of which he had not heard. I promised to send him a copy.

As to local works, Mr McGregor says there is little opportunity for such works, but he had thought upon the subject, and he would recommend a pier to be constructed in extension of the one at present useless at half-tide at the north-east end of the island at Ruardganish [Point] used for foot-passengers, horses, and cattle. Also a pier to be erected at Archnacroish, midway in the island on the east coast, for the convenience of passengers from Oban.

The poor would derive great advantage from encouragement as fishermen. Lines for cod fishing and nets for mackarel [sic] fishing are much required by many of the poor. If £2 worth of lines &c. were given to about 30 families it would set them up for the next spring fishing, so that they would get on through the next summer.

The herring fishing for the last three years has been a failure, but during the last fortnight a large shoal has been passing the island; the poor were at first unprepared for such abundance, but soon procured the necessary articles from Oban, and they have since been very successful.

There are two mills on the island; also two parochial schools, with about 100 scholars at each, and one adventure school.

Mr McGregor represents rents on the island to be exorbitant, the result of competition for the possession of land.

I conversed with the schoolmaster Peter McDougal at Balegrundle; many poor had applied to him for relief, saying that the allowance given by the Parochial Board was insufficient. These poor used formerly to beg round the island, but alms are now universally refused, because there is a rate for the poor. Peter McDougall stated he thought the poor better off before there was an assessment.

The Rev. Mr Wood informed me that rents could not be paid by the small farmer this year. Little or no arrears of rent are due at present. The potato crop used to pay half the rent.

I have thus placed before you the chief information derived from my visit to Lismore, which I may sum up in the following manner:

The potato crop is wholly gone
About 400 of the poor will shortly be destitute
No means of employment are available for the poor
At present no scheme is on foot by the upper classes to avert famine, or procure employment for the poor.

Appendix 13
Biographies of Cheyne's Tenants on Lismore

Tenants listed under the township where they were first recorded from 1841 onwards.

Sources: Census Records; Parish baptism records; Statutory Death Records; Estate plans; Barcaldine Rentals; 1834-6 Lists of Church Communicants; Inventory of James Cheyne 1853; Lismore Emigrant Register 2009; Lismore Museum Emigrant Records since 2009.

Fiart

James Black
Son of Duncan Black and Dorothy Black, born in Fiart in 1776.
Married to Catherine Black, children Mary (1830), Duncan (1832), James (1835).

A communicant and head of family in Fiart 1834-6. Aged 60, he was a farmer in Fiart in 1841 and, aged 72, was still farming 15 acres there in 1851 (he was still owing £12 arrears in 1853). His sons Duncan and Archibald were listed as tenants in Killean in 1853 (rent £18, no arrears; rent £6, arrears £16). James died (80) at Killean in 1856. Duncan and Archibald were farming 10 acres in Killean in 1861

Meals (Myles) Black [Miles = Maol-Moire in Gaelic]
Son of Duncan Black and Janet McKellaich, born in Achanard in 1821.

His father, Duncan Roy Black was a communicant and head of family in Fiart 1834-6. In spite of his apparent youth (15 but really 20), Myles is listed in 1841 as a farmer on Fiart, living with his widowed mother and three younger siblings. He left Lismore before 1851. In 1863 aged 40, described as an iron foundry scaffold man in Old Monkland, Lanarkshire, he was killed by a fall of bricks from the tunnel head of a furnace.

Niel and John Black
See Appendix 14

William Black
Son of Archibald Black and Catherine Black in Fiart. Unmarried. His father was communicant and head of family in Point of Fiart 1834-6. Aged 35, he was a farmer in Fiart in 1841 and, aged 45, was still farming 25 acres there in 1851. By 1853 he was a tenant in Craignich (rent £16 arrears £66). In 1861 (60), he was farming 15 acres in Craignich. 1871 (60) agricultural labourer in Achnacroish. 1881 (82) Died a pauper at Achnacroish.

John Campbell
Son of Archibald Campbell and Sarah Black in Fiart. Married to Ann McColl, children: Janet (1814), Archibald (1816),

Alexander (1819), Cathrine (1821), Sally (1825), Dugald (1829), Peggy (1832), Duncan (1834) all in Fiart. A communicant and head of family in Fiart 1834-6. Aged 65, he was a farmer in Fiart in 1841 and, aged 73, was still farming 25 acres there in 1851. By 1853 he was a tenant in Craignich (rent £62, arrears £45). In 1861, John (82) had retired and his son Archibald was farming 50 acres. In 1862, John (86) died at Tirlaggan, where his son Archibald was ground officer (1871 census).

No tenants in 1861.

Kilcheran

Donald Carmichael

The son of John Carmichael and Cathrine McColl, born in 1818 in Cloichlea. They were resident at Cloichlea at least up to 1827 but had moved to Kilcheran by 1834 (communicants list). Aged 20, Donald was a farmer in Kilcheran in 1841 (rent £60), with his widowed mother (45) and two brothers. The family emigrated to Ontario, Canada, probably in the 1840s.

James McNicol

James and his wife Mary Smith lived at Craignish on the Argyll mainland between 1818 and 1824. He would have been brought in by Campbell of Barcaldine to run the home farm (as he does not appear as an 1834 communicant). Aged 61, he was a farmer in Kilcheran in 1841 (rent £130) and, as an elder of the kirk, he gave evidence in 1842 to the Poor Law Inquiry. He must have died before 1851. On census day in 1851, his daughter Robina was a visitor at Bachuil on Lismore and, in 1872, his wife, Mary McNicol née Smith died in Rothesay, aged 83.

Myles Kieth

Son of Duncan Kieth/McKeich and Ann Black, born 1782 in Fiart. Married to Chirsty/Christian McGlashan, children: Duncan (1826), Archibald (1828), Ann (1832), John (1834), Peggy (1838) all in Achanard and Mary (1841 in Kilcheran). A communicant and head of household in Achanard 1834-6. Aged 60, he was a farmer in Kilcheran in 1841 and, aged 72, he was farming 20 acres in Craignich in 1851. By 1855 he was on the parochial poor list and by 1861, aged 79, he was a pauper, formerly farmer, in Killean where he died, aged 84, in 1863. Registered by his son Archibald, Mull.

John MacColl

Married to Janet McDugald, children Ronald (1828), Hugh (1830), Alexander (1832) all in Killandrist, Lismore. Communicant and head of family in Kilcheran 1834-6. He must have spent some of his life away from the island (wife from Kilbride and daughter born there in the 1820s). He was absent from home in Kilcheran at the 1841 census. Aged 58, he was farming 20 acres in Kilcheran in 1851, and the family emigrated to New York State, USA in 1852.

No tenants in 1861.

Craignich

Donald Black

Married to Chirsty/Christina Black, children Chirsty (1804), Colin (1809), Niel (1814), William (1812) all in Craignich. Duncan (around 1800) not recorded. A communicant and head of family in Craignich 1834-6. Aged 70 he was a tenant in Craignich in 1841. In 1851, aged 85, he was in the household of his son Duncan (52), farmer of 23 acres in Newfield. He must have died before 1855. By 1861, Duncan (62) was farming

18 acres in Craignich but, by 1871, aged 71, he was a general servant at Achuran. He died at Achuran in 1886, aged 88.

John Black

He had a croft of 2 acres on Craignich in 1836. Aged 40, he was a tenant in Craignich in 1841 and he was due to pay £6 rent in 1853 (arrears of £22). Aged 63 he still had a croft of 4 acres on Craignich in 1861.

Niel Buchanan

Aged 40, farmer of 12 acres in Craignich in 1861. He is likely to be the Niel Buchanan (8) son of Hugh Buchanan, tenant in Achnacroish in 1841 and, aged 20, ploughman in Kilcheran in 1851.

Donald Campbell

Aged 34, farming 15 acres in Craignich in 1861. He may be a son of John Campbell (Fiart) and brother of Archibald who was farming at Craignich in 1861 (see above).

James Campbell

Married to Bell Black, children: Lachlan (1820), Duncan (1821), Colin (1822), Charles (1825), Bell (1829), Archibald (1831), Mary (1834), Janet (1836) all at Achanard. Donald (1841 at Craignich). Communicant and head of family in Achanard 1834-6. Aged 50 he was a tenant in Craignich in 1841, and aged 70, he was farming 20 acres in Craignich in 1851. In 1853 he was still a tenant in Craignich (rent £23 arrears £65) but he must have died before 1855 (Valuation list). By 1861 he had been succeeded by his son Colin (37), farmer of 37 acres in Craignich.

Hugh Carmichael

Married to Mary McGregor, children Gilbert (1822), Dugald (1825, 1827), John (1828), Mary (1831), all at Killean. A communicant and head of family in Craignich 1834-6. Aged 60 he was tenant in Craignich in 1841 but, by 1845, his widow was on the poor list. His wife Mary was a widow/pauper in Craignich in 1851. His son Dugald was a crofter in Killean from 1871. The Gilbert Carmichael, 28, crofter of 2 acres at Port Ramsay in 1851 was probably his son.

John McCorquodale

Probably the John McCorquodale married to Cathrine Carmichael in Balimakillichan (Dugald born 1795). A communicant and head of family in Craignich 1834-6. Aged 65 he was tenant in Craignich in 1841 but, by 1851, his widow, Cathrine (80) and her adult sons were farming 40 acres in Tirlaggan. Her son Dugald is listed as a tenant on Craignich in 1853 (rent £56 arrears £84) but, by 1861, he was farming 35 acres in Tirlaggan.

John McGlassen, McGlashan or Gray

The son of Archibald McGlassen and Sarah McCallum, born in Craignich in 1804. His younger brother Donald (born 1806) was a tenant on Craignich in 1836 but, aged 30, John was a tenant in Craignich in 1841 (with Donald in his household). He married Peggy McIntyre from Killean in 1843. Aged 45, he was farming 20 acres in Craignich in 1851 and in 1853 he was still a tenant in Craignich (rent £27 arrears £60). In 1861 (57) he was an agricultural labourer in Killean and by 1871 he had moved to the Argyll mainland where he died in Muckairn parish in 1886.

Donald McGlassen, McGlashen or Gray

The brother of John McGlassen. He was a tenant on Craignich in 1836 but in the household of his brother in 1841. He married Sarah McCorquodale from Fiart in 1846. Aged 42, he was farmer of 13 acres in Craignich in 1851 and in 1853 he was still a tenant in Craignich (rent £22 arrears £41). By

1861 (54), he was a sailor in Killean (neighbour of his brother) where he died in 1874.

Fates of the 1861 tenants after the clearance:

Duncan Black
1871 (71) servant Achuran

John Black
Dead by 1871, widow in Portcharron

William Black
1871 (60) agricultural labourer in Achnacroish; 1881 (82) Died a pauper at Achnacroish

Niel Buchanan
1871 (45) fisherman in Kinlochspelvie, Mull

Archibald Campbell
1871 (50) Ground officer Tirlaggan

Colin Campbell
1871 (46) quarryman, living at Tirlaggan

Donald Campbell
1871 Not found

Baligrundle

Allan Black
See Appendix 14.

Dugald Carmichael
The son of Archibald Carmichael farmer in Baligrundle and Bell McGregor born around 1780. Married to Chirsty McColl, children: Bell (1820), John (1823), Ann (1828) all in Baligrundle. Communicant and head of family in Baligrundle 1834-6. Aged 50, he was a farmer in Baligrundle in 1841 (rent £21 7s, 10 bolls meal, 7 bolls barley). He does not appear in the 1851

census for Lismore but, by 1861 (84) was a pauper in Achnacroish. He died at Achnacroish in 1862 aged 84.

Archibald McColl

Married to Ann McColl, children: Anne (1806), Mary (1808), Duncan (1810), Malcolm (1812), Cathrine (1815), all in Baligrundle. Tenant and ground officer on Baligrundle (including the Kilcheran Islands). Communicant and head of family 1834-6. Aged 75, he was the principal tenant on Baligrundle in 1841 (rent £106 12s, 42 bolls meal, 24 bolls barley). He died by 1843, resulting in the deforcement crisis. His son, Malcolm, apparently avoided punishment, lived in Ardchattan at least between 1859 and 1863, reurned to Lismore in the mid-1860s, and then emigrated to Ontario, Canada, in 1870.

Donald McColl

Married to Ann Campbell, children: Donald (1832), James (1834), Cathrine (1835), Mary (1837), Archibald (1839), Alexander (1834) all in Baligrundle. He had been miller on the township for many years, possibly since 1815 (Baligrundle rental). He was a communicant and head of family in Baligrundle 1834-6. Aged 50 he was the Baligrundle miller in 1841 (rent £44, 12 bolls meal, 8 bolls barley) but, by 1851, he had been replaced by Malcolm McCallum who had been listed as a joiner in Balure in 1841. In 1851 Donald (70) was farming 25 acres at Achuran, but must have died before 1855. His son James (born 1834), a church minister, emigrated to Prince Edward Island, Canada, in the 1860s but was back in Scotland by 1880, finally settling in New Zealand.

Dugald McColl

Married to Mary McColl, with baptisms 1810-1819 at Baligrundle. Communicant and head of family in Baligrundle in 1834. Aged 60, he was a farmer in Baligrundle in 1841 (rent £33 8s, 12 bolls meal, 8 bolls barley). He is likely to be the Dugald McColl in the group of McCalls who landed in New York 6 October 1843 on the ship Hudson from Liverpool. He died in Ontario, Canada, in 1870.

Miller only in 1851, no tenants in 1861.

Achnacroish (with Newfield)

Donald Black
No Black households on Achnacroish in 1834. Aged 29 he was a farmer of 35 acres in Achnacroish in 1861. His location has not been traced in 1851 or 1871.

Hugh Buchanan (see daughter Mary Campbell under Killean)
Son of Niel Buchanan and Mary Black, born in Balimakillichan in 1792. Married to Cathrine Black, children: Mary (1823), Ann (1825) in Baleveolan, Neil (1830), Janet (1832) in Portcharron, Sarah (1835), Duncan (1838) in Achnacroish. Communicant and head of family in Achnacroish 1834-6. Listed as tenant in Achnacroish in 1841 (rent £32 16s, 12 bolls meal, 8 bolls barley), 1851 (57, 35 acres), 1861 (69, 35 acres) and 1871 (77, 43 acres, 30 arable). He paid £47 rent in 1853 and had £67 arrears. Retired farmer (89) in his daughter's household on Baleveolan in 1881. Died, aged 92, in 1883 in Baleveolan, registerd by his daughter Sarah Campbell. Hugh's son Neil married Catherine Keith from Achanard and emigrated to Australia in 1864.

Archibald Campbell
See Appendix 15.

Son of Colin Campbell and Chirsty Black, born in Achanard in 1813. Aged 25, he was living with his widowed mother in Kilcheran in 1841. Aged 34 he was farmer of 10 acres in Achnacroish in 1851 (paying £22 rent, £5 arrears in 1853).

He married Sarah Buchanan (Catherine born 1860) and became an innkeeper and farmer of 15 acres in Achnacroish in 1861, aged 45. Aged 50, he was a spirit dealer (not tenant) in 1871.

Hugh Campbell

He was probably the brother of Archibald Campbell, farmer in Achuran, Lismore in 1851. Aged 32, he was farmer of 20 acres in Achnacroish in 1861, but by 1871 he was an agricultural labourer there.

Alexander McColl

Married to Mary Carmichael, children: Ann (1844), Chirsty (1846), Catherine (1849) all Newfield. Communicant and head of family in Achnacroish 1834-6. Aged 35, farmer in Newfield in 1841. Present in Newfield at least up to 1849 (baptism records). Replaced by Duncan Black by 1851 (rent £35 arrears £36 in 1853), and not found in 1851 census of Lismore. His daughter Catherine (born 1849 in Newfield) has been identified as an emigrant to Ontario, Canada. It is likely that he emigrated to Canada around 1850.

Donald McColl

Son of Alexander McColl and Mary Campbell, born in Baligrundle 1785. Married to Mary McColl, children: Donald (1819), John (1820), Donald (1823), Dugald (1825), Archibald (1826), Duncan (1829), Hugh (1831), Angus (1833), Mary (1835), all in Achnacroish. Communicant and head of family in Achnacroish 1834-6. Aged 55 he was a tenant in Achnacroish in 1841 (rent £30 12s, 12 bolls meal, 8 bolls barley). As an elder of the kirk, he gave evidence to the Poor Law Inquiry in 1842. Not at home in the 1851 Census, but his wife Mary (not a widow) listed as the tenant. Their rent was £47 in 1853 and they had arrears of £61. Emigrated to Ontario, Canada, with his wife and four sons in 1859 (S.S. Glasgow from Glasgow).

John McIntyre
A Malcolm McIntyre is listed as a communicant and head of family in Achnacroish 1834-6. Aged 25, John is a tenant in Achnacroish in 1841 (rent £12 3s, 5 bolls meal, 5 bolls barley). He does not appear in the 1851 census of Lismore but a John McIntyre is listed as a Craignich tenant (rent £46 arrears £55) in the Cheyne inventory of 1853.

Tirlaggan

Archibald Black
Son of Donald Black and Sarah McPhail, tenants in Tirlaggan (baptisms 1821-1827). Aged 20 tenant in Tirlaggan in 1841 (rent £16 2s, 4 bolls meal, 2 bolls barley). In 1851 his mother Sarah/Sally was listed as farmer of 25 acres in Craignich with Archibald (31) in the household. In 1861 Sarah Black (77) was a "retired farmer" back in Tirlaggan, where she died in 1862 aged 81. Archibald witnessed her death but does not seem to have been resident on Lismore.

In 1871, he was a "flesher" (43) in Oban and he died there in 1889 aged 66.

Cathrine McColl
m.s. Campbell, widow of Archibald McColl, children: Archibald (1810), Jannet (1811), Dugald (1814), Cathrine (1816), Flora (1818), Donald (1820), Duncan (1825) all in Tirlaggan. Aged 45, she was listed as tenant (widow) in Tirlaggan in 1841 (rent £6, 2 bolls meal). Her later life has not been traced but her son Archibald (aged 25 resident in Tirlaggan in 1841) was a labourer in Baligrundle in 1851, and in Craignich in 1861.

Dugald McColl
Married to Ann McColl, children: Dugald (1821), Angus (1824), Archibald (1826), Ann (1828), Janet (1831), Peggy

(1834), all in Tirlaggan. Communicant and head of family in Tirlaggan 1834-6. Aged 50, he was tenant in Tirlaggan in 1841 (rent £6 6s, 2 bolls meal). Died at Tirlaggan in 1843, and most of his family moved to Glasgow

Dugald McColl

Communicant and head of family in Tirlaggan 1834-6. Aged 85, he was a crofter in Tirlaggan in 1841, and seems to have died soon after. In spite of his imprisonment for his part in the 1843 deforcement, Dugald's son Malcolm (40, mason in 1841) was, aged 50, farming 12 acres in Killean in 1851. By 1861 he was a labourer in Craignich and he died aged 70 in Killean in 1870.

Duncan McColl

Son of Dugald McColl and Janet Carmichael, born in Ardchattan. Married to Mary Livingstone, children: Dugald (1824), Mary (1825), Janet (1828), Ann (1830), Archibald (1833), Peggy (1835, 1837), Cathrine (1839), Duncan (1841), John (1844), all in Tirlaggan. Communicant and head of family in Tirlaggan 1834-6. Aged 45, he was tenant in Tirlaggan in 1841 (rent £17 8s, 6 bolls meal, 4 bolls barley) and, aged 58, he was farming 12 acres in Craignich in 1851. He was a tenant in Craignich in 1853 (rent £10 arrears £36). He died, aged 65, at Killean in 1855, leaving 9 living children (Dugald 31, Mary 29, Janet 27, Ann 25, Archibald 23, Peggy 21, Catharine 19, Duncan 17, John 15). His wife Mary was a cottar in Killean in 1861.

Hugh McColl

Son of Dugald McColl and Janet Carmichael born in Tirlaggan around 1795. Married to Mary McCorquodale, children: Archibald (1836), Cathrine (1838) in Tirlaggan. Communicant and head of family in Tirlaggan 1834-6. Aged 40, he was tenant in Tirlaggan in 1841. In 1851 (57) and 1861 (60) he was a labourer in Tirlaggan. He died at Tirlaggan in 1862, aged 68.

Killean

Donald Black
Aged 41, he was roadman in Killean in 1851. His wife had been born in Bonawe and his children on Lochaweside/Glenorchy. He was due to pay £1 10s rent in 1853 and had £6 arrears. In 1861 he was a farmer of 5 acres in Killean. Aged 60 he was listed as a road contractor in Killean in 1871.

Archibald Buchanan
Formerly a tenant in Baleveolan (see Chapter 3; Appendices 1,2)), aged 71, he was a farmer of 50 acres in Killean in 1861.

Duncan Buchanan
Son of Neil Buchanan and Euphemia/Effy McCallum born in Balimakillichan around 1790. Married to Sarah, who was probably his second wife. Communicant and head of family in Killean 1834-6. Aged 50 he was a tenant in Killean in 1841 (rent £14 8s, 6 bolls meal, 4 bolls barley) but, by 1851, aged 67, he was a labourer in Killean. One son, Hugh, emigrated to Nova Scotia before 1851. In 1861 (77) he was a grocer in Achnacroish. He died a pauper in Achnacroish aged 88 in 1870.

Mary Campbell
Daughter of Hugh Buchanan and Catherine Black (see above under Achnacroish), born in Baleveolan in 1823. Around 1850 she married Hugh Campbell, a joiner born in Salen, Mull. Aged 36, in 1861, she is listed as a farmer of 13 acres in Killean in the apparent absence of her husband. By 1871 she was living with her husband in Salen, Mull.

Jean Carmichael

Aged 43 she appears as a widow farming 16 acres in Killean in 1851, paying £20 rent (£51 arrears) in 1853. She had been living off the island for several years (children aged 5 to 15 born in Greenock). In 1861, Jean (55) is listed as the occupier of 7 acres in Killean and, at 65, she is still farming there in 1871.

Archibald McCallum

Married to Cathrine McGlashan, children: John (1834) in Killean in 1834. Communicant and head of family in Killean 1834-6. Aged 45, he was a tenant in 1841 (rent £10 8s, 6 bolls meal, 4 bolls barley). As his wife died a pauper widow (of tuberculosis) in Killean in 1858, he must have died before 1855. There is evidence that their son John emigrated to Minnesota, USA.

Donald McColl

Married to Ann Carmichael, children: Mary (1813), Janet (1815), Ann & Bell (1817) Dugald (1822), Archibald (1824), Cathrine (1827), Betty (1829), Duncan (1834) all in Killean. Communicant and head of family in Killean 1834-6. Aged 50, a widower, he was a tenant in Killean in 1841 (rent £5 14s). By 1851, only Donald's son Duncan (15) appears to be living in Killean. He later emigrated to Nevada in the USA, finally marrying Catherine Carmichael (originally from Lismore) and settling in Elgin County, Ontario.

James McColl

Son of Malcolm McColl and Mary McIntyre or McGregor born in Achnacroish 1796. Married to Euphemia/Effy McColl, children: Duncan (1839), John (1844) in Killean. Aged 40 he is listed as a tailor only in 1841 (rent £6 10s) but, aged 50, he is a tailor and crofter of 3 acres in 1851. He was due £5 rent in 1853 and had 17s arrears. In 1861 (63) and in 1871

(76), James is again listed as tailor only in Killean. He died in Killean in 1873 aged 79.

Malcolm McColl

Communicant and head of family in Killean 1834-6. Aged 65 he was tenant in Killean in 1841 (rent £30, 12 bolls meal, 8 bolls barley) with his married son Duncan in the household. Duncan and Kett/Catherine Carmichael had two children baptised in Baligrundle in 1843 and 1845. When Duncan died at Laggan on Lismore in 1860 (aged 51) Malcom is listed as deceased. Malcom probably died before 1843.

John McIntyre

Married to Bell Kieth, children: Duncan (1822), Bell (1825), Chirsty (1828) all in Killean. Communicant and head of family in Killean 1834-6. Aged 60 he was a farmer in Killean in 1841 (rent £11 4s, 6 bolls meal, 4 bolls barley) but must have died soon after because, by 1851, his widow Isabella (66) was farming 28 acres at Killean. The McIntyres were listed as tenants in Killean in the 1853 inventory (rent £54 arrears £30). Bell had left Killean by 1861.

Malcom McIntyre

Married to Cathrine Carmichael, children: Archibald (1813), Janet (1817), Mary (1821), John (1823) all in Killean. Communicant and head of family in Killean 1834-6. Aged 70, a widower, he was a tenant in Killean in 1841 (rent £14 8s, 6 bolls meal, 5 bolls barley). In 1851, his son Archibald (37) was a labourer in Killean, and in 1861 (46) an agricultural labourer in Killean, where he died in 1869. Malcom must have died in the 1840s.

Niel McIntyre

Probably born in Baligrundle 1776. Married to Janet Black, children: Archibald (1813), John (1814) both in Baligrundle, Janet (1816), Donald (1819) both in Killean. Communicant and head of family in Killean 1836. Aged 65, he was a crofter in Killean in 1841 (rent £4) and, aged 80 he had 3 acres in Killean in 1851. He is not listed as a tenant in the 1853 inventory but had arrears of £1 17s. He must have died before 1855. By 1861, his son John, a fisherman, was based in Baleveolan

Portcharron

Duncan McColl
Son of John McColl and Mary Black, born in Taylochan (Portcharron), Lismore in 1800. Aged 30, unmarried tenant in Portcharron with his widowed mother and brother in 1841 (rent £25). In 1845, Duncan and his brother John moved to be tenants in Portcastle on Baleveolan Estate (Chapter 3). Aged 46, Duncan was a farmer of 30 acres in Portcastle and John, 42, in the same household was a ground officer. Duncan died at Portcastle in 1861, aged 61, and John in 1878, aged 71.

Hugh Carmichael, 55, 1841 Tenant
See Appendix 14

No tenants in 1851 and 1861.

Appendix 14
Three Lismore Families

Niel Black, son of Duncan and Mary Black, born 1799 in Fiart

Married to Mary Black

Children born in Point of Fiart: Niel (1820); Hugh (1822); Mary (1824); Christina/Christian (1828); Isabella/Bell (1831); Archibald 1834)

1834-6 Communicant and head of family in Point of Fiart

1841 Aged 50, farmer in Fiart, his household of ten included his wife Mary (40); children Hugh (15), Christian (13), Dorathy/Dorothy (11), Isabella (9), Archibald (5) and Catherine (4); his widower brother John (45) and John's daughter, Isabella (20). Mary (17) had already left home.

1846 Niel's son Niel married John's daughter Isabella (children Donald 1846, Mary 1849, Helen 13 January 1850 – the last child born on Fiart). Niel Junior (nicknamed breachd/freckled in Rev. MacGregor's book, was absent from the island in 1841 and 1851 and does not appear in the Scottish death records from 1855). Niel's brother John needed emergency financial support from the parish.

1851   Aged 73, now farmer of 17 acres in Killean, his household of five included his wife Mary (60) and three unmarried children, Hugh (24, carpenter), Isabella (18, house servant) and Archibald (15, servant). Christina and Dorothy, in their early twenties, had left the island. His brother John, aged 63, had remained in Fiart as a cottar, with his married daughter Isabella (35) and four grandchildren (1-6). His niece, Catherine Black (14), is included as a visitor.

1853   Paying £26 rent (£70 arrears) in Killean (Cheyne Inventory).

1861   Niel and Mary Black had died and Hugh (34), unmarried farmer of 15 acres inKillean was now the head of a household of six, including his unmarried brother Archibald (24, ploughman) and his sister Bell (26) who was married to a sailor John McIntyre (absent at the time of the census). The McIntyres had a new baby (Mary, 9 months). Christina (27, now married to James Copeland, sailor), was resident in Govan with three children (4,6 & 9). A further child Mary Copeland (12) was back at the family home in Killean, together with James Black (9, Hugh's sister's son, born Lanarkshire).

1871   Hugh was still unmarried but was now a ship's captain, living in Achnacroish with the McIntyres and their daughter Mary (11). He was finally on his own, aged 54, working once more as a carpenter in Achnacroish in 1881, and his sister and husband were

APPENDIX 14

in their own house there. John Black (88) had meanwhile been off the island but had returned a pauper to Killean with his widowed daughter (56), his unmarried granddaughter and her 8-month old daughter, born in Glasgow.

1889   Christina, aged 61, died of tuberculosis in Glasgow.

1891   Dorothy, unmarried, aged 50, reappears as a domestic servant in Bathgate. It is likely that she had been in service in England.

1895   Mary, aged 68 widow of James Bryan, gardener, died at Achnacroish, witnessed by her brother Hugh.

1901   Hugh, aged 75, living in Achnacroish with his sister Dorothy as housekeeper (66). She died in 1902 aged 62.

1907   Hugh, still unmarried, died aged 85 at Achnacroish.

Allan Black, son of Duncan Black and Catherine McPhail, born in Baligrundle before 1800.
Married to Mary Black

Children born in Baligrundle: Cathrine (1828); Ann (1830); Bell (1832); Mary (1835); Duncan (1840); Archibald (1842).

1834-6   He had succeeded his father as communicant and head of family in Baligrundle.

1841   Allan Black (40) farmer in Baligrundle (rent £21 6s, 8 bolls meal, 6 bolls barley) his household of seven included his wife Mary (35) and his children Catherine (12), Ann (10), Isabella (8), Mary (4) and Duncan (3).

1845   Married Catherine McIntyre from Tirfuir, Lismore.

1846   Birth in Baligrundle of Flora.

1851 Allan (55) had lost his farm and was a labourer in Kilcheran. His household of five included his second wife, Cathrine (40), his children Mary (14) and Duncan (12 – the first child in the family to be described as a school attender). There was also a new infant Chirsty/Christian (3) born 1849 in Kilcheran. The older children had left home: Catherine (22) in Glasgow, Anne (21) and Isabella (19) appear to have been house servants elsewhere on Lismore.

1861 Allan (66) was now a shepherd in Kilcheran in a household of four including his wife Catherine (43), daughter Flora (14) and a grandson (7) born in Glasgow.

1871 Allan (74) and Cathrine (61) were living alone as paupers in Kilcheran.

1878 Aged 80, died at Craignich in 1878.

Hugh Carmichael, son of Archibald Carmichael and Isabella McGregor, born in Baligrundle around 1784.

Brother of Dugald and James Carmichael, tenants in Baligrundle.

Married to Elizabeth/Betty MacColl (born in Baleveolan)

Children born when a cottar in Baligrundle: Cathrine (1813, died young); Archibald (1816); Donald (1816); Mary (1820); and Alexander (1822, died young)

Children born when a tenant in Portcharron/Taylochan: Dugald (1824, died young); Isabella/Bell (1826, died young), Catherine (1829) and a second Alexander, the future folklorist, (1832)

1834-6 Communicant and head of family in Portcharron.

1837 Death of son Archibald, aged 21.

APPENDIX 14

1841   Hugh Carmichael (55) tenant in Portcharron (rent £16), head of a household of seven including his wife Betty (50), two sons Donald (20) and Alexander (7), a male servant, and two lodgers (a joiner and an 'independent' Carmichael relation). Cathrine and Mary had already left home, and Alexander attended school in Greenock, where Mary was living.

1851   Hugh Carmichael (68), farmer of 25 acres in Kilandrist (on Campbell of Airds estate), in a household of three, including his wife Betty (58) and Alexander (18) listed as a ploughman. On the day of the census, there was a young MacColl visitor.

1857   Daughter Cathrine emigrated to Canada.

1861   Hugh Carmichael (78), blind, farmer of 14 acres in Kilandrist, head of a household of nine including his wife Betty (70) and his daughter Mary (40) who had returned from living in Greenock with her husband and five children (1 – 15). Hugh died in 1862 and his daughter Mary emigrated to Canada with her family in 1871. His son Alexander (1932-1912), the celebrated folklorist, left Lismore in the early 1850s to pursue his career in the excise service.

Appendix 15
The Kilcheran Cottars

1841 Cottars

Alexander Black (deceased 1851, family gone 1861)
Aged 45, labourer in Kilcheran. Listed as head of household including his sister Jean Kieth (m.s. Black) and her husband Duncan Kieth (50). Kieth children Mary (1836, Point of Fiart), Cathrine (1838, Point of Fiart), Duncan (1841, Kilcheran).

1844	Death of Duncan Kieth – posthumous birth of Sarah, daughter of Duncan Kieth & Jane (Jean) Black in Fiart.
1851	Jean Kieth, 40, widow and pauper in Kilcheran with two daughters (8 and 12). Mary Kieth (16) was a housemaid in the Cheyne household in Kilcheran.
1861	Jean Kieth, 55, pauper in Killean with two unmarried pauper daughters (15 and 20), and a grandson (4).
1871	Jean Kieth, 68, widow and agricultural labourer in

Killean, with two daughters both listed as 'imbecile' and a 14 year old grandson.

Angus Black (deceased 1851, family gone by 1861)
Married to Eve Kieth, children: Ann (1821, Fiart), Alexander (1823, Kilcheran), William (1825, Fiart), John (1827, Fiart), Duncan (1829, Kilcheran), Colin (1831, Kilcheran), Mary (1835, Kilcheran), Anne (1839, Kilcheran).

1834-6   Communicant and head of family in Kilcheran.

1841   Aged 50, labourer in Kilcheran. Household wife and 3 children (5-10).

1847   Aged 66, died at Kilcheran.

1851   Eve Black, 56, widow and cottar in Kilcheran, with one son Colin (18).

1858   Son Duncan had an assisted passage to New South Wales on the *Forest Monarch*.

1861   The family had left Lismore.

1877   Eve Black died aged 76 in Glasgow, witnessed by her son William Black.

John Black (gone by 1851)
Married to Isabella/Bell Campbell, children: Donald (1840), Ann (1841), Archibald

(1843)   Cathrine (1846), all Kilcheran.

1841   Aged 35, publican in Kilcheran. Household Isabella (25), Donald (1) and a female servant (12).

Between 1846 and 1851 the family left Lismore.

Mary Black (McKellaich) (gone by 1851)
Married to John Black, children: John (1818), Mary (1819), Ann (1823), Dorothy (1825), Donald (1827), James (1831), Cathrine (1831), all Kilcheran.

| 1841 | Aged 45, widow cottar in Kilcheran. 2 children (9 and 12). |
| 1851 | Aged 60, widow cottar in Craignich. Adult daughter and pauper sister (54). Not traced further. |

John Brown (gone by 1851)

| 1841 | Aged 30, Preacher missionary of the United Secession Church in Kilcheran. Fluent in Gaelic. |
| 1843 | Succeeded by William Wood. |

Archibald Campbell (gone by 1851) Son of John Campbell and Ann Black in Achinduin, Lismore. Married to Peggy Kieth, children: Ann (1829, Craignich), Dugald (1832, Craignich), Duncan (1833, Achanard), William (1835, Achanard), Amelia (1837, Achanard), Peggy (1840, Kilcheran). Births of Archibald and Colin (1840s) not recorded on Lismore.

1834-6	Communicant and head of family in Achanard
1841	Aged 50, quarrier in Kilcheran. Household Peggy (35) and 5 children (1-12).
1851	Aged 70, cottar in Craignich. Household Margaret (48), two adult unmarried servant children, and 4 children (5-12).
1852	Aged 72 died in Craignich. Reported by his brother Colin Campbell farmer in Achinduin.

Christian (Chirsty) and Margaret (Peggy) Campbell (gone by 1851)

Chirsty Black was married to Colin Campbell. Children: Peggy (1812), Archibald (1813), Lachlan (1815), Bell (1816), Mary (1818), Ann (1820), Hugh (1822), James (1825), Ann (1827), all born in Achanard.

Peggy McColl was married to Duncan Campbell. Child unnamed (1822), Archibald (1824), Lachlan (1827), Lachlan (1829), all born in Achanard.

1834-6   Archibald Campbell communicant and head of family in Achanard.

1841   Christian (50) and Margaret (45) were living in a joint cottar household in Kilcheran with Donald (14), Lachlan (11), Archibald (25), Ann (13) and two McIntyre children (3 and 8). It is likely that they were sister-in-law widows.

1851   Chirsty (62), a widow, was in the household of her unmarried son Archibald (34) farmer of 10 acres in Achnacroish, with his unmarried sisters Bell (31) and Ann (20), and unmarried brother Hugh (27), all servants, and a McIntyre herd (11).

1861   Archibald (45) was an innkeeper and farmer of 15 acres in Achnacroish, with his new wife Sarah (26) and one child.

1871   Archibald (50) was a spirit dealer, not tenant, in Achnacroish.

Duncan Carmichael (present 1861)
Son of Dugald Carmichael and Dorothy McColl, born Balnagown, Lismore, 1794. Married to Mary Demster/Dempster, children: Dugald (1832), Peggy (1834), James (1836), John (1838); then to Cathrine McDonald, children: Mary (1843), Dorothy (1848), John (1850), Flory (1852). All born Kilcheran.

1834-6   Communicant and head of family in Kilcheran.

1840   Death of wife Mary Dempster

1841   Aged 40, cottar, apparently widower, in Kilcheran, with two children (5 and 9).

1851   Aged 54, store keeper in Kilcheran. Household, wife Cathrine (33), four children (3-7) and a house servant (16).

1861   Aged 66, 'woodplanter' [forester] in Kilcheran. Household Cathrine (46), son James, house carpenter (25), and 3 children (8-13).

1864   Aged 71. Died at Killean. Registered by his son John.

John Carmichael (present 1861)

Son of Dugald Carmichael and Ann McGregor, born in Balimakillichan

1834-6 Communicant and head of family in Kilcheran.

1841   Aged 55, cottar in Kilcheran, living with his widowed sister Flory (60) (who was on the parochial poor list 1846-51) and one child, Dugald Black (10).

1851   Aged 70, labourer in Kilcheran. Sister Flora (77) a pauper.

1855   Parochial poor law list.

1861   Aged 80, Pauper, formerly farmer, in Kilcheran.

1862   Aged 84, Pauper, formerly farmer, died at Kilcheran. Registered by Duncan Carmichael, Kilcheran.

Anne Demster (Dempster) (gone by 1851)

1841   Female servant and head of single household in Kilcheran. Presumably a sister of Mary Demster, wife of Duncan Carmichael. Not traced further.

Hugh Fletcher (deceased by 1851, family gone by 1861)

Married to Catherine Black, child: Flory (1825) in Kilcheran.

1834-6 Communicant and head of family in Kilcheran.

1841   Aged 50. Household: Catherine (55) and Christian McCallum (not born on Lismore).

1851   Catherine Fletcher (72) widow and cottar in Kilcheran. Daughter Ann, unmarried (38) and grandson John (9).

Catherine McColl (Kieth) (gone by 1851)

Married to Donald McColl, children: John (1820, Craignich), Malcolm (1822, Craignich), Duncan (1824, Craignich), Donald (1835, Kilcheran).

1841   Aged 45, widow in Kilcheran. Three children (6-15).

1847-51 Parochial poor law list.

1851   Aged 58, widow, cottar in Craignich. One son (16). Not traced further.

Dugald McColl (gone by 1851)

The son of Donald McColl and Janet Black, born 1802 in Craignich. Married to Ann McColl, children: Mary (1845), Ann (1847) in Craignich.

1834-6 Communicant and head of family in Kilcheran.

1841   Aged 30, wright in Kilcheran. Household of mother (75) and a McColl child (12).

1851   Aged 47, wright in Craignich. Wife Ann (34), three children (1-5) and his pauper/widow mother in law (79).

1856   Aged 54, died of tuberculosis in Tirlaggan; posthumous birth of daughter Catherine in Craignich.

Alexander McCorquodale and Alexander McKinnon (gone by 1851)

1841   Aged 20 and 15, sailors in Kilcheran. Not identified

John McCorquodale (present 1851, family gone by 1861

Son of Archibald McCorquodale, weaver in Kilcheran and Ann McPhail. Married to Mary McKillop, children: Archibald (1809), Anne (1811), Chirsty (1813), John (1817), Cathrine (1822), Hugh (1824), Dugald (1828), Allan (1830), all Kilcheran.

1834-6 Communicant and head of family in Kilcheran.

1841 Aged 50, weaver in Kilcheran. Household wife, adult male relation, two children (10 and 14), and a young McKillop relation (8).

1851 Aged 65, weaver in Kilcheran. Household: Mary (60), Archibald, unmarried labourer (30), Bell, unmarried (24), Cathrine, unmarried (22), Hugh, unmarried (20), Allan (17) and a grandson (4 months) born in Dumbarton.

1860 Death, aged 74, at Port Ramsay, of consumption. Witnessed by Hugh McCorquodale, his son, who was illiterate.

1861 Mary McCorquodale, aged 74, widow and crofter of 4 acres in Port Ramsay.

Household: Catherine and Hugh and 2 grandchildren, one born Glasgow.

1863 Death of Allan Kirkwood, illegitimate son of Isabella McCorquodale, farm servant, born in either Dumbarton or Glasgow. Death witnessed by Archibald McCorquodale, uncle.

Niel McDonald (probably deceased by 1851, family gone from Kilcheran by 1851)

Married to Flory/Flora McKellaich/McDonald, children: Duncan (1810), Donald (1814), Janet (1815), Ann (1817), Mary (1820), all Point of Fiart; Allan (1824), Cathrine (1827) both Achanard.

1834-6 Communicant and head of family in Achanard.

1841 Aged 50, carpenter in Kilcheran. Household Flory (50), Duncan, carpenter (25), Donald, carpenter (20), Mary (15), Allan (14), Catherine (10).

1843 Son Duncan, resident in Kilcheran, married Cathrine McColl.

1845-47 Children born in Kilcheran to son Donald, married to Dorothy McCorquodale.

1845-48 Duncan and Cathrine McDonald had children but not on Lismore.

1851 Duncan McDonald, aged 42, boat builder in Achnacroish. Household Cathrine, wife (40), three children (3-6) and an apprentice from Appin (18).

All of the other members of the family had died or left the island by 1851 (*but see Donald below*).

1861 Duncan McDonald, aged 52, boat builder in Port Ramsay. Household Cathrine (50), son John (16) boat builder, and 3 other children (8-14).

1869 Donald McDonald, ship carpenter, aged 56, died at Point, Lismore.

1871 Duncan McDonald, aged 58, boat builder in Port Ramsay. New wife Isabella (50), daughter and stepson, apprentice boat builder.

1881 Duncan McDonald, aged 70, boatbuilder employing 1. Household Isabella (62), daughter Mary, stepson boat builder and granddaughter, both born Glasgow.

1888 Duncan McDonald, aged 79, died at Port Ramsay.

Malcolm Sinclair (gone by 1851)

Born on the mainland (Ardchattan or Dalavich)

1841 Aged 40, lime burner in Kilcheran. A single man in a household of 3 Sinclairs.

1851 Aged 63, lime merchant, resident on Sheep Island with a 12 year old niece.

1867 Aged 69, lime merchant, single, died of starvation on Sheep Island. Reported to have been insane, refusing food. Reported by his brother John Sinclair.

Cottars from 1851

Donald McIntyre

Born c1796. Married to Ann McColl, children: Cathrine (1821), John (1826), Mary (1831), Janet (1834), Alexander (1836), Ann (1839), all Sailean.

1841　Aged 40, carpenter in Sailean. Household Ann (40), John (15), Janet (6) Alexander (4), Ann (2).

1851　Aged 56, carpenter in Kilcheran. Household Ann (54), Janet (16), Alexander (14)

1861　Aged 63, ship carpenter in Achnacroish, master employing 2. Household Ann (62) and a 21 year old apprentice

Allan Black
See Appendix 14
Angus McDonald

Born c 1805. Married to Janet Black, children: John (1849), (Janet 1851), Duncan & Hugh, twins (1853), Catherine (1858) at Kilcheran.

1851　Aged 42, labourer in Kilcheran. Household Janet (26), John (1½)

1861　Aged (56), ploughman in Killean. Household Janet (32), John (11), Duncan (7), Ketty (2). Not traced further.

Donald Black

Born 1806, son of Duncan Black and Isabella Keith in Baligrundle. Married to Janet Campbell, children: Mary, Duncan, John, Malcolm (Isabella).

1841　Aged 35, mariner in Killean. Household James, brother (30), Bell, mother (70).

1851　Aged 48, boatman in Kilcheran. Household Janet (35), Mary (6).

1861 Aged 58, boatman in Kilcheran. Household Janet (45), Mary (16), Duncan (7), John (5).

1871 Aged 68, widower, ferryman in Kilcheran. Household Mary (27), Duncan (16), Malcolm (6).

1881 Aged 80, retured mariner in Kilcheran. Household Isabella (31).

1890 Aged 88, died at Kilcheran.

Selected Bibliography

Black, D. 2006. *Sgeul no Dhà às an Lios: A Tale or Two from Lismore*. Glasgow: Cadispa at the University of Strathclyde.

Correspondence Relating to the Measures Adopted for the Relief of the Distress in Scotland [Treasury Correspondence]. (1847). London: HMSO.

Devine, T.M. (1994). *Clanship to Crofters' War*. Manchester University Press.

Devine, T.M. (1994). *The Transformation of Rural Scotland*. Edinburgh: John Donald.

Devine, T. M. (1995). *The Great Highland Famine*. Edinburgh, Birlinn.

Gray, M. (1957). *The Highland Economy*. Glasgow: Oliver & Boyd.

Hay, R.K.M. (2009). *Lismore. The Great Garden*. Edinburgh: Birlinn

Hay, R.K.M. (2010). Improvement not clearance: A factor's instructions to his ground officers on the Isle of Lismore, 1831-46. *Review of Scottish Culture* 22, 99-109.

Hay, R.K.M. (2011). Crops and livestock in the Improvement era. In *Scottish Life and Society. Farming and the Land*. Edinburgh: John Donald, 244-266.

Hay, R.K.M. (2012). Keeping the peace on Lismore. *Historic Argyll* 17, 37-48.

Hunter, J. (1976). *The Making of the Crofting Community*. Edinburgh: John Donald.

Lobban, M.D. (2004). *Lachann Dubh a' Chrògain: Lachlan Livingstone and his Grandsons, Bards of Mull and Lismore*. The New Iona Press.

MacDougall, J. (1984). *Highland Postbag*. London: Shepheard Walwyn.

McGeachy, R.A.A. (2005). *Argyll 1730-1850*. Edinburgh: John Donald.

Smith, J. (1798). *General View of the Agriculture of the County of Argyll*. Reprinted by the Grimsay Press, Glasgow, 2003.

Statistical Accounts of Scotland (1791-9, 1845). Accessible at: http://stat-acc-scot.edina.ac.uk/

The Royal Commission of Inquiry into the Conditions of Crofters and Cotters in the Highlands and Islands [The Napier Report] (1884).

Walker, S.P. (2003). Agents of dispossession and acculturation. Edinburgh accountants and the Highland Clearances. *Critical Perspectives on Accounting* 14, 813-853.

Sources

Primary Sources

National Archives of Scotland
Principal Sources

GD13 Campbell of Baleveolan

GD112 Breadalbane Muniments

GD170 Campbell of Barcaldine

GD241 Thomson & Baxter WS

GR Sasine Records

SC52, 54, 57 Argyll Sheriff Court

Argyll Papers, Inveraray Castle

MacDougall of MacDougall Papers, held in the 1745 House at Dunollie (Dunollie Archive)

The Bachuil Ground Officer Letters, held at Bachuil House, Lismore. Transcriptions available in Lismore Museum archive. (Bachuil Letters).

Introduction

In 1925, 16 years after his death, Hugh Anderson's daughter organised a private publication of eleven of his most popular songs in "Measan Millis as an Lios" (Sweet Fruit of the Garden) (Glasgow: Gilleasbaig Mac-na-Ceardadh). A copy is held in the Lismore Museum archive. The translation of the verse is by Ronnie Black. An account of Anderson's life can be found at www.lismoregaelicheritagecentre.com . Livingstone and MacDonald bards: Lobban M D. (2004).

Chapter One

Background: Gray (1957); Hay(2009); Hunter (1976); McGeachy (2005). MacDougall family affairs: MacDougall (1984). Argyll Highlanders: McElwee, W. (1972). *Argyll and Sutherland Highlanders*. Oxford: Osprey. Peninsular War: Bryant, A. (1944). *Years of Victory, 1802-1812*. London, Collins. Esdaile, C. (2002). *The Peninsular War. A New History*. London: Allen Lane; Urban, M. (2001). *The Man Who Broke Napoleon's Codes*. London, Faber & Faber. Campbells at Waterloo: Dalton, C. (1904). *The Waterloo Roll Call*. London: Eyre & Spottiswoode. The military history of the Barcaldine Campbells and Duncan Campbell's management of his finances: Nenadic, S. (2006). The impact of the military profession on Highland gentry families, c1730-1830. *The Scottish Historical Review* 85, 75-99. Army commissions: Bruce, A.P.C. (1980). *The Purchase System in the British Army, 1660-1871*. Royal Historical Society. Barcaldine Lismore rents: GD170/569/2. Argyll Houses: RCAHMS Canmore ID Barcaldine House 86375, Lochnell House 22997. Reduction in number of Argyll landowners: Gray (1957) p194. Letters: MacDougall (1984). Argyllshire Valuation Roll, 1751: NRS E106/3/2. Lismore estate sales: GR 2127/90 (1842); GR2296/141 (1845); 1853 GR 2644/65. Rev. Gregor MacGregor's Private Record Book. MacGregor archive, Lismore Museum. 1629 tack for Baleveolan: GD112/10/7. 1707 tack for Baligrundle: GD112/10/7. Emigration: Lismore Register of Emigrants published in CD format, Lismore Museum, 2009. Carmichaels in the USA: Carmichael, R.L. (1935). *The Scottish Highlander Carmichaels of the Carolinas.* Privately published. Reprinted in 1978 by The R.L. Bryan Co., Columbia, S Carolina. Archibald Black Nova Scotia Deed 1812: Lismore Archive, Box 1800-1849. The Story of Achanard at: www.lismoregaelicheritagecentre.com Baligrundle Mill 1817: NRS GD170/564. The Baligrundle deforcement 1843: SC51-41-5-00267; www.inverarayjail.co.uk ; Hay (2012). Rev. MacGregor: NSA for Lismore & Appin Parish, 1841. Agricultural Improvement: Hay (2011). Environmental limitations: Fraser Darling, F. (1945). *Crofting Agriculture.* Edinburgh: Oliver & Boyd. Improvement in Argyll parishes: NSA. Campbell of Barcaldine and sheep farming: Bangor-Jones, M. Sheep Farming in Sutherland in the Eighteenth Century. *The Agricultural History Review* 50, 181-202 (2002). Emigration from Argyll: OSA for Argyll parishes. Lismore tenancies: Hay (2010). Combie estate maps: Lismore museum archive. Arrears: Inventory of J A Cheyne NRS. Cattle numbers in 1846: Treasury Report p58. Cheyne on cattle: Blackwood's Edinburgh Magazine 67, 240 (1850). Horses: Caledonian Mercury, 1 December 1851. Whisky distilling on Lismore: Hay (2009) pp128-135. Collected papers on Lismore ferries: Lismore Archive Boxes, 1800-1849, 1850-1899. Coseguina Volcano 1835: Bradley R.S. & Jones, P.D. (eds). (1992). *Climate since AD 1500.* London: Routledge. Bradley, R.S. *et al.* (1992). The climate of the last millennium. In Alverson, K.D. *et al.* (eds) (2003). *Paleoclimate, Global Change and the Future.* Heidelberg: Springer Verlag, p105.

Food distribution on Lismore 1839/40: Treasury Report p58. The potato crop: Salaman, R. (1985). *The History and Social Influence of the Potato*. Cambridge University Press. Blight in Nova Scotia: Lismore archive. Emigrant letters LISDD:2009.N. Free Church Relief of Potato Famine: 1847 Report of the Destitution Committee. Minutes of the Presbytery of Lorn: NRS CH2/984/6. Situation on Lismore 1846: Treasury Report p58-9.

Chapter Two

Details of the lives of the MacDougall family: MacDougall (1984) and Dunollie Boxes E, P, R, LA, LC. Fostering of Patrick MacDougall: *Records of Argyll*, Blackwood & Sons, Edinburgh, 1885, p163. Louisa MacDougall's piety: *Highland Post* p149, 173. Allan's private notebooks: Dunollie Archive AWCB Boxes 1&2. Supply of provisions: AWCB Box 4. Baxter & MacDougall WS: Edinburgh Postal Directories 1830s, 1840s. Indebtedness: Dunollie Box LC. New partnership: Dunollie Box LA. Edmund Baxter's life traced through Edinburgh Census Records. Death of Patrick Campbell of Baleveolan: Letter Charles Stewart to Duncan Campbell of Barcaldine, 11 June 1830. GD170/2737. Livestock judge: Transactions of the Highland and Agricultural Society in 1830, p 26. Diary of Allan MacDougall for 1845: Dunollie Box LB. Lodgings in the 1840s and 1850s from the ground officer letters to John MacColl on Lismore: Dunollie Box R. Serious debt in the 1850s: Dunollie Box LC. List of potential wool suppliers: Dunollie AWCB Box 3. Search for employment: Dunollie Box R.

Chapter Three

Background: Hay (2009, 2010). Most of the ground officer correspondence can be found in: The Bachuil letters

1831-1845; Ground Officer letters 1846-1857, Dunollie Box R. Baleveolan evictions c1800: Baleveolan Papers GD13 letters 173, 178, 183-5,187,191-2. The MacDonald letters from Cape Breton (1843-1857): Lismore Museum Archive, LISDD:2009.N. Emigration: The Lismore Emigrant Register, 2009. John MacDougall's correspondence: Gifted by the MacDougall MacCallum Foundation to Lismore Museum Archive (2012). 1831 Rental: Dunollie Box P. 1844 Rental: GD241/424. Petition of Mary Stewart: GD241/424. 1834 Rental and 1840 arrears: Hay (2010). Competition for land: Treasury Report p59. Lime burning: Martin, C. & Martin, P. (2006). *The Lismore Limekilns*. Unpublished Report to Historic Scotland.; GD17/552; GD241/408; Dunollie Box R. Lime analyses: GD241/408. MacIntyres as employers: Napier Report paragraphs 36906-36914, 36942, 36967-36981, 37081-37084. Drainage: Smith, J. (1831). *Thorough Draining and Deep Working*. Bere barley: Hay, R. (2012). Bere barley: rediscovering a Scottish staple. *Review of Scottish Culture* **24**, 126-139. Grievance about rotations: Napier Report 36949. Captain Pole's correspondence: Treasury Correspondence 58-59. Poor Law Records: Argyll & Bute Archives CO6/7/30. MacCorquodale spuilzie: Dunollie Box R. Donald Campbell and arrears: Dunollie Box R. The Buchanan brothers: Dunollie Box R,S.

Chapter Four

The Cheyne family and JAC: Cheyne, A.Y. (1931). *The Cheyne Family in Scotland*. Edinburgh; Cheyne-MacPherson, W.D. (1843). *The Cheynes of Inverugie, Esslemont and Arnage and their Descendants*. Kirkwall. JAC Trust Deed NRS RD5/939/595. Will of Mrs Frances Charlton Sprot or Cheyne, 1873. *Lismore archive*; SC70/4/146. *Register of the Society of Writers to her*

Majesty's Signet. Edinburgh, 1983. Brown, R. (ed.) (2004). *A History of Accountants and Accounting* Cosimo: New York. Negligence: Miss I Brown etc Pursuers vs. J.A. Cheyne & John McKean W.S, Defenders. 1 March 1833. *The Scottish Jurist*. V. 1833. Edinburgh. Inventory of JAC 1853: Register of Inventories (Dunoon) SC51/32/8. Inheritance: *Services of Heirs in Scotland*, 1819, 1829. National Bank of Scotland: www.bankingletters.co.uk/page11.html Fife Banking Company: www.banking-history.co.uk/fife.htm; *Edinburgh Gazette* 15 July 1829; CS228/A/9/45. Railway holdings: *Edinburgh Advertiser* 30 November 1824; House of Commons Parliamentary Papers 48 (1837). Factor for Kellie estate: GD124/15/1802. Standard Life: Moss, M. (2000). *Standard Life 1825-2000*. Edinburgh. Slaves: Records of the Slave Compensation Commission, 1833-42. See www.ucl.ac.uk/lbs/project/scottishdata.pdf Tax commissioner: Collection of the Public General Statutes, 1836. London. Kilmaron Castle: Canmore ID 100435. Accountants and Clearance: Walker (2003). Highland and Agricultural Society: *Transactions* 1829. Inferiority of Highlanders: Bruce, J. (1847). Destitution in the Highlands. Letters on the present condition of the Highlands and Islands of Scotland. Reprinted from the Scotsman newspaper. Edinburgh. See Devine (1995) pp129-130. Genetics: Sykes, B. (2006). Blood of the Isles. Bantam: New York. Coffin Letter: Treasury Correspondence p46. Land acquisition: Sasine Records GR 2127/90; GR 2296/141. Baligrundle Church: MacKelvie, W. (1873). Annals and Statistics of the United Presbyterian Church. Lismore Kirk: Presbytery of Lorn, 26 July 1848. CH2/984/6. Cattle Prices: Blackwood's Edinburgh Magazine (1850) 67, p240. Moving bones: Alexander Carmichael's Notebooks: CW106 fo21r. Trust Deed: RD5/939/595. *Services of Heirs*, 1854. Court cases: NRS CS228/B/21/13 Summons of Declarator of Non Entry. The

Marquess of Breadalbane vs James A Cheyne Esq Dunedin 22 June 1857; CS232/C/55/4 Mrs F C Cheyne or Sprot vs Cheyne's trustees.

Chapter Five

Lismore Emigrant Register, 2009. Mull ferry: Minutes of the Commissioners of Supply of Argyllshire, 7 May 1752. 1834-6 Parish Church Communicants: CH2/814/3/61. Militiamen: List of Men within the Subdivision of Lorn and County of Argyll liable to serve in the Militia. Argyll Papers, 24; Lismore Historical Records 1800-1850. The MacKillop letter: NRS GD170-1640-7-00002. Combie Estate Maps: NRS RHP 5261, 5263. Cheyne purchase of Combie lands: The Scottish Jurist V p1 (1833), XI p74 (1838); Sasine records GR 2127/90. Highland Seminary: MacWilliam A S (1958) *The Innes Review* 8, 30-38. Cheyne purchase of Barcaldine lands: Sasine Records GR 1744.45, GR2319/202, GR2296/141. JAC Trust Deed NRS RD5/939/595. Dòmhnall an Dansair: Lobban (2004), Black (2006). Baligrundle tenants: GD170/568/17. Alexander Carmichael's early years: Lismore in Carmichael's Childhood & Youth: the 1830s and 1840s. Paper to the Edinburgh University Alexander Carmichael Conference, June 2011 (*In press*). 1843 Deforcement: see chapter 2 sources. Paupers: Poor Law Inquiry(Scotland) 1843. Appendix Part II. 377.002. Parish Records: CH2/814/3. 1838 famine: Captain Pole's correspondence. Treasury Correspondence p 58. Napier Report 1884. Croft size: Hunter 1976. Railway Companies: www.avoeo05.dsl.pipex.com/scotrlys.htm Parochial Boards: Blackden S. (1986). The Board of Supervision and the Scottish Parochial Medical Service, 1845-98. Medical History 30, 145-172. Argyll & Bute Archive: CO6/7/30. Treasury Correspondence, 1847. Repeal of the Corn Laws: Importation Act 1846 (9 & 10 Vict.

c. 22). Public Money Drainage Act 1846 (9 & 10 Vict. c. 101). Great Protection Meeting: Blackwoods Magazine 67, 239-40, 1850. Cheyne's drainage loan: Edinburgh Gazette 10 February 1847; GR2436/50. Marches and drainage GD241/408. JAC Inventory: SC51/32/8. Mrs Cheyne's houses: Valuation 1865/6, Argyll Archive CA/4/2/16. Barcaldine finances: GD170/2333. Argyll Sheriff Court Records, 1840s & 1850s: SC28/1/2; SC52/4/3; SC57/1/1; SC54/5/1; SC54/2/297. Ownership by Mrs Cheyne: Sasine G.R. 3308.191. Letting of Craignich: Valuation 1865-6.

Chapter Six

Lismore Emigrant Register, 2009. Linen: GD170/395. Kelp: Argyll Papers Bundle 290. Report, May 1847, Destitution Committee Scotland Free Church. Pole's Report: Treasury Papers p232. Letters of John McDougald: Lismore Archive. Lismore school curriculum: NSA, Lismore & Appin Parish. Dissent as a factor in migration: Donald Meek, personal communication. Duke of Argyll & Napier Commission: *Crofts & Farms in the Hebrides*. David Douglas, Edinburgh, 1883. Background to Scottish Land Reform: Hunter (1976); Devine (1994). 1885 General Election: Glasgow Herald, 15 August. Proposed break up of Frackersaig: Glasgow Herald 31 Nov 1907. Fair Rents and Petitions for land: Lismore Historical Documents 1850-1899; 1900-1949; Argyll Papers bundle 132. The Resettlement: File on the Resettlement of Ballygrundle and Craignish, Isle of Lismore, 1913-1916, under the Small Landholders (Scotland) Acts of 1866-1911, Argyll Papers, Imveraray Castle. The Campbell papers, 1 Baligrundle: Lismore Archive

Chapter Seven

Letter from the Carmichael Watson Archive, Edinburgh University: CW MS527. For an analysis of the destruction of the social order in a lowland setting, see Hay (2005) *Lochnavando no More. The Life and Death of a Moray Farming Community, 1750-1850*. Edinburgh: John Donald. Captain Hugh Anderson: www.lismoregaelicheritagecentre.com

Acknowledgements

The research for this book started with the archive initiated in the 1990s by the pioneers of the Lismore Museum; there is a particular debt of gratitude to Murdo MacDonald, formerly Argyll & Bute archivist, who supplied copies of documents important to the island, and continues to support the museum. The vision of the pioneers has now (in 2013) been recognised by the award of full accredited status. I am grateful to the directors of Comann Eachdraidh Lios Mòr (The Lismore Historical Society) for access to the archive; to my fellow curators Jennifer Baker, Margaret Black, Freda Drysdale, Lorraine King, Anne Livingstone and Barbara McDougall for their help over the years; and to Laura Gloag, the island genealogist, for her collaboration, over five years, in compiling the information in the appendices.

Much of the core of the book relies on the rich archive of MacDougall family papers held in the new 1745 House archive at Dunollie. I am grateful to Madam Morag MacDougall, Chief of the Clan MacDougall, for acces to the archive, and permission to quote extensively from it. Catherine Gillies and Linda Fryer have been my guides in the search to understand Allan MacDougall, even discovering his personal diaries at a late stage in the writing, in an attic chest. It is unfortunate that we were not able to uncover a portrait. Extracts from Baleveolan ground officer letters to Coll and Alexander Livingstone are presented with the permission of Niall Livingstone of Bachuil. I am also grateful to Ishbell MacKinnon, archivist of the Argyll archive at Inveraray, for access to documents on the 1913/4 resettlement; and to Jim Cheyne for advice on Cheyne family history. Jill Bowiss kindly provided information on the Barcaldine Campbells from the Ardchattan archive. The generous gift of the letters of John McDougald, the Balimakillichan weaver, to the Lismore archive by the MacDougall MacCallum Foundation has provided a rare insight into cottar life on the island.

The Carmichael Watson Project at Edinburgh University is an unfailing source of unique information about Lismore in the nineteenth century, and I am particularly grateful to Donald William Stewart for alerting me to the work of Steve Walker of the Cardiff Business School on the role of accountants in Highland clearance events. Professor Walker was kind enough to read parts of the book in draft and provide valuable advice. I am also grateful to Donald Meek for his continued inspiration in all things Gaelic, and interest in Lismore; his knowledge of the land reform movement on Tiree has illuminated Chapter Six. Margaret Lobban is pleased to see her father's song featured in the Introduction, and Ronnie Black kindly provided the translation of the verse from Hugh Anderson's *Oran do Lios Mòr*.

As in previous projects, I would acknowledge the courteous help of staff at the National Records of Scotland and the National Library of Scotland. A particularly helpful librarian at the Central Library in Edinburgh uncovered an unpublished and uncatalogued family history, which shed new light on James Cheyne and his brothers.

ACKNOWLEDGEMENTS

As ever, Chris Small, my learned and literary neighbour at Park, provided encouragement throughout the project and was the first person to read the whole manuscript. Bob Chambers also read the manuscript, drawing on his extensive knowledge of land reform to provide valuable advice, particularly on Chapter Six. In writing this book, I have benefited enormously from the knowledge and generosity of many people. Nevertheless, any errors of fact, judgement, interpretation or transcription must be my responsibility alone.

Finally, I must express my gratitude to John Randall of the Island Book Trust for his help and encouragement, and to Alayne Barton for efficiently seeing the manuscript through to publication. By their quiet and diplomatic work over the years, they have built an outstanding list of titles that might otherwise have gone unpublished.

Index

Other individual Lismore tenants and cottars can be traced through the Appendices

Accountants and accountancy 11, 22, 102-9, 113, 123, 280, 286, 292
Achallader 39
Achanard township 21, 24-6, 30, 110, 115-7, 120-3, 126, 133, 142-3, 152, 156-7, 161-2, 169-70, 177, 184, 248, 250-1, 255, 271-2, 275, 283
Achinduin township 20, 117, 121, 271
Achnacroish township 20, 26, 62-3, 64, 110-1, 113, 115, 118-9, 123-6, 138, 142, 152, 155, 157-9, 178-9, 186, 221-3, 248, 251, 253-7, 259-60, 264-5, 272, 276-7
Achuran township 20, 155, 157, 165, 186, 251, 253-4, 256
Actuary 105-6
Age structure 153, 173, 175
Airds House 18
Alastrath 30
Anderson
   Hugh 9, 191
   Dr Thomas 71
Appin 62, 116, 123, 130-1, 148, 151, 164, 178, 183, 276
Appin murder 62, 123

Arable farming 12, 28-30, 64, 71, 74, 77, 85, 100, 116, 121, 126, 135, 137, 139, 140, 142, 163, 170, 175, 255
Ardincaple, Seil 53-4
Ardnamurchan 172
Argyll,
   Colin, 1st Earl 62, 115
   George, 7th Duke 47
   John, 3rd Duke 20
   John, 9th Duke 184, 192
   George, 8th Duke 16, 179, 182, 288
Arithmetic 103, 180
Army Regiments
   69th Regiment of Foot 17
   91st Regiment of Foot 16
   94th Regiment of Foot 23
   98th Argyll Highlanders 16
   Scots Guards 16-7
Arrears of rent 15, 23, 32, 61, 68-70, 76, 78, 83-5, 87, 89, 91, 96-9, 107-8, 141, 151, 156, 162-4, 167, 190, 245, 248, 249, 251-2, 255-62, 264, 283, 285

Bachuil 66, 67, 179, 249
Baptist Chapel 131, 183

Ground Officers (see Coll and Alexander Livingstone) 12, 281, 284
Land 21, 66, 195
Baligarve township 20, 133, 191
Baleveolan estate 11, 12, 30, 32, 37, 49, 53, 54, 61-100, 115, 138, 140, 151, 164, 172, 175-7, 190, 193-9, 244, 262
Baleveolan township 24, 25, 31, 61-100, 125, 133, 138, 147, 157, 158, 164, 175-7, 186, 193-9, 255, 259, 262, 266
Baligrundle township 20, 24, 26, 62-3, 66, 71, 110-1, 113, 117-9, 123-4, 126, 128, 136, 143, 149, 152-6, 159, 164-5, 171, 177, 182-7, 190, 192, 217-9, 253-7, 261, 265-7, 277, 283, 286, 287, 288
Balimakillichan township 21, 61-100, 125, 151, 159, 175-7, 190, 195-6, 198-9, 252, 255, 259, 273, 292
Balnagown township 20, 64, 66, 87, 272
Banns 130-1
Baptist 131, 183
Barcaldine Castle 18
Barcaldine House 18
Bard 9, 11, 192, 280, 282
Bath 18, 19
Baxter, Charles 47, 48, 53-4, 99
Baxter, Edmund 47, 98, 284
Baxter C&E 53, 55, 56, 58
Baxter & MacDougall W.S. 47, 48, 52, 284
Beet 80
Begging 42, 58, 128-9
Bellman 131
Black
    Allan, tenant, Baligrundle 123, 155, 159, 213-5, 217, 253, 265-6
    Archibald, Achanard and Cape Breton 24, 170
    Donald, boatman, Kilcheran ('The Dancer')123, 163, 178, 213-5, 277-8

    Miles, tenant, Baleveolan 74, 83-4, 97, 194, 197
    Niel, tenant, Fiart 158-9, 164, 201, 231, 248, 263-5
Blackwoods Magazine 150, 283, 284, 286, 288
Boat and boatbuilding 32-3, 110, 122, 133-4, 161, 163, 172, 177, 178, 202, 213, 214
Board of Agriculture for Scotland 12, 182-4, 187, 190-1, 192
Bolivar, General Simon 102
Book-keeping 180
Borthwick,
    Archibald 108, 113, 167
    Patrick 108
Breadalbane, Earls/Marquess of 28, 39, 62, 113, 145, 287
Bronze Age cairn 124
Brown, James 107-8
Brown and Pearson 107, 110, 123, 124
Bruce, James 109, 286
Buchanan
    Alexander, labourer, Killean 133, 138-41
    J&A, tenants, Baleveolan 68, 84, 98-9, 158, 176, 194, 197, 233, 285
Bute 88, 166
Butter 51, 135

Cameron, Sir Donald of Lochiel 132
Campbell
    Sir Alexander 16
    Alexander of Clenamachrie 24
    Charles of Combie 21, 110, 122, 133, 162
    David of Combie 120
    Lt Gen Sir Colin (Colin Melfort) 16-7
    Colin Lord of Glenorchy 62
    Colin of Glenure (The Red Fox) 20, 62, 123
    Donald of Airds 20
    Captain Donald of Baleveolan 21, 49, 55, 68, 96-7, 140, 151, 244

INDEX

Duncan, 8th of Barcaldine 16, 18, 20, 26, 110, 122, 123-4, 142, 162, 249, 282, 283, 284
Sir Duncan of Glenorchy 24
Of Dunstaffnage 23, 120
Sir John, 7th of Airds 20, 244
John of Baleveolan 49, 62
John of Combie 21, 115, 120
Neil of Dunstaffnage 21, 122
Vice Admiral Patrick 16
Patrick/Peter of Baleveolan 49, 65, 284
Of Lochnell 16, 18, 244
Canada 24, 26, 35, 117, 124, 153, 155, 160, 181, 189, 249, 254, 255, 256, 267
Cape Breton Island 24, 36, 67, 169, 285
Carmichael
Alexander, folklorist 111, 124, 125-6, 159-60, 170, 180, 191, 235, 266-7, 286, 287
Duncan, tenant, Portcastle 84, 91-2, 195, 198
Hugh, tenant, Creckanbreck 74, 84, 87-8, 196, 199
Hugh, tenant, Portcharron and Kilandrist 125, 159-60, 235, 262, 266-7
Carolinas 24, 116, 169, 283
Carpenter 67, 122, 133, 158, 163, 195, 212, 214, 223, 264, 273, 275, 276, 277
Carrot 80
Castalla, Battle 17
Castle Stalker 18
Cattle 28, 31, 35, 75, 77, 79, 89, 107, 111, 115, 135, 141, 143, 150, 186, 244, 245, 283, 286
Ayrshire 31, 150
Highland 31, 111, 150
Shorthorn 31
Ceilidh house 191
Census 12, 53, 66, 67, 90, 91, 99, 111, 117, 122, 124, 128, 138, 151-62, 166, 167, 171, 172, 181, 193, 197, 198, 201-37, 247-78
Central Belt of Scotland 11, 25, 28, 36, 153, 160, 170, 173, 175, 181, 189
Cheese 135
Cheltenham 18, 46, 49
Cheyne
Frances Charlton 102, 103, 111, 112-3, 167, 171, 285
Frank Auchinlech 113
James Auchinleck W.S. 11, 12, 20-21, 22, 25, 31, 32, 36, 41, 61, 100, 101-13, 115-67, 174, 185, 190, 214, 244, 247, 257, 264, 269, 283, 285-8
James Auchinleck junior 102, 111, 112-3
Ninian Richard 102
Ninian Richard, junior 102
Chisholm, Bishop John 122, 177
Church
Episcopal 101,
Established/Parish 35, 117, 128, 130, 148, 160, 241, 247, 287
Free (from 1843) 35, 172, 284, 288
Roman Catholic 122
United Presbyterian/Secession 111, 127, 128, 143, 271, 286
Clachan, Lismore 125, 191
Claycombie 116
Cloichlea township 20, 117, 185, 249
Coal 29, 179
Coffin, Sir Edward Pine 81, 110, 144-7, 243, 286
Communicants (church) 117, 127, 247-75, 287
Corn Laws 31, 97, 111, 149, 287
Coseguina Volcano in Nicaragua 33, 68, 283
Craignich township 21, 30, 32, 87, 110, 115-21, 143, 152-8, 161-7, 171, 173, 175, 177, 181, 182-7, 190, 192, 204-9, 248-9, 250-3, 257, 258, 266, 271, 274, 288
Craignish, Argyll 249
Creckanbreck 62-3, 64, 65, 87-8, 176, 196, 199
Crofters' Act, 1886 143, 171, 183

Crofters' Party 132
Crops
  Barley 26, 29, 82, 135, 244, 253, 254, 255, 256, 257, 258, 259, 260, 261, 265
  Bere barley 29, 31, 32, 76, 77, 285
  Black oats 29
  Cereals 11, 27, 29, 31, 33, 76, 77, 78, 99
  Clover 31, 77, 78, 244
  Grass/grassland 12, 27, 29, 31, 77, 98, 120, 126, 135, 137, 138, 139, 142, 165, 175
  'Green' 27, 77, 83, 172
  Hay 29, 77, 80, 139
  Oats (white) 29, 31, 66, 76-7, 82, 135
  Potato 9, 11, 27, 29, 31, 32, 33-5, 53, 61, 70, 76-80, 81-3, 93, 97, 98, 99, 104, 108, 109, 111, 127, 128, 129, 131, 135, 136, 138, 139, 142, 143-7, 149, 160, 163, 165, 171, 172, 174, 240, 241, 243, 244, 245, 246, 284
  Turnips 27, 31, 77, 78, 79, 80, 82, 85, 86, 99, 244
  'white' 76, 77, 78
Cuidad Rodrigo, Storming 17, 23, 38

Dalnarrow 116, 117, 189
Death 9, 40, 164, 175, 247, 264
Debt 18, 22, 38, 42, 45, 48, 53, 55, 58, 70, 88, 93, 98, 107, 112, 141, 164, 172, 244, 284
Deforcement 26, 65, 124, 155, 165, 254, 258, 283, 287
Demography 118, 175, 176, 179
Dennistoun 182
Disruption of the Church of Scotland, 1843 148
Distilling 32, 76, 283
Diversification 27, 76, 78, 80
Downing Street 150
Drainage, subsoil 29, 54, 55, 71-4, 83, 87, 88, 98, 151, 285
Druimavuic 49, 54, 55, 62, 64, 66, 69, 90, 92, 93, 97
Dumbarton 23, 25, 166, 170, 174, 275
Dunollie 12, 18, 37, 39, 40, 41, 42, 43, 46, 47, 51, 52, 53, 54, 56, 61, 81, 101, 102, 281, 284, 285
Dunstaffnage 21, 23, 54, 120, 122
Dyke 64, 74-6, 120, 151, 187

Edinburgh 11, 18, 22, 37, 38, 41-7, 49, 50, 51, 53, 54, 55, 57, 58, 97, 101-6, 107-9, 112, 132, 148, 151, 160, 166
Edinburgh Advertiser 103, 286
Eilean Musdile 116
Elder (church) 129, 249, 256
Electricity 190
Elgin County, Ontario 170, 181, 260
Emigration 24, 28, 33, 36, 67, 100, 108, 109, 112, 116, 124, 150, 152, 153, 155, 157, 159, 160, 163, 165, 166, 169, 170, 171, 177, 179, 181, 247, 249, 250, 254, 255, 256, 259, 260, 267, 283, 284, 285, 287, 288
"Empty Quarter" 189-91
Enclosure 32, 64, 69, 70, 74, 75, 85
English reading, writing 180
Eviction 9, 11, 26, 65, 66, 69, 86-92, 93, 97, 98, 108, 120, 124, 133, 134, 142, 164, 167, 184, 285

Fell, Rev. James Alexander of Penkridge 22, 183
Fence 187
Fennachrochain township 20
Ferry 32, 115, 116, 123, 167, 177, 178, 179, 215, 278, 287
Fertiliser 27
Feudal tenure 62, 113
Fiart township 21, 30, 32, 110, 115-22, 123, 125, 126, 136, 142, 143, 152-6, 157, 158, 162, 164, 165, 169, 177, 178, 184, 187, 189, 190, 201-3, 247, 248, 249,

INDEX

250, 251, 252, 263, 264, 269, 270, 275
Fife Banking Company 104
Fine 130, 148
Fire station 179
Fishing/fisheries 25, 33, 81, 127, 128, 147, 152, 170, 172, 173, 179, 198, 232, 245, 253, 262
Fixation of nitrogen 77
Food aid 35, 68, 131, 172, 244, 284
Fort William Sheriff Court 164
Frackersaig township 21, 183, 185, 288
Fraser-Mackintosh, Charles 132, 138

Gaelic 11, 39, 109, 124, 132, 180, 191, 248, 271
Gillespie Graham, James 18, 105
Gladstone, Willam, Prime Minister 132
Glasgow 23, 25, 56, 58, 59, 68, 71, 75, 79, 82, 86, 103, 104, 105, 124, 144, 147, 157, 158, 159, 160, 166, 170, 174, 180, 181, 182, 244, 256, 258, 265, 266, 270, 275, 276, 279, 288
Glasgow Herald 103, 288
Government 35, 82, 105, 113, 132, 144, 145, 148, 149, 150, 151, 187
Grassum 65
Grazing 27, 31, 64, 74, 77, 134, 136, 138, 140, 142, 164, 184, 189, 190
Great Protection Meeting, 1850 150, 288
Greenock 23, 25, 159, 166, 170, 174, 180, 181, 260, 267
Ground Officer 12, 31, 50, 53, 54, 56, 61, 66, 68, 70, 72, 78, 87, 97, 98, 99, 143, 167, 227, 249, 253, 254, 262, 284, 285
Guano 79

Haig, Alexander of Blairhall 20-2
Harvest 25, 28, 33, 34, 68, 70, 78, 107, 160, 162, 170

Hawthorn House 67
Head dyke 64, 74
Health 27, 52-3, 58, 81, 98, 127, 163, 165, 174, 181
Herd 31, 193, 196, 197, 201, 211, 213, 217, 222, 231, 235, 240, 272
Heritage Centre 179
Herring 25, 81, 245
Highland and Agricultural Society 31, 51, 80, 101, 104, 106, 284, 286
Highland Seminary, Roman Catholic 23, 71, 111, 122, 177, 287
Horse and horsemanship 16, 25, 31, 32, 33, 49, 66, 111, 141, 182, 245, 283
House/Housing 27, 67, 74, 79, 89, 92, 94, 95, 96, 121, 127, 129, 130, 135, 160, 161, 165, 177, 187, 189, 190, 191, 239-41, 288
Hunger 162, 170, 172, 180

Idle labourer 144, 147, 149
Illegitimacy 42, 174, 275
Illicit still 32
Improvement, agricultural 11, 27-33, 51, 54, 61-100, 149, 151, 172, 190, 244, 283
Industrial Revolution 25, 170
Infield 29, 30, 63
Inn 109, 155, 122, 157, 161, 163, 178, 272
Insurance 56, 104, 106, 112
Inveraray 65, 144, 147, 244
 Sheriff Court 26, 65, 124, 164, 283
Inverness 79, 132
Iron Age dun 124
Islay 28, 29, 107, 108, 146

Joiner/joinery 67, 180, 222, 254, 259, 267
Jupiter of Larne 116

Kellie, Fife 104, 109, 286
Kelp 33, 107, 170, 288
Kerrera 39

Kilandrist township 20, 159, 185, 267
Kilcheran township 21, 23, 110-1, 115, 117-9, 121-3, 125, 126, 127-8, 133-4, 142, 143, 150, 152, 153, 154, 155, 156, 157, 161-2, 163-7, 171, 177-9, 185, 186, 189, 211-5, 249-50, 254, 255, 266, 269-78
   Islands 254
   Lime kilns 30, 71
   Loch 116, 117
Killean township 20, 62-3, 99, 110, 113, 115, 118-9, 123, 125, 126, 127, 136, 138, 139, 142, 150, 151-8, 161, 164-5, 178-9, 185-6, 229-34, 248, 250, 251, 252, 253, 255, 258, 259, 260, 261, 262, 264, 265, 269, 270, 273, 277
Kilmaron, Fife 105, 112, 154, 163, 286
Kingairloch 25

Lambert, Alexander, Writer in Oban 49
Lanarkshire 86, 155, 182, 203, 248, 264
Latin 180
Law, James, grieve, Kilcheran 154, 213
Liberal Party 132, 183
Lighthouse 116, 297
Lime and liming 29, 32, 71, 89
Limeburner 83, 161, 178
Limekiln 29, 71, 115, 122, 161, 177, 285
Limestone, Dalradian 29
Linen 170, 288
Linlithgow 102, 105
Lismore and Appin parochial board 148, 161, 172, 287
Lismore emigration register 152, 181, 247, 283, 285, 287, 288
Lismore kirk 111, 129, 249, 256, 286
Livingstone (MacLea/Macleay) of Bachuil 21, 67
   Alexander 21, 76-92, 97, 292
   Coll 66, 69-73, 93-96, 292
   Duncan, tenant in Balimakillichan 66, 198
Locke, George 50, 54, 85, 93, 97

MacColl/McColl
   Archibald, ground officer, Baligrundle 26, 124, 143, 155
   Archibald, carter in Glasgow 181-2
   Donald, tenant Achnacroish 157
   Duncan, tenant in Tirlaggan 166, 181
   John, ground officer, Baleveolan estate 56, 79-86, 96, 98
   John, grocer, Govan 182
   Malcolm, deforcer, Baligrundle 26, 124
   Samuel, schoolmaster 180
MacCorquodale family, tenants, Balimakillichan 83, 89-90
MacDonald, Duncan, carpenter, Port Ramsay 133-8, 141-3, 161, 222, 275-6
MacDougall
   Alexander (Sandy) (brother of Allan) 16, 17, 18, 37
   Allan Duncan 11, 12, 22, 36, 37-59, 61-100, 101, 133, 147, 151, 156, 161, 175, 177, 190, 192, 284
   Ann Colina (Campbell and Locke) (sister of Allan) 37, 49-50, 51, 55, 66, 68
   Coll 21
   Dugald of Gallanach 19
   Sir John 25th Chief 16, 22, 35, 39, 40, 46, 48, 49, 50, 53, 59, 87
   Louisa Maxwell 19, 37, 39, 40, 41, 51
   Lt Neil of Ardentrive 17
   Patrick 24th Chief 16, 37, 41, 42, 43
   Patrick (brother of Allan) 37, 38, 47, 52
McDugald/MacDougall, John, weaver, Balimakillichan 67, 90,

INDEX

93, 175, 196, 199
MacGregor, Rev Gregor 23, 25, 35, 73, 81, 88, 94, 95, 96, 111, 128, 131, 149, 156, 171, 180, 243-5, 283
MacKean, John W.S. 103, 105, 112, 286
   Margaret Blair 103
Mackenzie, Sir Kenneth of Gairloch 132, 134
McKillop, John, tenant, Achanard 120-1, 287
MacKinnon, Donald, Professor of Celtic at Edinburgh University 132, 140
McNicol, tenant, Kilcheran 129-30, 154, 249
Machair 28
Mackerel 81, 245
Mangel 80
Manse 156, 179, 191
Manure 58, 74, 76, 77, 79, 85
Martinmas 57, 65, 68, 83, 91, 151, 184, 186
Mason 67, 185, 198, 258
Mathematics 180
Meal (oat) 31, 66, 68, 93, 94, 98, 129, 135, 172, 243, 253, 254, 255, 256, 257, 258, 259, 260, 261, 265
Merchant 47, 67, 93, 127, 160, 179, 194, 276
Micronutrients 29
Militia 117, 121, 287
Milk 27, 129, 135, 138
Mills and millers 24, 26, 31, 34, 66, 67, 116, 117, 123, 125, 155, 177, 217, 218, 245, 254, 255, 283
Minnesota 68, 177, 260
Moluag 66
Mortcloth 130, 148
Morvern 122
Mull 10, 29, 108, 116, 123, 146, 172, 178, 250, 253, 259, 280, 287
Multiple tenancy 30, 63, 74

Napier Commission 12, 78, 122, 131-43, 147, 152, 161, 165, 171, 177, 182, 183, 280, 285, 287, 288
Napoleonic War 16-7, 18, 102, 117, 149, 169, 282
National Bank of Scotland 48, 104, 108, 286
Newfield 62, 118-9, 125, 157, 178, 185, 221, 222, 250, 255, 256
New Zealand 112, 113, 166, 254
Nicolson, Alexander, Sheriff of Kircudbright 132
Norse 49, 124
Nova Scotia 17, 24, 169, 259, 283, 284

Oban 31, 33, 37, 49, 53, 56, 57, 81, 82, 86, 94, 104, 110, 116, 121, 123, 128, 144, 147, 148, 166, 178, 243, 244, 245, 257
Ontario 155, 157, 159, 165, 170, 180, 181, 249, 254, 255, 256, 260
Outfield 29, 30, 64
Oxendean 104, 163

Paisley 25, 104, 170, 180
Park 177
   Lime kilns 30, 71
Parish minister 31, 35, 68, 69, 72, 81, 94, 97, 128, 130, 172
Parsnip 80
Passbook 74, 86
Pasture 10, 32, 74, 77, 85, 121, 136, 138
Paterson, David, and sons 166, 182, 187
Pauper 36, 83, 90, 93, 115, 125, 127, 128, 130, 148, 150, 155, 159, 160, 161, 162, 164, 178, 194, 198, 199, 203, 207, 213, 214, 215, 218, 223, 226, 227, 229, 231, 232, 233, 234, 236, 237, 248, 250, 252, 253, 254, 259, 260, 265, 266, 269, 271, 273, 274, 287
Peel, Robert, Prime Minister 149
Peninsular Campaign 16, 23, 282

Phosphate 79
Ploughman 154, 158, 167, 182, 185, 186, 202, 213, 214, 215, 222, 233, 251, 264, 267, 277
Point, Lismore 245, 276
Point of Fiart 116, 117, 136, 142, 169, 189, 201, 202, 248, 263, 269, 275
Pole, Captain 81, 144-6, 149, 172, 243, 285, 287, 288
Police 26, 124
Poor Law Inquiry 128-31, 148, 154, 239-41, 249, 256, 285, 287
Poor Law (Scotland) Act, 1845 148
Port Appin 32, 82
Portcastle 61, 62, 63, 64, 66, 87, 91, 92, 176, 195, 198, 262
Portcharron township 20, 62, 63, 92, 110, 111, 113, 118-9, 123, 126, 127, 136, 151, 152, 153, 154, 156, 159, 165, 235-7, 253, 255, 262, 266, 267
Postman 186
Potato blight (*Phytophthora infestans*) 34, 36, 83, 143, 284
Potato famine 9, 11, 31-36, 53, 61, 81-4, 97, 104, 108, 109, 110, 111, 127, 128, 138, 139, 142, 143, 146, 148, 149, 160, 163, 165, 171, 172, 174, 284, 287
Preacher 123, 212, 271
Precentor 131
Premium 57, 80, 95
Procurator fiscal 26, 124
Public Money Drainage Act, 1846 149-151, 288
Publican 66, 67, 122, 160, 161, 194, 212, 270

Quarry 71, 160, 177
Quarryman 67, 88, 138, 253
Quay 71
Quebec 169

Railway Companies 286, 287
   Callender to Oban 148
   Edinbugh and Glasgow 104, 105
   Edinburgh Leith Glasgow Paisley Ardrossan and Troon 104
   Scottish Grand Junction 104, 112, 144-7
   Stirling 104
Relief 38, 70, 104, 107, 109, 110, 128, 130, 131, 144, 145, 148, 149, 172, 244, 245, 279, 284
Religion 39, 40, 101
Rent 15, 18, 23, 31, 32, 38, 49, 65, 66, 68, 69, 70, 74, 78, 80, 83, 84, 86, 87, 91, 93, 94, 95, 96, 97, 98, 99, 107, 108, 110, 113, 116, 120, 123, 125, 126, 129, 130, 133, 134, 136, 137, 139, 142, 143, 151, 156, 161, 162, 163, 164, 166, 183, 184, 185, 186, 193, 194, 195, 196, 197, 217, 222, 223, 240, 241, 244, 245, 247-67, 272, 276, 277, 282, 285, 288
Resettlement 182, 187, 192, 288
Rig and furrow 27, 30, 71, 72
Road man/contractor 179, 186, 231, 259
Rotation 27, 31, 32, 74, 76-80, 172, 285
Royal Bank of Scotland 104
Runrig 29, 63
Russell, Lord John, Prime Minister 145
Ryegrass 78, 135, 142

Sailean 30, 62, 63, 64, 116, 176, 179, 185, 186, 194-5, 198, 277
   Lime kilns 71, 160
Sailing smacks 71, 133
Sailor/Seaman 121, 123, 125, 127, 158, 178, 179, 186, 212, 222, 234, 253, 264, 274
School 19, 41, 51, 67, 102, 103, 124, 132, 133, 140, 149, 159, 174, 179, 180, 182, 218, 245, 266, 267, 288
Scotsman newspaper 109, 286
Scott, Sir Walter 39-40
Scottish Protective Association 150

INDEX

Scottish Widows Fund 105
Seed 78, 79, 80, 82, 83, 85, 99, 136, 244
Sequestration 91-2, 107
Shankland, William and John 187, 215
Sheep 10, 31, 75, 77, 86, 134, 136, 139, 155, 158, 160, 178, 183, 186, 190, 244, 283
Sheep Island 161, 276
Sheepwalk 15, 28, 36, 69, 100, 142, 143, 156, 163, 164, 187
Shelter 74, 75
Shepherd 67, 121, 135, 155, 157, 159, 160, 163, 167, 178, 186, 198, 203, 209, 214, 218, 219, 226, 266
Shettleston 182
Shoemaker/Cobbler 67, 125, 160, 177, 178, 194, 226, 227, 230, 232
Shop 66, 177, 179, 182, 186
Signature 41
Six year shift 27, 76-7
Skye 108, 132
Slavery 105
Small Landholders (Scotland) Act 1911 183, 288
Smith, blacksmith 67, 125, 157, 177, 178, 230, 232, 233
Smith, James of Deanston 72, 285
Soil acidity 29, 71
Sprot
    Frances Charlton (see also Frances Cheyne) 103, 285, 287
    Thomas W.S. 104, 113
Spuilzie 90, 98, 285
Standard Life Assurance Company 105, 108, 109, 113, 286
Steamer 23, 33, 75, 82, 83, 179
Stewart
    John Hope Johnstone, farmer 154, 166, 214
    Mary, merchant, Baleveolan 67, 93, 94, 194, 285
Straw 79
Subsistence 29, 144, 146
Sugar 105, 159, 180, 181

Tacksman 24, 116
Tailor 67, 124, 125, 160, 161, 178, 218, 219, 223, 230, 231, 233, 260, 261
Talavera, Battle 16, 123
Taylochan 118-9, 125, 262, 266
Tax commissioner 105, 106
Tea 180
Timmins, Sophy 46
Tiree 146, 181
Tirefour township 21
Tirewin 62, 123
Tirlaggan township 21, 62, 63, 110, 113, 118-9, 123, 125, 126, 138, 153, 154, 156-7, 165, 166, 167, 178, 179, 181, 185, 225-7, 249, 252, 253, 257, 258, 259, 274
Tobermory Sheriff Court 164
Toronto 24, 170
Tory Party 132
Treasury, Her Majesty's 109, 143-9, 243, 279, 283, 284, 285, 286-8
Tree planting 39, 70, 74, 75, 163
Trevelyan, Sir Charles 110, 143-7

Uist 108, 186
United Secession/United Presbyterian Church 111, 127, 128, 143, 271, 286
Upper Canada 24

Valuation Roll 20-2, 125, 161, 197, 208, 209, 251, 282, 288
Village 93, 115, 136, 177-9, 182, 189

Waterloo, Battle 16, 24, 282
Weaver 67, 90, 93, 94, 122, 125, 127, 160, 162, 175, 178, 194, 196, 199, 212, 213, 230, 232, 236, 274, 275
Weed 72, 77, 99, 137
Wellington, Lord 16
Whisky 22, 32, 283
Whitsunday 65, 93, 95
Widow/er 89, 124, 127, 130, 133,

152, 154, 165
William Roy's Military Map 116
Wintertown 29, 74
Wood/woodland 93, 189
Wood, Rev William 128, 227, 271
Woodcockdale 102, 104, 112, 163
Wool 57-8, 67, 156, 163, 177, 284

Wright 67, 122, 161, 163, 178, 212, 274
Writer to the Signet 37, 47, 101, 102, 286

Young, John W.S. 42-7

THE ISLANDS BOOK TRUST
– high quality books on island themes in
English and Gaelic

The Islands Book Trust are a charity committed to furthering understanding and appreciation of the history and culture of Scottish islands in their wider Celtic and Nordic context. We do this through publishing books, organising talks and conferences, visits, radio broadcasts, research and education on island themes. For details of membership of the Book Trust, which will keep you in touch with all our publications and other activities, see www.theislandsbooktrust.com , phone 01851 880737, or visit Ravenspoint at the address below where a full selection of our books is available.

Our publications include substantial conference volumes on island themes such as St Kilda, Alexander Carmichael, Whaling, Emigration, and the School of Scottish Studies; and books in English and Gaelic by leading scholars and writers such as Donald Meek and James Hunter.

The Islands Book Trust, Ravenspoint, Kershader, South Lochs, Isle of Lewis, HS2 9QA (01851 880737)

A SMALL SELECTION OF OTHER TITLES FROM THE ISLANDS BOOK TRUST

See www.theislandsbooktrust.com for a full list of our publications

History of Skye	A new edition of the Classic book by Alexander Nicolson edited by Cailean Maclean
From the Low Tide of the Sea to the Highest Mountain Top	Community Ownership of Land in the Highlands and Islands by Jim Hunter with photographs by Cailean Maclean
Alexander Macdonald Bard of the Gaelic Enlightenment	Edited by Camille Dressler and Dòmhnall Uilleam Stiùbhart
Tiree – War among the Barley and Brine	By Mike Hughes and John Holliday. A snapshot of Tiree during the Second World War when there was a high presence of personnel based on the island
Destination St Kilda From Oban to Skye and the Outer Hebrides	By Mark Butterworth, including 67 rarely seen original magic lantern slides from the 1880s from the collection by Aberdeen photographers George Washington Wilson and Norman Macleod

Stroma – The Island in the Stream	By Roddy Ritchie, Alistair Murray and George Gunn, including 71 beautiful images of Stroma
Foula – The Time of my Life	By Chris Mylne with over 90 illustrations. A valuable record of island social life in Foula in the 1950s
The Island Lighthouses of Scotland	By John A Love, a biologist and illustrator who has been fascinated by lighthouses ever since visiting the Bass Rock over 50 years ago
The French MacDonald	Edited by Jean-Didier Hache, based on the journal of a Marshal of Napoleon in the Highlands and Islands of Scotland in 1825
Dualchas àraid agus Prìseil Oighreachd ar Sinnsearan	Two volumes of unique photographs from a collection by Dr Kenneth Robertson, catching the spirit and changing face of South Uist and Eriskay from the late 1950s
Exploring the Islands of the West	By Marc Calhoun, two volumes covering Skye and Tiree to the Outer Isles and Firth of Clyde to the Small Isles

Return to Patagonia	By Greta Mackenzie, following up the best selling 'Why Patagonia'? tracing many family connections between Lewis and Patagonia from over a century ago.
From Cleits to Castles – A St Kildan Looks Back	The autobiography of Calum MacDonald